Japan's Unequal Trade

JAPAN'S
UNEQUAL
TRADE

EDWARD J. LINCOLN

THE BROOKINGS INSTITUTION
WASHINGTON

Library of Congress Cataloging-in-Publication Data
Lincoln, Edward J.
  Japan's unequal trade / Edward J. Lincoln.
    p. cm.
  Includes bibliographical references.
  ISBN 0-8157-5262-8 (alk. paper)   ISBN 0-8157-5261-X
(pbk. : alk. paper)
    1. Japan—Commercial policy.   2. Balance of trade—Japan.
3. United States—Commercial policy.   I. Title.
HF1601.L56 1990
382'.17'0952—dc20   90-30760
                                                           CIP

        9 8 7 6 5 4 3 2 1

The paper used in this publication meets the minimum requirements of the American National Standard for Information Sciences—Permanence of Paper for Printed Library Materials, ANSI
Z39.48-1984.

Set in Trump with Trump Gravur and Floreal Haas display
Composition by Graphic Composition, Inc.
Athens, Georgia
Printing by R. R. Donnelley and Sons Co.
Harrisonburg, Virginia
Book design by Ken Sabol

℟ THE BROOKINGS INSTITUTION

The Brookings Institution is an independent organization devoted to nonpartisan research, education, and publication in economics, government, foreign policy, and the social sciences generally. Its principal purposes are to aid in the development of sound public policies and to promote public understanding of issues of national importance.

The Institution was founded on December 8, 1927, to merge the activities of the Institute for Government Research, founded in 1916, the Institute of Economics, founded in 1922, and the Robert Brookings Graduate School of Economics and Government, founded in 1924.

The Board of Trustees is responsible for the general administration of the Institution, while the immediate direction of the policies, program, and staff is vested in the President, assisted by an advisory committee of the officers and staff. The by-laws of the Institution state: "It is the function of the Trustees to make possible the conduct of scientific research, and publication, under the most favorable conditions, and to safeguard the independence of the research staff in the pursuit of their studies and in the publication of the results of such studies. It is not a part of their function to determine, control, or influence the conduct of particular investigations or the conclusions reached."

The President bears final responsibility for the decision to publish a manuscript as a Brookings book. In reaching his judgment on the competence, accuracy, and objectivity of each study, the President is advised by the director of the appropriate research program and weighs the views of a panel of expert outside readers who report to him in confidence on the quality of the work. Publication of a work signifies that it is deemed a competent treatment worthy of public consideration but does not imply endorsement of conclusions or recommendations.

The Institution maintains its position of neutrality on issues of public policy in order to safeguard the intellectual freedom of the staff. Hence interpretations or conclusions in Brookings publications should be understood to be solely those of the authors and should not be attributed to the Institution, to its trustees, officers, or other staff members, or to the organizations that support its research.

Foreword

THE TOPIC OF U.S.-Japan trade relations has generated much heated debate in recent years. Even the core of the problem is a subject of disagreement: is it Japan's global trade surplus, the bilateral trade imbalance, or competitive practices in particular markets? Are American or Japanese practices responsible for the lopsided imbalances and specific industry outcomes? Because Japan is a powerful industrial nation with which the United States maintains important strategic and economic ties, the answers to these questions have serious implications for American policy toward Japan.

In this study, Edward J. Lincoln focuses on the unusual patterns that have distinguished Japanese trade from that of other industrial nations—a low level of manufactured imports and a relative absence of the two-way flow within particular industries known as intra-industry trade. He argues that these unusual characteristics cannot be explained away as the result of standard economic factors and that they are the outcome of attitudes, policies, and institutions that emerged from Japan's determined effort to catch up with the West. Now that Japan has joined the ranks of the advanced industrial nations, these features of the economy have proved to be difficult to change.

Since 1985, however, the large appreciation of the yen against the dollar has prompted the Japanese to reassess their import policy and the economic relationship of Japan to the world in general. Lincoln argues that American trade policy toward Japan must incorporate this new atmosphere; now is not the time to abandon the liberal trade principles embodied in the GATT for a system of managed trade. The developments since 1985 imply that U.S. pressure will be more successful in opening Japanese markets to imports than it has been in the past because domestic groups in Japan favoring greater openness have become stronger and more vociferous. Sanctions or other harsh negotiating tactics may be necessary occasionally, but they should be applied carefully and rationally.

Edward J. Lincoln is a senior fellow in the Brookings Foreign Policy Studies program. He is grateful for valuable comments and suggestions on the manuscript from Kent E. Calder, Stephen Cohen, Donald J. Daly, Eleanor M. Hadley, Robert Z. Lawrence, Marcus Noland, Hugh T. Patrick, John D. Steinbruner, Kenji Takeuchi, and Philip H. Trezise. The author also thanks Jeanette Morrison for editing the manuscript, Christine C. de Fontenay and Carole H. Newman for providing computer assistance, Susan Nichols and Yvonne S. Sabban for making the many changes to the text, Yasuo Konishi, Patricia Nelson, and Yuko Iida Frost for research assistance, and Fred L. Kepler for compiling the index.

Brookings gratefully acknowledges the financial support for this project provided by the John D. and Catherine T. MacArthur Foundation, the Andrew W. Mellon Foundation, and the Rockefeller Brothers Fund.

The views expressed here are those of the author and should not be ascribed to any of the persons acknowledged above or to the officers, trustees, or other staff members of the Brookings Institution.

BRUCE K. MAC LAURY
President

January 1990
Washington, D.C.

Contents

Tables

xi

Figures

Japan's Unequal Trade

CHAPTER ONE

Introduction

THESE ARE HEADY TIMES for the Japanese. The nation is in the midst of profound economic, political, and social changes that are fundamentally altering its relationship to the rest of the world. Affluence, rapid acquisition of foreign assets, and a strong currency are the key elements driving these changes. As a major world creditor, as a provider of billions of dollars of foreign aid, and as the possessor of important advanced technologies, Japan has the resources to be a principal actor in world affairs, moving to center stage from its peripheral roles of seller and trader. Tentatively and cautiously, Japan is exploring what it wants to do with its newfound international status.

In a number of ways, Japan has lived a very insular existence since the end of the Second World War, remaining aloof from international political and economic developments while concentrating on domestic growth. Insularity has included a basic hostility to importing manufactured products from other nations and a set of institutional features that have actively discouraged such imports, features that are the focus of this study. As Japan now moves into an era of greater interaction with the world on many fronts, that hostility is beginning to wane. But this encouraging development does not mean that the United States or other nations should end their pressure on Japan to continue opening its markets. Left to itself, Japan's behavior on imports will remain peculiar and unsatisfactory to its trading partners. Nevertheless, the atmosphere of change should make Japan more receptive to pressure. Japan may never be as open to, and as enthusiastic about, imports as other nations, but its behavior could well come much closer to international norms.

Economic relations between Japan and the United States are multidimensional, and on many of these fronts the news of the past decade has been mainly of increased problems accompanied by a rising tone of competition and antagonism. These problems could be dismissed as the inevitable noise in a successful relationship with

I

constantly mounting levels of trade and investment, a relationship now so intertwined that, as some have put it, divorce is virtually unthinkable.[1] But the news generated over the past decade gives the impression of an incipient trade war rather than bickering between close allies; as intertwined as the two nations may be, foolish responses to the problems could unravel the fabric of relations.

The spring of 1989 brought a further heightening of visible tension when the U.S. government named Japan, along with Brazil and India, an unfair trading nation under the "Super 301" provision of the Trade Act of 1988. This signaled the start of negotiations on three particular products specified in the complaint (satellites, forest products, and supercomputers) and broader talks on structural barriers to access to the Japanese market.[2] Japanese officials and the media expressed shock that the United States could label an ally so bluntly. As undiplomatic and crude as this approach may be, the decision to apply Super 301 to Japan accurately reflected the high level of frustration in Washington in dealing with Japan.

What is the core of the problem, or "friction," as the Japanese call it? At one level the problem is the growth of global Japanese trade and current-account surpluses, coupled with a U.S. move to large deficits. From a deficit of $11 billion in 1980, Japan's current account exploded to an unprecedented surplus of $87 billion in 1987. Viewed less broadly, the problem is a lopsided U.S.-Japan bilateral component within these global developments. Over the same period, the U.S. merchandise trade deficit with Japan deteriorated from $10 billion to $60 billion.[3] At a microeconomic level, the difficulty lies in American perceptions and accusations of "unfair" Japanese business practices in the U.S. market, which have been used to justify protectionist reactions, and in allegations of visible and invisible barriers to the Japanese market.

This study focuses mainly on the question of access to Japanese markets, a question marked by great controversy and considerable confusion. Japanese government officials and business executives often deny that any barriers exist, and academics in both countries disagree about the existence or effect of access problems. The data in this study, however, lead to the strong conclusion that Japan's pattern of trade on imports has been and remains very peculiar when compared with those of other countries—a peculiarity that cannot be explained through standard economic factors. Japan does indeed exhibit an aversion to manufactured imports and avoids the two-way trade in many manufactured products that characterizes the international trade of other nations. Neither the defensive arguments put forth by Japanese government officials nor those of academics are convincing.

Why focus on these microeconomic questions of market access? In recent years most of the bilateral discussion has concerned the serious imbalance in macroeconomic conditions at the root of the huge and stubborn trade surpluses and deficits. This part of the relationship is now fairly well understood and has been treated in other studies.[4] The macroeconomic policies each country followed in the first half of the 1980s, for what appeared to be perfectly good domestic reasons, had the unfortunate consequence of greatly increasing the trade and current-account imbalances. Reduction of the trade surpluses and deficits requires continuing the macroeconomic policy corrections that began in 1985 but still have far to go—especially in the United States. However, reductions in trade imbalances by themselves will not improve bilateral relations appreciably; they must be accompanied by a change in U.S. perceptions of Japanese trade practices.

Why? Microeconomic problems are largely separable from macroeconomic developments and have their own logic and consequences. Improving access to the Japanese market will not move overall trade imbalances very far in any direction, but that is not the point. These issues are serious and significant in their own right and involve a need for change on Japan's part. Of course, all nations have some trade barriers or business practices that others find disagreeable. Why not accept them as small irritants in a by and large profitable partnership? This is certainly one option, but, for several reasons, downplaying these problems would be a mistake.

First, Japan is now an economic superpower. Its policies and behavior greatly influence the entire international trading system. That system, constructed in the early postwar years in the form of the General Agreement on Tariffs and Trade (GATT), has been guided by the belief that import barriers in general are undesirable, and that concessions granted to one participant in the system should be granted to all (the most-favored-nation principle). While the GATT has not produced perfect free trade, it has led to the dismantling of many formal barriers and enabled world trade to expand rapidly over the past 40 years. Japan could undermine that system if it is perceived as achieving continued economic success through protectionist trade policies. If, on the other hand, Japan chooses to support the system by example, through demonstrably opening its markets to imports, and by playing a stronger role in multilateral negotiations, the system will be more secure and viable.

Second, economic ties are at the core of bilateral relations. As a matter of diplomatic priority, the strategic military relationship has generally outweighed economics; trade issues have been downplayed or submerged when larger security issues have been at stake. Japan remains a close and quite supportive strategic ally of the United States. U.S. bases in Japan, for example, unlike those in the Philippines, are not controversial (the Japanese even provide half their financial support), and Japan has joined most American diplomatic initiatives toward the Soviet Union and other countries. But this necessary strategic priority does not mean that economic issues can be ignored; ultimately, they determine the success or failure of bilateral relations. The perception of unfair Japanese trading practices, for example, is a key element in explaining why congressional support for liberal trade has declined. Furthermore, it is largely Japan's economic success, and not a new assessment of the Soviet military threat, that has driven the bilateral discussion on defense burden-sharing. If Japan's behavior on imports fails to change, or if the U.S. government fails to press Japan on market-access issues, rising dissatisfaction with Japan could undermine the strategic relationship.

Third, a central feature of Japanese economic policy has been the protection of emerging high-technology industries from import competition. Even without this policy, Japanese corporations are highly competent, aggressive world competitors. With de facto protection of their domestic market, they gain an advantage in international competition that puts an unduly large share of advanced industrial assets and production under Japanese ownership. American corporations are among the principal losers in this process. Although the long-term implications of such developments are not well understood, and remain an area of great controversy among scholars, the case cán be made that the United States should maintain an American-owned industrial capability in emerging technologies both for security reasons and for its long-term prosperity.[5] Protectionism in Japan is by no means the only issue involved in American competitiveness, but it is one issue, and one that should not be ignored in the broader consideration of how the U.S. government should act to promote future American prosperity and industrial strength.

For all these reasons, trade issues are a crucial element in U.S.-Japan affairs. Continuation of the liberal trading framework that has contributed to world growth and development over the past 40 years is by no means certain. That system could collapse if the United States feels that Japanese companies have unfairly gained control of important emerging high-technology industries to the detriment of American economic interests. If other nations (such as South Korea and Taiwan) believe that the Japanese strategy has been successful, they may try to emulate it rather than the liberal trade model embodied in the GATT. Even if American perceptions are exaggerated and one-sided, the sense that Japan gains at American expense in the current trade system will further erode support for the system. Thus the questions of Japanese trade behavior and trade policy assume great importance. Determining if Japan's behavior is protectionist, however, is not a simple exercise, and some observers have concluded that Japan has been unfairly accused.

American and Japanese views of bilateral economic problems naturally differ, and their differences are considered in chapter 2. Much of the Japanese writing on this topic places more emphasis on the size of trade imbalances or Japanese penetration of U.S. markets as the core of the problem rather than unfair trade practices or barriers to entry in their own market. This emphasis reinforces the Japanese sense that most criticism from the United States is unjustified scapegoating—blame for problems that are really the fault of the United States. Even most American economists agree that the size of the trade and current-account imbalances is largely a product of macroeconomic factors and that American macroeconomic policy mistakes are a key element in explaining the outcomes. Furthermore the Japanese can point to unfavorable long-term trends in American business practices, such as low productivity growth and inadequate quality control, to reinforce their argument.[6]

The American criticism of Japan is basically an antitrust view. Implicit in the thicket of positions and verbiage is a belief that success by Japanese corporations or industries—measured in terms of market share in U.S. or third markets—is acceptable, so long as it is truly the product of the sort of economic factors claimed by the Japanese. The problems, then, stem from the conviction that in many cases market outcomes are shaped by Japanese business practices considered unfair—predatory pricing, patent infringement, industrial espionage, and explicit or implicit protection of Japanese markets from import competition. Not all American analysts share this conviction (see chapter 2), but this is the basis on which the problem must rest: Japanese success in blocking imports into their own country or in penetrating U.S. markets comes, at least in part, from anticompetitive behavior rather than from competitive ability.

The Japanese focus on trade imbalances as the core of the problem is partially correct. American politicians and others have indeed emphasized the size of the trade imbalances, and have tied the existence of import barriers in Japan to the size of those imbalances. The unsuccessful amendment offered by Representative Richard Gephardt to the 1988 omnibus trade bill epitomizes this tendency; it mandated protectionist retaliation against countries with large trade surpluses vis-à-vis the United States deemed to stem from their barriers to American goods.[7] The Super 301 provision in the Trade Act of 1988 is commonly thought to retain this emphasis on the impact of trade barriers on bilateral imbalances, but the actual language of the law carefully avoids this, placing the emphasis on increasing U.S. exports without reference to the impact on imbalances.[8] The Japanese are perfectly justified in denying that the imbalances are the product of microeconomic trade barriers; to a large extent macroeconomic outcomes and microeconomic issues are separable. Since the mid-1980s the Japanese have been vigorously pushing the macroeconomic side of the argument because the United States is so obviously at fault. But at best this blinds the Japanese to the microeconomic problems and, more likely, represents an attempt to direct the dialogue away from an area in which they would have to admit they are at fault themselves.

This study challenges the notion that Japan's pattern of behavior on trade is normal. To do so, chapter 3 emphasizes intra-industry trade (the two-way flow—exports and imports—of similar products, such as automobiles), a form of international trade most industrial countries engage in heavily, but not Japan. Intra-industry trade flows have received relatively little attention in the debate over Japan's trade policies and practices. The prevalence of intra-industry trade is distinctively lower in the case of Japan than for other nations, and the disparity has not changed much since the beginning of the 1970s. Furthermore, intra-industry trade is especially low in those

Japanese industries that export the most—a pattern unique among the nations studied here. Japan's intra-industry trade is also especially low (and usually because exports are far greater than imports) in those industries that supply most U.S. exports to the rest of the world; that is, Japan accepts few imports from the United States in precisely those areas of U.S. worldwide competitive strength.

A distinctive pattern of trade does not necessarily imply a pernicious set of import barriers, and chapter 4 explores the reasons why Japan's pattern of intra-industry trade has been peculiar. That explanation rests primarily on the catch-up mentality caused by Japan's position as an industrial latecomer, in which the desire to produce virtually all manufactured products at home was very strong. This desire spawned institutions, policies, and behavior patterns in industry and government that have frequently sought to exclude or minimize imports. Successful industrialization by a latecomer must necessarily involve the substitution of domestic production for imports, but in Japan's case the process has been pushed too far and for too long. In fact, the Japanese argument that the share of manufactures in total imports must be low because Japan depends on imported raw materials is partially circular; Japan has such a high share of raw materials in its imports partly because it has deliberately chosen to rely on imports of those materials in their crudest forms, and has restricted imports of processed goods using those raw materials as part of the drive to produce those goods domestically. Once the institutions and policies skewing production toward domestic firms are in place, they become difficult to change. This is especially true because many of them—such as product standards, the relations among firms, the primacy of big business, and the dominance of manufacturers over distributors—are outside the realm of traditional trade barriers.

Since 1985, however, important changes have begun in Japan, and these deserve equal attention. The rapid appreciation of the yen, up 100 percent against the dollar, has brought serious changes in attitude. Government, business, and academe are beginning to articulate a new set of concepts, discussed in chapter 5, in which manufactured imports are regarded more positively. Indeed, manufactured imports are growing rapidly, a trend that promises to continue. This raises important questions. Is the protectionist past gone? Will the problems of access disappear? How far will the new trend go? Several more years must pass before the answers become clear. At present the evidence is mildly encouraging. Intra-industry trade has not risen much yet, but modest policy changes in such areas as the distribution sector, plus the rise of foreign direct investment by Japanese manufacturers and other forms of new corporate behavior, indicate that some real change is taking place.

Recently, some analysts have portrayed Japan as unchanging, either out of a lack of political leadership or a lack of broad public support for change.[9] Such views are too extreme, and this study is cautiously optimistic; the real changes taking place in Japan are far less than many Japanese government officials would have foreigners believe, but neither are they so trivial as to be dismissed. The caution in this assessment stems from the dynamics of Japanese society. Economic changes necessary to bring major structural shifts in the economy imply a redistribution of economic benefits in society—away from export manufactures or import-competing industries and toward distributors and other service industries, plus consumers. Within the context of Japanese societal norms, these shifts cannot be left to market forces alone. This is often true for economic shifts in the United States as well, but the group dynamics that are engendered in Japan when issues are moved from the economic to the political and social realms will moderate the pace and extent of change more than would be the case in the United States. Japan is not unchanging, but the need to compensate losers or opponents to maintain group cohesiveness is a powerful force that works against decisive change.

What should the United States do about Japan, given evidence of both de facto protectionism and recent improvements in market access? This question assumes a greater urgency under the Trade Act of 1988, which gives the U.S. executive branch greater latitude to act in a protectionist fashion if it so desires. Many Japanese spokesmen would have the United States drop its pressure on the ground that the recent changes imply the market is sufficiently open. At the other extreme, some Americans propose that liberal trade be abandoned as a principle, in favor of a general system of managed trade.

Those who see protectionist behavior as unchanging and unchangeable in Japan argue that pushing for more liberal trade is doomed to failure. Barriers removed through negotiation will simply be replaced with other, more subtle barriers. The social or cultural forces that yield protectionist outcomes in Japan, according to this argument, are simply too strong to be modified through outside pressure.[10] A number of proposals have emerged over the past several years suggesting that the United States should abandon the free trade ideal and simply negotiate trade outcomes with Japan, either on an overall basis (defining acceptable levels for the bilateral trade imbalance and making Japan achieve the target) or on an industry basis (defining acceptable levels by product for imbalances or for U.S. exports to Japan).[11] A recent report to the U.S. Trade Representative by an advisory group of high-level business leaders called for a microeconomic version of managed trade, labeling it a "results-oriented" bargaining strategy.[12] This concept recognizes the problems with trying to manage the entire bilateral imbalance (mainly that Japan would restrict exports rather than increase imports) and attempts to stick with the liberal goal of expanding trade and raising the market share of imports in Japan. But the report despairs of achieving this solely through removal of trade barriers and calls for targets on Japanese purchases in areas subject to negotiation.

Now is not the time to abandon free trade principles in favor of a general set of draconian measures to dictate trade outcomes. Chapter 6 argues that the current liberal trade regime embodied in the GATT is still in our national interest, and that the changes under way in Japan imply a greater chance for success in pushing for openness, although they most certainly do not mean that problems will disappear. Problems will remain complex and difficult, especially in high-technology industries, and resolving them will require realistic use of sanctions or retaliation as a bargaining tool. In some cases, managed trade or results-oriented negotiation may be unavoidable, but it should not become an ideal and should be chosen as a tactic only with great reluctance and caution. The Trade Act of 1988 certainly provides the authority for the U.S. government to retaliate or seek managed trade outcomes, an authority that could be easily abused. Pursued carefully, however, credible pressure on Japan, based on this law, to continue opening its markets should produce positive results.

Both nations will benefit from continued efforts to open Japanese markets. Japan is a strong economic power with a large trade surplus; it does not need protectionist practices. Especially because the economy continues to grow at a healthy pace, Japan can readily afford the short-term adjustment costs involved in reallocating production resources away from those areas adversely affected by imports. More imports, reflecting a higher level of intra-industry trade, need not jeopardize Japan's ability to be a major player in leading or emerging industrial sectors.

Japan will be better off economically by making these adjustments. Often the dialogue within Japan on market opening has emphasized the sacrifice or cost to domestic interests in reducing import barriers. But Japan today is an anomaly; it has an unusually large and productive manufacturing sector that continues to expand exports even at the current strong value of the yen, while the standard of living lags behind that of other industrial nations. Low productivity in agriculture and services, deficiencies in basic elements of social infrastructure, as well as tax and land-use policies that restrict housing space unnecessarily have all constrained the standard of living in Japan. This skewed pattern is not immutable and is improving slowly, but why the Japanese public has tolerated it for so long remains a puzzle.

Were Japan the only nation hurt by its protectionism and skewed economic structure, and the only one to gain from liberalization, the United States would have little reason to push Japan in a liberal direction. But benefits accrue to the United States as well. In a narrow sense, American manufacturers benefit from increased production and export of those products in which they are internationally competitive. In a broader sense, the United States benefits from the long-term considerations already mentioned; to the extent that exclusion from Japanese markets damages the long-term competitiveness of American industries, greater access increases their ability to drive down costs, attract investment funds, stay abreast of technological advances, and thereby survive international competition. If America considers these industries important to its future prosperity, then an international trade environment that reduces artificial impediments to their survival is desirable.

A more complex, and more political, factor comes into play here also. All other factors being equal, an increase in Japan's imports implies a rise in exports as well (since the balances are largely macroeconomic phenomena). In reality other factors do not remain equal, but the proposition that rising imports of manufactures will yield rising exports as well remains a valid one. Would the United States be willing to absorb more exports from Japan? A central tenet of this study is that it would; if frustration with Japan has resulted from one-sided relationships in which Japan exports, but takes few imports, then more imports by Japan should facilitate more exports to its partners. This consideration has been conspicuously absent in industry behavior and government policy in Japan. In a sense the Japanese have been their own worst enemies; formal and informal barriers have frustrated Japan's trading partners and eroded the willingness to absorb more manufactured products from Japan.

Uniqueness is a popular theme in Japan. This study finds Japan's trade patterns to be distinctive. But rather than assuming this distinctive pattern flows from some immutable, unique culture, this study calls for Japan to change, to behave more like other industrial nations, and for the United States to continue to apply pressure in this direction. Should Japan successfully change, through continuation of recent liberalizing trends, then trade tensions should lessen and trade flows expand to the benefit of all. Should Japan fail to change, as some predict, then the prognosis for trade relations must be pessimistic.

CHAPTER TWO

Peculiar Trade Patterns

ANECDOTAL EVIDENCE abounds on protectionist Japanese import policies and aggressive export behavior in the postwar period. American and other business executives believe that they have faced, and continue to face, a variety of formal and informal barriers to entry into the Japanese market, as well as predatory pricing, patent infringement, and other practices that damage their ability to compete against Japanese products in third markets and at home. If they are correct, demonstrating the peculiarity of Japanese practices ought to be a straightforward job of assembling facts. And yet the issue is not so simple, because formal import barriers in Japan—tariffs and quotas—are no longer very significant in most cases, and the existence of many informal barriers has been vehemently denied by the Japanese government. Nevertheless, one approach to the question is to catalog import barriers and estimate their probable impact on trade.

Economists have generally sought to analyze the questions through general tests: if Japan behaves in a protectionist fashion on imports and in a predatory fashion on exports, its trade patterns should differ distinctly from those of other countries. Do they? On the export side, Japan's overall behavior is quite normal; Japan does not export an unusually large share of its economic output. The distribution of exports across industries, however, shows a somewhat unusual concentration in a narrow range of products—a point explored later in this chapter. On the import side, the statistical data (reviewed later) clearly show Japan imports far fewer manufactured goods than other industrialized nations. No one disputes the trade figures. The dilemma arises in interpreting why Japan imports so much less, with some economists arguing that economic factors involved in creating comparative advantage—variations across countries in labor and capital inputs, geographic distance from markets, energy costs, and others—account for most or all of the difference. According to this argument, Japan's behavior is not peculiar, since it can be explained by these standard economic variables. But other analysts have rejected this conclusion, arguing that economic factors fail to explain fully Japanese trade behavior, and that the evidence suggests a pervasive protectionist pattern. This chapter reviews the debate and finds the latter position more convincing.

Existing studies have generally looked at the overall level of imports or asked whether the pattern of imports conforms to that predicted by comparative advantage theory. But there is another way of addressing the issue—intra-industry trade, a pattern of trade in which nations both export and import the products of the same industry. This pattern of trade, which is extensive among most industrial countries excluding Japan, is attracting increased attention from economists. A brief discussion of existing studies is included in this chapter, but because intra-industry trade is a central and complex element in understanding the peculiarity of Japan's trading patterns, the main analysis is the subject of chapter 3.

Most of the academic debate has taken place in the United States, partly because many Japanese have simply refused to acknowledge any problem in their own trade behavior and have tried to redirect the discussion. They believe that Japan's markets are as open as those of other countries, that any remaining problems are due to the failure of foreign firms to understand their market, and that the central issues are macroeconomic. The failure of most mainstream Japanese economists and government officials to acknowledge a market-access problem is both discouraging and a measure of how far they are from comprehending the nature of their own protectionism.

Cataloging Japanese Trade Barriers

Reviews of Japanese trade barriers are now widespread.[1] In brief, early in the postwar era Japan erected very stiff tariff and quota barriers. Under the authority of the 1949 Foreign Exchange and Foreign Trade Control Law, all imports required import licenses and thus were subject in principle to government control. The Ministry of International Trade and Industry (MITI) exercised enormous power through its control of the foreign exchange budget, from which import licenses were granted, the licenses in effect amounting to a quota on all imports.[2] The government decontrolled some items in the 1950s (by granting automatic licenses), but the system of direct control remained extensive. Not until Japan came under increasing pressure within the General Agreement on Tariffs and Trade and the International Monetary Fund to dismantle its stiff import barriers did any real change take place. Most quota restrictions were eliminated in the early 1960s, although in many cases liberalization of quotas on products was offset by the imposition of high tariffs on those same products. According to Japanese calculations at the time, 59 percent of all Japanese imports were subject to quotas in 1960, and liberalization reduced that figure to only 12 percent by 1963.[3]

Formal quota and tariff barriers have continued to fall since that time. By the 1980s Japan had lower average tariffs and fewer quantitative restrictions on industrial products than other industrial nations. No one denies that Japan has made impressive progress in dismantling the vast array of formal barriers that characterized the earlier postwar period, although the few instances of high tariffs or quotas that remain often happen to be on products of importance or interest to Japan's trading partners. Relatively high tariffs continued in the 1980s on whiskey, biscuits, chocolates, and plywood, while stringent quotas remained on beef, citrus fruit, and several other agricultural products. Still, even these remaining formal barriers are being negotiated away, with the quotas on beef and citrus fruit, for example, to be lifted in 1991.[4] Despite this continued formal opening of the market, however, the sense of pervasive restrictions through informal means has persisted. These are the implicit restraints that are so difficult to verify and to remove because they are so deniable.

Table 2-1 lists the principal types of informal import barriers that attracted the attention of American negotiators in the 1980s and examples of products they have affected. The list includes only those actions by government or industry that are obvious policy decisions; it omits general cultural or business behavior patterns that can restrict imports (these are considered in chapter 4). Problems related to some of the specific products in the table have been partially or fully solved, but others have not, and those included are only a selective list.

The Japanese rebut accusations of informal barriers with claims that foreigners are trying to change Japanese culture, or that many of the policies in question are domestic ones with no original intent to block imports. In some cases those arguments may be correct, but the record includes many examples in which policy decisions have been specifically aimed at limiting imports. Standards have been

TABLE 2-1. INFORMAL BARRIERS TO IMPORTS, JAPAN, 1980S

Problem	Nature	Examples of affected products
Standards	Product standards set differently from international standards and specified in a way deliberately to exclude foreign products	Metal baseball bats, formaldehyde levels in infant clothing, processed food
Testing and certification processes	Difficulty in obtaining either broad type certification or self-certification at foreign factories, necessitating expensive and time-consuming individual inspection	Automobiles, metal baseball bats, medical equipment, telecommunications equipment
Customs procedures	Delays and arbitrary actions by customs officials, sometimes in opposition to liberalization measures announced at a higher level	Automobiles
Intellectual property right protection	Inadequate protection of intellectual property rights and fears that patent approval processes for foreign technology are delayed to benefit Japanese competitors; trademark approval delays	Computer software, fiber optics, sound recordings
Government procurement practices	Manipulation of procurement by government and government-funded organizations to benefit domestic suppliers, despite a 1979 agreement in the Tokyo Round agreement to open procurement	Communications satellites, tobacco, super computers, TRON operating systems
Industry collusion	Collusive actions by industry with or without government sanction to inhibit imports through joint exercise of market power or direct control of import channels	Soda ash, chemical fertilizer (urea), integrated circuits, silicon wafers, auto parts
Administrative guidance	Informal advice from government to importers or users to inhibit imports	Textiles, gasoline
Other government regulation	Use of product regulations that inhibit the use of foreign goods (size and weight limits in road transportation, procedures under the national health insurance system, retail promotion guidelines, others)	Kidney dialysis machines, high-cube containers, cigarette advertising, processed food

SOURCES: Office of the U.S. Trade Representative, *1989 National Trade Estimate Report on Foreign Trade Barriers*, pp. 97–114; and Japan Economic Institute, *Yearbook of U.S.-Japan Economic Relations in 1981* (Washington, 1982), pp. 46–47.

shaped in cooperation with domestic industries specifically to exclude foreign products; testing agencies have been controlled by domestic manufacturers or have refused to visit foreign factories; patent approvals have been delayed deliberately to allow domestic firms
to create a competing product; government-funded agencies have
been told bluntly that purchase of foreign items would jeopardize
their funding; and trading companies have been warned to moderate
their purchases of certain foreign products. Even the medfly infestation of citrus fruit in California in the early 1980s, which provided
legitimate grounds for Japan to restrict certain imports, brought an
attempt to block fruits not subject to the infestation as well as unnecessarily expensive and time-consuming fumigation procedures.[5]

Several attempts have been made to measure the impact of trade
barriers on Japanese imports. In 1985 the U.S. Department of Commerce estimated that removal of all known barriers would have increased U.S. exports to Japan by $16.9 billion in 1982, based on the
assumption that American market shares in an open Japanese market would equal American shares in the world market. C. Fred Bergsten and William Cline reestimated the Commerce data, dropping
the assumption that market shares would necessarily be as high as
in world markets; they arrived at a figure between $5 billion and $8
billion in additional U.S. sales to Japan.[6] Even that more modest estimate represented an increase in U.S. exports to Japan of 20 to 34
percent—a substantial amount. More recently, Robert Lawrence estimated through a different methodology that Japanese imports of
manufactures from the world would increase by just over 40 percent
in the absence of import barriers.[7] The precise dollar impact of trade
barriers is not particularly important beyond the general agreement
of all these estimates that the amount is substantial.

Besides limiting the quantity of imports, barriers have biased the
structure of flows. Complete liberalization of wood product markets
in Japan would lead to much higher imports of manufactured wood
products and fewer imports of logs and wood chips. Liberalization of
beef markets may lower imports of feed grains while meat imports
rise rapidly. In general, formal and informal barriers have pushed Japan's import structure toward raw materials and crude manufactured materials and away from more sophisticated or higher value-
added products. (The impact of this biased pattern on the structure
of imports is considered in more detail in chapter 4.)

One American economist has suggested that the anecdotal evidence on Japanese trade barriers is highly selective and may represent only one tail of a normal distribution that ought to include many success stories as well.[8] Robert Christopher, in fact, has written about American success stories in Japan, and some of the problems American firms create for themselves.[9] Success stories exist, but they are rather few in number, and many of them concern specialty consumer products in niche markets.[10] No one argues that Japan is a completely closed market; it does import manufactured goods from the rest of the world, even though the levels are low. And certainly the successful firms are often pleased with their sales and profits in Japan. But the documented evidence on informal trade barriers compiled for government negotiations clearly shows they are more than a publicized fringe phenomenon, and have even adversely affected many of the companies that have been successful in Japan. In some cases, negotiations have prompted substantial liberalization, but many other barriers remain.

New data based on direct evidence of business practices by Japanese firms strongly contradict the idea that complaints about Japan come from one tail of a normal distribution. Looking at the purchases of capital equipment and industrial supplies in Japanese, American, and European manufacturing subsidiaries operating in Australia, Mordechai Kreinin finds that Japanese subsidiaries exhibit a strong preference for Japanese products.[11] He finds no analogous preference for products of their own (or any other) nationality at American subsidiaries. These disparities are visible in both the actual purchasing patterns and the criteria listed by managers of these subsidiaries for deciding which products to buy. Such evidence implies that even when stripped of a protective home government, Japanese firms still demonstrate a national buying preference that firms of other countries do not display.

A different perspective on the problems in penetrating Japanese markets comes from a comparison of unit labor costs in manufacturing. According to detailed calculations by Donald Daly, a combination of exchange-rate movements, rapid productivity growth, and low wage growth kept unit labor costs in Japanese manufacturing well below those in the United States, Canada, or European nations through the 1970s and first half of the 1980s. He finds that costs were so much lower in Japan that the limited ability of foreign products to penetrate the market is not particularly surprising.[12] Nevertheless, the rapid movement in exchange rates since 1985 has more than offset Japan's advantage in unit labor costs. Thus evidence on unit labor costs, while adding another dimension to the argument, fails to supply a complete explanation, especially in light of the other evidence on the existence of barriers and national buying preferences.

A Low Level of Manufactured Imports

Economic analysis of Japan's position begins with a very broad question: does Japan import less than it "should"? The basis of comparison must be the behavior of other nations, all of which follow some protectionist policies of their own.[13] Thus the standard is a relative one and not an absolute one: is Japan more protectionist than other countries? Adopting a comparative standard complicates the issue somewhat. For one thing, a comparative standard makes economists somewhat skeptical about the anecdotes of businessmen, since businessmen can tell of barriers in most countries—including the United States. Furthermore, with what countries ought Japan to be compared—only other industrial nations, or a broader set of countries including developing Asian countries? Any such analysis must also adjust for economic differences across countries that can affect import patterns: raw material endowment, income levels, overall economic size, and others.

The simple facts are presented in table 2-2. Japan imports substantially fewer manufactured goods than other nations, regardless of whether the measure is the ratio of manufactured imports to gross domestic product or to domestic manufacturing output. In 1987 the ratio of manufactured imports to GDP was only 2.4 percent, with the United States (7.3 percent), Italy (10.0 percent), and Spain (10.9 percent) the only other industrial nations on the list at all close to Japan. Among the developing countries listed, only India is close to Japan. The disparities are even more stark for imports as a share of domestic manufacturing output (GDP originating in the manufacturing sector), with Japan the only nation on the list below 10 percent. Japan's figures are not just lower, they are startlingly lower than those of any other country in this table.

Furthermore, many of the nations in this table have greatly expanded their imports of manufactured goods over time. As a share of GDP, manufactured imports in the United States almost tripled, from 2.5 percent to 7.3 percent, from 1970 to 1987. France, West Ger-

TABLE 2-2. IMPORTS OF MANUFACTURED GOODS, SELECTED
COUNTRIES, SELECTED YEARS, 1970–87

| Country | Manufactured imports as a percent of | | | | | | | | | | | |
| | GDP | | | | | | GDP in manufacturing | | | | | |
	1970	1973	1978	1980	1985	1987	1970	1973	1978	1980	1985	1987
Japan	2.3	2.4	1.9	3.0	2.6	2.4	6.5	6.9	6.3	10.3	8.6	8.3
United States	2.5	3.3	4.7	4.8	6.5	7.3	10.1	13.5	20.2	22.1	32.1	37.8
Other industrial nations												
Australia	11.1	9.6	11.0	11.7	12.6	13.7	45.8	43.7	57.6	61.1	73.5	80.6
Austria	17.1	18.7	20.2	21.9	22.3	22.0	50.9	61.0	72.3	78.8	82.0	83.7
Belgium	26.4	30.5	32.5	35.7	42.1	41.4	82.1	99.8	124.4	146.2	187.7	187.3
Canada	13.4	15.4	17.1	17.4	19.2	18.8	66.9	77.2	93.9	97.0	83.1	109.9
Denmark	19.3	18.9	17.0	17.1	20.4	18.3	104.4	105.8	103.2	99.3	121.8	107.6
Finland	17.0	15.9	13.9	17.1	15.2	16.6	71.4	65.9	57.7	67.8	68.5	77.6
France	7.7	8.9	9.8	11.0	12.3	12.9	28.4	33.1	37.8	45.4	55.4	59.2
Germany, West	8.9	8.9	11.1	12.6	15.0	14.4	23.1	24.5	32.7	38.5	47.0	44.7
Italy	6.0	7.2	8.1	10.1	10.0	10.0	22.3	26.0	29.0	35.0	42.0	43.1
New Zealand	16.1	15.9	16.7	16.4	20.3	18.8	n.a.	72.8	74.7	74.4	90.8	n.a
Netherlands	26.0	23.2	23.9	24.8	30.0	29.4	100.4	93.5	122.4	138.6	169.2	157.2
Norway	23.5	23.9	20.7	19.7	19.5	21.0	108.7	111.1	117.5	123.2	139.2	140.9
Spain	6.8	7.2	5.4	6.1	7.8	10.9	n.a.	n.a.	n.a.	21.7	28.7	37.5
Sweden	14.4	14.5	15.3	16.7	19.4	20.0	56.5	59.6	71.9	78.8	89.9	96.2
Switzerland	22.7	20.6	21.1	25.2	25.1	24.4	n.a.	n.a.	n.a.	n.a.	n.a.	n.a.
United Kingdom	7.9	11.3	15.1	13.6	16.4	17.0	27.4	40.3	56.9	57.7	78.0	78.0
Developing countries												
India	2.0	2.2	3.3	3.3	5.0	5.6	15.7	17.5	22.1	20.5	30.3	31.0
South Africa	17.6	11.3	15.0	22.3	19.4	16.9	81.1	51.7	74.8	109.7	95.7	79.1
South Korea	12.2	17.0	17.5	15.4	20.6	20.8	57.8	67.7	62.5	52.0	73.1	68.5
Thailand	14.4	14.2	14.6	16.8	15.9	16.2	88.3	73.1	72.7	79.1	71.6	67.0

SOURCE: World Bank, *World Tables* (Washington, 1989).
n.a. Not available.

many, Spain, and the United Kingdom also substantially increased
their imports. Even South Korea, a nation actively pursuing industrial policies to build its domestic manufacturing sector, shows a
large increase in import penetration.

Several trends in the postwar era are responsible for this greater
import penetration. Formal trade barriers around the world have
fallen, consumption patterns have converged somewhat, and transportation costs have shrunk. Countering these trends, oil prices rose
dramatically in the 1970s, and one of the rebuttals often heard concerning the low level of manufactured imports in Japan is that the
rising cost of oil (and the weakening exchange rate that accompanied

it) prevented Japan from moving in this diretion. From 1980 to 1987, however, the price of oil dropped precipitously, while the yen rose. Despite these developments, imports as a share of both total GDP and of value-added in manufacturing fell. The only other nations showing such a trend in the share of manufactured imports to value-added in manufacturing are South Africa and Thailand. Even without turning to more sophisticated economic measures, the failure of manufactured imports to penetrate Japan's economy more robustly over this long 17-year period is highly suggestive that protectionism remains. One factor alone, the very extensive reductions in formal trade barriers over the past 25 years, should have led to increased imports. The crude data, therefore, paints a picture of very peculiar import behavior, and one that needs some explanation.

The only economists disputing this general picture are Bergsten and Cline, who choose to compare Japan to other nations on the basis of the ratio of total imports to GNP, rather than manufactured imports to GNP.[14] Because Japan lacks many important raw material inputs (especially crude oil and iron ore), its total imports contain large quantities of raw materials. The Bergsten-Cline analysis implicitly assumes that because Japan must import raw materials, its imports of manufactured goods will necessarily be limited. The alternative assumption is that if Japan's imports of manufactured goods were more in line with those of other nations, its total imports relative to GNP would be larger than those of other countries. There is no persuasive economic argument why larger raw material imports should necessarily limit manufactured imports, and no other analysts have adopted the Bergsten-Cline approach. The focus should be on manufactured imports, and the role of natural resource positions can be tested as explanatory variables.

Those economists attempting to explain the simple variation in the ratio of manufactured imports to GNP or to manufacturing output generally conclude that Japan's behavior is unusual, even after adjustment is made for economic factors. These studies follow the lines first used by Hollis Chenery, positing that the level of imports (relative to total domestic output) in a nation will vary with per capita income (as an indicator of economic development) and population (as a size indicator).[15] For example, Kazuo Sato, looking at manufactured imports relative to domestic manufactured output, uses population, the ratio of net imports of raw materials to GDP in manufacturing, plus dummy variables for European Community members, non-EC European nations, and Japan. This formulation assumes that more populous nations import relatively fewer manufactured goods (because they have larger, more developed domestic manufacturing sectors), while the need to import raw materials could affect the ability to absorb manufactured imports. It also assumes that the institution of the European Community, as well as common land borders among European nations (regardless of EC membership), is a relevant factor in explaining the level of manufactured imports. His regressions show a negative coefficient for the Japan dummy variable that is significantly different from zero, implying that Japan's import level is unusually low; the other variables are insufficient to account completely for the low level of Japan's imports.[16]

Bela Balassa and Marcus Noland reach similar conclusions with slightly different equations. Explaining manufactured imports as a ratio to GNP, they use GDP per capita, population, raw material imports as a share in total imports, transportation costs, plus dummy variables for Europe and Japan as explanatory variables. They, too, conclude that Japan's low level of imports cannot be adequately explained by the economic variables. Their conclusion stands even when alternative dependent and independent variables are used in the equations.[17]

Lastly, a study by Lucia Barbone runs similar regressions, using per capita GNP (plus GNP squared), population (plus the log of population squared), as well as an estimate of transportation costs and the usual dummy variables.[18] This analyst, too, finds that the dummy variable for Japan is negative and significantly different from zero.

Hence the various specifications of the Chenery approach to explaining imports of manufactured goods overwhelmingly conclude that Japan is unusual. Whereas the distinctiveness of European countries—with import levels higher than predicted by economic factors—stems from their participation in the relatively free trade area of the European Community and from their common land borders, the distinctively low level of Japan's imports must stem from implicit protectionism.

A different approach to analyzing the low level of imports comes from Robert Lawrence, who uses a very specific set of assumptions related to intra-industry trade.[19] This model, developed by Helpman and Krugman, hypothesizes that the share of imports of a particular product relative to total domestic consumption of that product will be a function of the share of that nation's production of the product relative to total consumption of it in all other countries. A variant of this model relates import shares in an industry to that nation's exports as a share of world consumption. Testing both versions of this hypothesis, Lawrence finds that Japan remains distinctive, just as the Chenery-type models on overall manufactured imports find. The assumptions in the Lawrence approach are quite restrictive and have been challenged, but it has added another way of looking at Japan's distinctive import pattern.[20]

Defenders of Japan's normality have relied on studies of trade by industry, looking for conformity to comparative advantage theory. Put simply, this theory states that among the array of products that a nation can produce at a given time, it exports those in which it is relatively more efficient compared with other nations. Conversely, it imports those products in which it is relatively less efficient. As currently developed, the theory goes on to state that nations should have a comparative advantage in exporting products that use intensively the factor(s) of production they possess in relative abundance. This theory has great intuitive appeal; nations with abundant labor but not much capital stock export labor-intensive products, while nations with limited labor but abundant capital export capital-intensive goods. With some increase of complexity, the theory can accommodate other factors of production—especially land and technology.[21]

According to comparative advantage theory, a nation could be more efficient at producing all products than other nations and still benefit from trade—the key word is *comparative*. A nation more efficient at producing all products than other nations benefits by exporting those in which its relative lead in efficiency is the largest and importing those in which its relative lead is the least. For raw materials, on the other hand, absolute advantage may determine many world trade patterns; nations export or import these materials depending on whether or not they have a natural endowment of them. Thus Japan imports oil because it has an absolute disadvantage in oil production (it has virtually no oil reserves), but it imports labor-intensive cotton textiles because it has a comparative disadvantage in such products.

If a nation is unusually protectionist, or engages in unusually predatory policies to push exports as part of an overall strategy of industrial policy, its trade pattern should look different from those determined purely by market forces. Since static comparative advantage is the principal theory to explain the international trade result that should follow from smoothly functioning competitive markets, comparative advantage becomes the norm against which actual trade results should be measured.* Thus if protectionism or other aspects of industrial policy in Japan have distorted the allocation of resources toward certain industries and away from others, the actual pattern of exports and imports may differ from what a comparative advantage model would predict. Since the basis for developing a statistical model must be the actual data of other countries, the conclusion must be relative; all nations may depart somewhat from comparative advantage theory, so the question is whether Japan departs more than others.

The main proponent of explaining Japan's trade behavior through comparative advantage theory has been Gary Saxonhouse, who has explored this concept in a number of writings.[22] In this model, net exports (exports minus imports) in a set of 109 industries are hypothesized to be the result of capital, labor, raw material, and land endowments in each of the countries included in the sample; distance from markets is also a variable. The production relationship for each industry is assumed to be a standard Cobb-Douglas production function, in which no economies of scale exist. Using this model, Saxonhouse finds that as a highly industrialized, high-wage nation with a high capital-to-labor ratio, Japan has a preponderance of its net exports in capital-intensive industries and a preponderance of its imports in labor-intensive industries, just as one would expect from comparative advantage theory. By estimating the model across a sample of countries and over time without the Japanese data, and then comparing the actual results for Japan to the predictions of the estimated equations when applied to Japan's values for capital, labor, and the other factors, he finds only a small list of industries in which

---

*The assumptions involved in the simple theory of comparative advantage are unrealistic—perfect competition and an absence of economies of scale in production. The basis for evaluating conformity to comparative advantage—static efficiency—is also overly simplistic. The real world is dynamic rather than static. The theory has come in for criticism: see, for example, Joan Robinson, *Economic Heresies: Some Old-Fashioned Questions in Economic Theory* (Basic Books, 1971), pp. vii–viii. Relaxation of some of those strict assumptions leads to intra-industry trade, considered in chapter 3.

a dummy variable for Japan is significant. Other nations in the sample also have some industries with significant country dummy variables, so that Japan does not appear peculiar at all.

This controversial approach to analyzing Japan's trade structure has sparked a vigorous debate. The original model was criticized for its use of net exports, for a simplistic distance measure as one of the explanatory variables, and for the assumption of no economies of scale. Use of net exports is especially troubling, since this measure fails to address the question of Japan's import structure directly. Widely differing patterns of imports are compatible with net trade outcomes that conform to comparative advantage.

Saxonhouse has responded to these criticisms with a new model that measures imports of particular products (as a share of GNP) rather than net trade, and also drops distance from markets as an explanatory variable. His basic approach remains the same—estimation of equations for each of 62 industries over a cross section of nations, in which capital and labor stocks in each country, as well as educational levels, oil and coal reserves, and land area, are the explanatory variables. Japan is excluded in estimating the equations, and then predictions for Japan from the equations are compared with actual results. His conclusions for Japan remain the same; in only 8 of the 62 industries do Japan's import levels differ significantly from the prediction, and for all industries together the hypothesis that the actual import levels differ from the prediction is rejected.[23]

These new results are interesting and do address some of the criticisms of Saxonhouse's earlier work yet are unlikely to end the controversy. First, the list of products includes many raw materials, but no one argues that Japan imports too few of those goods. Second, among the manufactured products, the greatest detail is provided on chemicals, one of the few industries in which Japan's behavior is less distinctive (as will be discussed in chapter 3). Third, the countries used to estimate the equations include a number that are heavily protectionist, such as Australia, India, Indonesia, and Norway. Indeed, many of the countries are developing nations, which are likely to have protectionist policies and somewhat peculiar import patterns generated by incomplete manufacturing sectors. Conservatively estimated, at least 17 countries out of the 41 fall in this category. Finally, this research gives us a snapshot at one moment in time. As noted earlier, Japan's manufactured imports as a share of GNP have not risen over time, while those of other countries have.

If Japan's import patterns were normal in 1979, then did it have unusually high imports in earlier years?

The debate over this econometric approach will continue and will generate further studies. As interesting as the Saxonhouse approach is, it does not seem fully convincing. At the least one wonders why this disaggregated work on imports yields such different results from the models discussed earlier that analyze overall manufactured imports.

Japanese Views

Whereas Americans have attempted to test for the existence or importance of Japanese trade barriers, much of the discussion of trade issues in Japan itself has curiously avoided or denied nontariff barriers. The sense that foreign complaints must be misinformed, always a popular approach in Japan, is quite strong. Not all writing in Japan adopts this view; Japan is a large nation with a diversity of opinion. Nevertheless, the following examples represent a strong mainstream view in the 1980s.[24]

In a recent book specifically focused on bilateral trade problems, Takashi Eguchi and Manabu Matsuda, two Ministry of Finance officials, devote an entire chapter to debunking every argument that the Japanese market is not open, with extensive use of material from the Bergsten-Cline study and from Saxonhouse. These authors, who are actually at the more liberal end of the discussion in Japan, propose that Japan should do more to open its markets, but only to appease foreign opinion, not because import barriers are a problem.[25] Similarly, Ryutaro Komiya, a senior and respected academic economist specializing in international trade, comments that Americans have many "misunderstandings" about Japanese trade barriers, so that most of their complaints are invalid.[26]

When the Japanese do discuss trade problems, they tend to focus on the macroeconomic aspects of the issue or on episodes of protectionism in the United States rather than on protectionism in their own nation as the root of the problem. Koji Kobayashi, president of the NEC Corporation, when asked about bilateral problems in a recent interview, addressed his entire answer to episodes of Japanese competitive success in the United States causing a protectionist backlash, without a single word on problems of access to the Japanese market.[27] As another senior academic economist, Sadayuki

Sato, put it, "Since the principal cause of U.S.-Japan economic friction, and especially U.S.-Japan trade friction, is not a closed Japanese market, but instead the sinking base of the American economy (the loss of international competitiveness), it will be difficult to achieve any drastic solutions despite numerous bilateral negotiations."[28] Sato sees the American decline as structural, a long-term deterioration that will not be solved by the depreciation of the dollar since 1985. He fails even to mention the question of access to the Japanese market until late in his article, and then only in passing (in reference to the negotiations concerning Nippon Telegraph and Telephone Corporation procurement practices in 1979). Like Eguchi and Matsuda, he supports larger purchases from the United States only for the purpose of assuaging American feelings to prevent retaliation against Japanese exports. Hajime Karatsu, a respected but outspoken Japanese engineering and quality control expert, echoes Sato, arguing that "without fear of exaggerating, America's propensity to blame others for this slow recovery [from the oil shocks of the 1970s] can be called the real reason for its criticisms of Japan."[29]

Komiya also places his entire emphasis on macroeconomic developments, postulating that the trade imbalance leads Americans to make misguided complaints about the Japanese market. Starting from the proposition that Americans mistakenly believe Japanese trade barriers have caused the imbalance, he rightly argues that the imbalance is a macroeconomic phenomenon. The implicit but invalid conclusion is that Japanese trade barriers are not a problem.[30] Komiya is not alone in this reasoning; Reijiro Hashiyama makes the same logical connections, without ever testing the initial proposition that the bilateral problem exists mainly because Americans attribute the trade imbalance to Japanese barriers.[31]

The macroeconomic argument is convenient because it neatly transfers the blame for the problem and the responsibility for its solution from Japan to the United States. Not only is the blame transferred, but American economists largely agree with the macroeconomic analysis, so that the Japanese can find ample support from their American colleagues for their macroeconomic analysis. Indeed, Komiya says that if only the "common sense" of American economists (meaning macroeconomists) were spread to the American public, bilateral problems would diminish.[32] This shift in focus becomes, therefore, a clever and effective debating tactic for the Japanese. Not surprisingly, such analysis is widely accepted in Japan;

many nations prefer to blame their problems on others. But the entire line of reasoning rests on the fallacious assumption that Americans (and others) are at odds with Japan entirely or primarily because of the trade imbalance; if trade were more in balance, they believe, no one would complain about informal barriers.

To be sure, rising bilateral trade imbalances have certainly been one element in the criticism of Japan. Trade statistics have reinforced the argument made by Americans that Japan must alter its behavior; nations with large trade surpluses do not need to pursue protectionist policies. But the United States has had rising trade deficits with many countries in the 1980s, and Japan has faced more criticism than most of the others. The missing ingredient in these Japanese analyses is the combination of trade imbalances with the widespread perception that Japan behaves unfairly.

Eguchi and Matsuda also see the problem as centering on the trade imbalance but offer a somewhat more sophisticated version of the logical connections involved. They emphasize that the speed with which the trade imbalances widened in the 1980s imposed an exceptional adjustment burden on the United States because so many industries had to contract simultaneously in the face of increased import competition. In their view the widening trade imbalances in the 1980s did not represent a disequilibrium situation that must be corrected, but simply imposed short-run costs on the United States, costs that created disaffected groups clamoring for protection. The conclusion: rather than look at its domestic markets, Japan should do something to help other countries cope with the reallocation of resources or placate the disaffected groups in those countries.[33] Once again, the source of the problem is neatly shifted from Japan to the United States.

Professor Yutaka Kosai, a well-known economist who made his career in the Economic Planning Agency, extends this position a bit further. Claiming that the key to bilateral problems has been the shift of the United States from a free trade ideology to a fair trade (that is, protectionist) ideology, he concedes that the United States still dominates the formation and interpretation of international trade rules. Therefore, he argues, rational self-interest implies that Japan must open its markets further to placate the United States, or else Japanese exports could be jeopardized.[34]

Eguchi, Matsuda, and Kosai all belong to the camp that thinks Japan must do something, but only to appease unfair foreign pressure. Japan is the victim or scapegoat who must make sacrifices in a world where the United States remains the largest player. Nowhere does the notion appear that Japan might really have serious trade barriers itself, or that economic efficiency in Japan might be substantially improved by eliminating those trade barriers. This line of argument has a considerable history in Japan. Even when Japan had visible and stringent import barriers in the 1960s, many claimed that Japan had to liberalize, not because liberalization would directly benefit Japan, but because foreign pressure was irresistible and might harm Japan.[35]

The white papers on international trade issued by the Ministry of International Trade and Industry did discuss benefits to Japan to some extent back in the 1960s, when overt barriers were strong and steps were beginning to dismantle quotas and lower tariffs. For instance, they noted that lower import barriers would control domestic inflation, influence domestic industry in positive ways through increased international competitive pressure, and expand consumer choice.[36] But these statements played only a minor role in the official analysis of trade policy contained in these volumes. The dominant theme was the need to expand exports and limit the impact of import liberalization on domestic industry.

By the 1980s many of those who had admitted that Japan had been protectionist in the past now claimed that liberalization was largely complete, so that trade problems must be the fault of other countries, as Eguchi and Matsuda claim. The official white papers on international trade joined in this exercise. In 1982, for example, the white paper devoted a number of pages to justifying the low level of manufactured imports and emphasizing the inadequate effort of foreign firms to meet the competitive market conditions in Japan.[37]

Even when Japanese writers acknowledge that a market-access problem exists, they quickly deflect attention away from it. A recent article on American "unilateralism" spotlighted the Reagan administration's decision in the fall of 1985 to use section 301 of the U.S. trade law (which concerns retaliation for foreign unfair trade policies) to press for access to foreign markets. The article concludes that "the determination of 'fair' or 'unfair' is up to the United States, and such a high-handed negotiating style will make trade problems more political."[38] The focus thus becomes U.S. negotiating tactics rather than the substantive issue of access to the Japanese market. Whenever a market-access issue is under negotiation, the coverage of the problem in the Japanese media tends to follow these lines, largely ignoring the possibility of a substantive problem, and focusing on American strong-arm tactics.

Only occasionally do exceptions to these dominant positions appear. For example, Shigenobu Yamamoto—a professor of international trade and finance at Osaka University—takes a position quite close to the American one. After noting that the formal trade barriers in Japan are now roughly on a par with those of other industrial nations, he acknowledges that formal liberalization has nevertheless failed to lead to greater penetration of the market by foreign products—making him one of the few Japanese writers to recognize the simple facts on the ratio of manufactured imports to GDP or to manufacturing output considered earlier in this chapter. Rather than emphasizing continuing import barriers, however, he attributes the failure to natural market barriers arising because Japanese firms managed to build dominant domestic positions when import barriers were strong, making entry by foreign firms difficult.[39] His view is interesting, although the manner in which Japanese firms have built and now maintain market dominance can include practices that deserve to be called import barriers rather than competitive market forces.

As these examples of Japanese analyses of trade problems demonstrate, American and Japanese perceptions of the issue and its solutions have been far apart. Despite continuing controversy and debate among American analysts, there is now a strong case made by many that Japan imports too few manufactured goods. The dominant Japanese writings on the subject, though, generally fail to acknowledge even this dimension of the problem. To be sure, the macroeconomic aspect of bilateral relations and the protectionist pressures in the United States are legitimate targets of Japanese concern. But to ignore or deny that barriers to imports in Japan are also a legitimate and important aspect of bilateral problems does little to further a fruitful dialogue.

Export Concentration

Most of the debate on bilateral problems at the microeconomic level has concerned questions of protectionism, either in Japan or the United States. Yet there is another dimension of Japanese trade behavior at this level that deserves analysis by economists. U.S. business analysts have pointed out that the Japanese seem to target a narrow range of products in exports. In semiconductor devices, for example, Japanese firms have roughly 48 percent of world markets, but they have taken 90 percent of the market for one-megabit random-access memory devices.[40] At a broader level, textiles were the overwhelming Japanese export of the 1950s, steel of the 1960s, and automobiles of the 1970s and 1980s. The question, then, is whether Japan's export pattern appears unusual relative to other nations.

The structure of Japanese exports matters greatly, because the Japanese view of trade problems is that other nations have adopted protectionist policies in response to the success of Japan's exports. Saxonhouse, in his defense of Japan's trade structure, argues that if Japan's manufactured imports are unusually low, it may be because of the constraints on Japan's exports.[41] That is, the level of Japan's trade surplus is a result of macroeconomic factors. Any given surplus can be the result of large exports and imports, or low levels of exports and imports. If foreign trade barriers seriously constrain Japanese exports, macroeconomic conditions imply that imports will be constrained as well, according to this argument. At a broad level, Japanese analysts certainly express concern over the size of exports or their rapid growth as a cause of problems.[42] But insofar as Japanese exports per se are a problem, the answer may lie in the concentration of exports in a relatively narrow range of products compared with the export patterns of other countries.

This question has few theoretical underpinnings, although the same general hypotheses that apply to a nation's import levels might be relevant. Concentration of exports could be greater as distance increases, as the transport-related costs of entry into foreign markets reduces the range of products that can be profitably exported. On the other hand, concentration might lessen as a nation develops, reflecting the broader range of the domestic manufacturing base capable of exporting. But whether or not there are any theoretical justifications, the theme of Japan's unusually concentrated export structure is a recurring one.

If Japanese exports are unusually concentrated in a narrow range of products, such a finding would not necessarily imply that Japan resorts to "unfair" export practices, although why Japan should be different from the pattern of other nations would certainly be a puzzle. In this explanation, the overall level of exports from Japan may be normal, but the brunt of the competition falls on a small number of industries in the importing nation, with the competitive tactics and resulting large Japanese market shares stirring protest in those industries.

Export concentration can be measured in several ways. A study by the GATT in the early 1970s looked at the ratio of exports to production in different industries, finding that Japan had a higher average level of exports to production for manufacturing as a whole, but from fewer individual industries than West Germany, for which the ratio was exceptionally high. The same study also asked how many Standard International Trade Classification (SITC) three-digit or four-digit industry categories had exports exceeding an arbitrary dollar amount, finding that West Germany had a more diversified export structure according to this measure. Finally, the report calculated, for particular products, Japanese exports as a share of total exports from members of the Organization for Economic Cooperation and Development (OECD), finding nine products in which Japan generated more than a third of OECD exports. These nine products amounted to 37 percent of Japan's total exports. By contrast, only four West German products exceeded the one-third level, accounting for only 6 percent of total West German exports.[43]

Arranging exports in descending order by dollar value, table 2-3 shows how many three-digit industries are needed to account for 25 or 50 percent of each nation's total exports. Perhaps the most striking feature of this table is that all the countries included in the sample have rather concentrated export structures. However, by this measure, only two or three of these industries account for 25 percent of Japanese exports in all four years. By contrast the range is three to six industries for the other countries in the sample. If the frame of reference is expanded to the 50 percent level, the picture remains essentially the same, with Japan appearing more obviously concentrated. Whereas Japan reaches the 50 percent level with 10 or fewer industry categories, the others are generally above 10.

These data suggest that exports from Japan have tended to be more concentrated than those of other nations. Looking at the number of products needed to reach the 50 percent level shows that Japan's exports have become substantially more concentrated over time, with the number of industries falling from 10 to 6 (although a trend in the same direction can be pointed out for the United States). While the disparities among nations are not large, the fact is that Japan has

TABLE 2-3. EXPORT CONCENTRATION, FOUR INDUSTRIALIZED
COUNTRIES, SELECTED YEARS, 1970–85[a]

Country	1970	1975	1980	1985
	Number of three-digit export categories needed for 25 percent of total exports			
Japan	3	2	2	2
United States	4	3	4	3
France	6	6	5	6
West Germany	3	3	3	3
	Number of three-digit export categories needed for 50 percent of total exports			
Japan	10	7	8	6
United States	12	10	12	9
France	21	20	19	18
West Germany	13	13	14	13

SOURCE: United Nations trade data tapes.
a. Table shows the number of three-digit SITC industries (arranged in descending order by size, in dollars, of exports) needed to account for 25 percent or 50 percent of total exports of each country. The total number of three-digit industries in the exports of each country varies slightly by country and over time (from 179 to 183).

been consistently the most concentrated. During much of this period, and especially from 1980 to 1985, the yen was undervalued
(compared with what it would have been on the basis of purchasing
power parity comparisons for manufactured goods), and this tendency ought to have broadened rather than contracted the pattern of
successful exports. Thus, while the slight rise in U.S. export concentration in the 1980s makes intuitive sense (with the strong dollar
narrowing the range of export products retaining international competitiveness), the rising concentration in Japan does not.

The United Nations also provides summary statistics on export
concentration, shown in table 2-4 for a sample of 10 countries. This
calculation uses a Hirschmann index—a statistic often used to measure concentration—in which larger numbers imply greater concentration. The picture from these data, calculated using three-digit industry categories, is mixed. Nevertheless, in 1984 Japan's export
concentration was considerably higher than that of the United
States, the United Kingdom, France, Italy, and West Germany (and
higher than most of these in 1970). Canada is higher than Japan, but
this may come from its unusual position as a raw material supplier
to the United States.

Another perspective on this question is provided by figure 2-1. Because each nation has exports distributed across more than 100 sepa-

TABLE 2-4. SUMMARY STATISTICS ON EXPORT CONCENTRATION, SELECTED COUNTRIES, 1970 AND 1984[a]

Country	1970	1984
Japan	0.131	0.209
United States	0.099	0.110
United Kingdom	0.098	0.152
France	0.087	0.085
West Germany	0.133	0.136
Italy	0.113	0.100
Canada	0.184	0.225
Australia	0.191	0.180
South Korea	0.271	0.193
Hong Kong	0.342	0.310

SOURCE: UN Conference on Trade and Development, *Handbook of International Trade and Development Statistics, 1987 Supplement* (New York, 1988), pp. 237–40.

a. The concentration index numbers are a Hirschmann index normalized to the range [0,1].

$$H_j = \frac{\sqrt{\sum_i \left(\frac{x_i}{X}\right)^2} - \sqrt{\frac{1}{n}}}{1 - \sqrt{\frac{1}{n}}}$$

where j = country, x_i = exports of commodity i, X = total exports by country j, and n = number of traded products (182 in this sample).

rate three-digit categories, most of which generate far less than 1 percent of total exports, the figure includes only the top 15 exports for each country. The striking feature is that, at the three-digit level, all the sample countries have a sizable share of exports in a single industry category. Japan, however, has a much larger share of its exports in this single industry. In 1985 an astounding 24 percent of all Japanese exports were in a single category, compared with 18 percent for West Germany, 13 percent for France, and 12 percent for the United States. This single category is the same for all four countries: motor vehicles. Beyond this largest export industry, Japan does not appear distinctive.

For 1970 the picture was essentially the same, except that Japan was not quite as unusual as in 1985. In 1970 only 18 percent of Japan's exports were in the largest single category, but this still exceeded the figures for any of the other countries in the sample. Even at this earlier date, that category was motor vehicles, so the increasing concentration of Japanese exports has come as the result of the rapidly rising share of automobile exports, which has now come to occupy an extraordinarily large position in Japan's export structure.

Turning the focus to the bilateral relationship, figure 2-2 shows

FIGURE 2-1. TOP 15 EXPORTS AS SHARE OF TOTAL COUNTRY
EXPORTS, FOUR INDUSTRIALIZED COUNTRIES, 1970 AND 1985

Percent of country total, manufactured exports

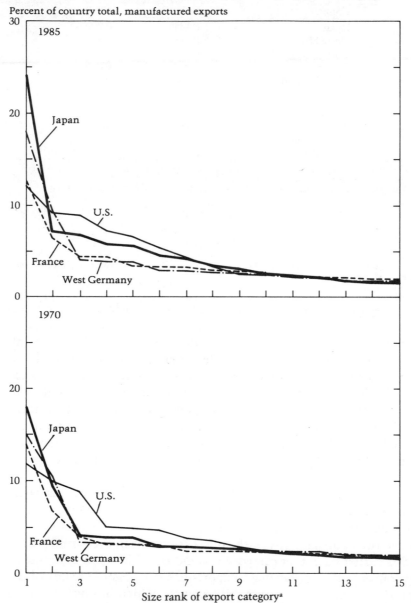

Size rank of export category[a]

SOURCE: Author's calculations based on United Nations trade data tapes.
a. Three-digit SITC categories in descending order by size (dollar value).

FIGURE 2-2. TOP 15 EXPORTS AS SHARE OF TOTAL COUNTRY
EXPORTS TO THE UNITED STATES, THREE INDUSTRIALIZED
COUNTRIES, 1970 AND 1985

Percent of country total, manufactured exports

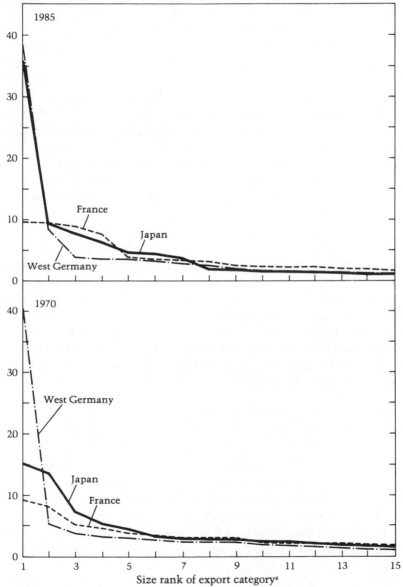

SOURCE: Author's calculations based on United Nations trade data tapes.
a. Three-digit SITC categories in descending order by size (dollar value).

the share of exports to the United States by Japan, France, and West Germany. In 1985 an astounding 36 percent of all Japanese exports to the United States consisted of motor vehicles. Far more dramatically than on a global scale, then, Japan's exports to the United States have become dominated by a single three-digit industry category. In this case, however, West Germany outranks even Japan, with 38 percent of its exports to the United States in this same category. Thus Japan is not alone in having unusually concentrated exports to the United States, although Japan's concentrated exports take place in the context of much higher overall levels of exports to the United States than is the case for West Germany.[44] France, lacking the same degree of success in exporting automobiles, has a much less concentrated export pattern, with only 10 percent in the top export industry. In 1970 also West Germany (with 40 percent of its U.S.-bound exports in motor vehicles) was the unusual country, while Japan's behavior did not stand out at all (with only a 15 percent share for its largest export category).

The notion that Japan's pattern of export concentration might be caused by distance from its principal markets (mainly the United States) is belied by the bilateral pattern. Whereas figure 2-2 shows the largest export from Japan to the United States accounts for 36 percent of total exports, a similar ranking of U.S. exports to Japan shows the largest category represents only a 13 percent share. Indeed, the concentration of U.S. exports to Japan closely mirrors the concentration pattern of U.S. exports globally. If distance from the U.S. market narrowed the range of successful Japanese exports, then why did distance from the Japanese market fail to narrow U.S. exports?

These data on export concentration do show Japan to be more concentrated than the other countries in the sample as a general conclusion, although this finding is more obvious on a global basis than in bilateral trade with the United States. All these comparisons and conclusions rest on the position of a single industry that has grown to occupy a disproportionate share of Japanese exports: motor vehicles. In this sense, the casual impression of business executives is correct, though the three-digit level of aggregation may be too broad to address the issue of heavy penetration of very narrow product categories.

The success of Japanese automobiles in the American market as well as in Canada and Europe has led to contention and de facto import quotas. However, these problems surfaced only when import penetration reached a historically high level (more than 20 percent) and were triggered in large part by the second oil shock (shifting demand toward smaller, more fuel-efficient cars) rather than by Japanese competitive tactics. Nevertheless, the higher concentration of Japanese exports may have some relevance to explaining trade disputes. Were Japan to develop a broader range of successful export industries, it might escape some of the criticism that has followed in the wake of its success in autos and a few other industries.

Conclusions

Evidence from a variety of measures identifies Japan as a nation with peculiar trading patterns. The level of manufactured imports in Japan relative to the size of the economy or to the size of domestic manufacturing output is very low; trade roughly conforms to comparative advantage expectations, but does so with limited imports; and exports are somewhat more highly concentrated in a single industrial category than is the case for other countries. Some of the difference can be passed off as the product of ordinary economic variables: capital and labor endowments, the lack of raw materials, or lack of participation in a customs union like the EC. But these variables fail to explain all the peculiarities. The one aspect of Japanese trade behavior not yet considered in any detail, intra-industry trade, is also unusually low (see chapter 3), adding another dimension to Japan's peculiarity. Virtually every approach to the question of Japan's trade behavior yields a distinctive picture: Japan simply does not import many manufactured products.

The most creative defense of Japan comes from the comparative advantage approach, in which economists have been more or less successful in demonstrating that Japan conforms to an expected pattern of behavior. However, this approach—whether using net trade or import levels directly—remains controversial, and the results hinge on assumptions or estimation procedures that can be challenged. The relative normality demonstrated through the comparative advantage approach also is entirely at odds with the considerable anecdotal evidence on trade barriers in Japan. The examples of barriers—both formal and informal—and the incidence of negotiating problems with Japan are so widespread that a conclusion of normality is difficult to sustain.

Even if the incidence of import barriers in Japan were not un-usually high, the attitude of many Japanese toward those barriers has been unhelpful, exacerbating the problems. The steadfast refusal to countenance even the possibility of access problems, and the deter-mined effort to shift attention to other issues, complicates the reso-lution of these issues and undercuts Japan's credibility abroad. To be sure, many factors influence the U.S.-Japan trading relationship. Nevertheless, because these attitudes produce defensive, drawn-out negotiations, they have certainly added to the high visibility and ten-sion that marked bilateral trade issues in the 1980s.

CHAPTER THREE

Intra-Industry Trade

INTRA-INDUSTRY TRADE—imports and exports of similar products—has been a puzzle in economics; the concept does not neatly
fit the dominant theory of why or how international trade takes
place, and yet intra-industry trade accounts for a considerable
amount of the actual trade flows in the world today. A variety of
theories have emerged over the past two decades to account for the
existence of intra-industry trade, but it is primarily the empirical
observations that concern this study. Broad international comparisons of intra-industry trade consistently show Japan to be at or near
the bottom, whereas a fairly high level of such trade characterizes
the United States and other nations (see table 3-1). This fact is a critical element in understanding why Japan has aroused so much ire
among its trading partners.

All cross-national studies of intra-industry trade identify Japan as
an outlier. Most of them, however, have not focused on Japan per se;
they either are intended to establish empirical support for some hypothesis concerning the theory or are investigating European behavior. In Japan only one major academic economist has focused extensively on intra-industry analysis, and her work generally agrees with
other studies in establishing that Japan has not engaged in much
intra-industry trade.[1] This chapter explores in greater depth the distinctive features of Japanese trade—the low level of intra-industry
trade, its failure to rise over time, the strong correlation between Japan's successful exports and extremely low intra-industry trade, and
the consistency of these patterns at a bilateral level. In a variety of
ways, Japan's behavior in intra-industry trade is startlingly different
from that of other countries.

The low level of Japan's intra-industry trade is a disturbing puzzle.
Why does Japan not conform to the patterns observed for other industrial nations? Even if the answer lies in some set of standard economic factors (which does not appear to be the case), Japan's consist-

39

TABLE 3-1. INTRA-INDUSTRY TRADE LEVELS, SELECTED COUNTRIES, 1980

Country	Intra-industry trade index number[a]	Country	Intra-industry trade index number[a]
France	82	Switzerland	61
Belgium	79	United States	60
Netherlands	78	Norway	51
United Kingdom	78	Finland	49
Canada	68	South Korea	48
Sweden	68	Japan	25
Germany	66	Australia	22
Italy	61		

SOURCE: Robert Z. Lawrence, "Imports in Japan: Closed Markets or Minds?" *Brookings Papers on Economic Activity*, 2:1987, p. 520.
a. Based on 94 industries. The intra-industry trade index is scaled here to vary between zero (no intra-industry trade) and 100 (complete intra-industry trade). The calculation of this index is specified more fully in appendix A.

ently low participation in intra-industry trade is important for understanding trade conflict.[2] Rather than accepting an international division of industry in which Japan both exports and imports capital-intensive and technology-intensive products, it tends to export but not import. This behavior imposes an adjustment burden on Japan's trading partners quite different from the pattern among other nations. American displeasure, in particular, is heightened by the fact that Japan's intra-industry trade is especially low in precisely those industries in which American firms are major world exporters, and in which other industrial nations have high levels of intra-industry trade.

Are these features contradictory to the conclusions drawn by economists who believe that Japan's trade patterns conform to comparative advantage theory? Not necessarily. A nation can conform to comparative advantage theory models and still carry on a high degree of intra-industry trade. Indeed, other industrial nations usually included in comparative advantage models transact much more intra-industry trade than does Japan.[3]

Why Intra-Industry Trade?

Comparative advantage has been the dominant theory of why and how international trade occurs since David Ricardo. Comparative advantage, however, implies that trade should be dominated by the movement of goods among nations with differing endowments of land, labor, capital, and technology. According to theory, developed (capital-intensive and technology-intensive) nations should trade with developing (labor-intensive) nations; developed nations with a comparative advantage in the same product areas should have little or no trade with one another. In the real world, though, a great deal of international trade is among these nations; about a third of total U.S. trade (exports plus imports) in 1987 was with two other industrialized nations, Canada and Japan, and another quarter was with the European Community. Similarly, about half of Japan's total trade in 1987 was with the United States, Canada, and the Community.

When economists investigated this seeming anomaly, they discovered that much of the extensive trade among developed nations consisted of two-way trade (that is, both exports and imports) of products belonging to similar industrial classifications.[4] The United States, for example, both exports and imports large quantities of office equipment—technology-intensive and capital-intensive products in which it ought to have a comparative advantage. This two-way trade in similar products was labeled intra-industry trade, and economists began searching for theories to account for its existence.

To be sure, the measurement of intra-industry trade depends on how industries are defined, since such trade disappears if each differentiated product is declared to be a separate industry. The measurement of intra-industry trade, therefore, is partially a statistical artifact that hinges on the choice of industry classification schemes, all of which are inherently arbitrary and imperfect. Yet regardless of the deficiencies or disparities among industrial classifications, enough evidence has accumulated to see that intra-industry trade is a real and significant phenomenon requiring explanations that are quite distinct from the traditional theory of comparative advantage.[5]

As noted earlier, the two concepts are not mutually exclusive; a combination of differentiated products within an industry coupled with comparative advantage and economies of scale provide the underpinning for intra-industry trade. If the products of an industry are absolutely identical and transportation costs are not a factor, comparative advantage should determine the flow of goods. As soon as these unrealistic explanations are relaxed, though, the possibility of intra-industry trade arises. Even with identical products (for example, raw materials), high transportation costs can bring about cross-border trade. The more interesting case, and one more applicable to manufactured goods, comes from the combination of product differentiation and economies of scale. Producers facing these conditions choose to specialize in mass production of particular differentiated products. If the scale of efficient production exceeds domestic demand, then this strategy is economically rational only if the industry can export. Simultaneous moves to specialize in separate differentiated goods and achieve economies of scale in production then lead to two-way trade in products similar enough to be grouped in the same industry in standard industry classification schemes.[6]

Intra-industry trade may also be related to the product cycle or to variations in factor requirements at different stages of production. Different products within an industry may be at varying stages within the product cycle—for example, black and white versus color television sets (or now high-definition television)—so that nations import one product and export the other. In other cases, inputs or intermediate goods in an industry may involve differing degrees of labor or capital intensity, so that parts are imported (exported), while the finished product is exported (imported).[7]

Hence intra-industry trade does not invalidate the theory of comparative advantage, which remains a useful tool for explaining how differing factor endowments affect international trade patterns. Intra-industry trade is best understood as an extension of the theoretical explanation of trade flows rather than a negation of comparative advantage; it explains the sizable portion of trade that does not fit neatly into comparative advantage.

Economists are still unsure if the effects of intra-industry trade are as desirable as those derived from comparative advantage. Comparative advantage has had great appeal as a theory because it has desirable welfare properties. By postulating that an international division of industry based on comparative advantage allows each nation to allocate its resources in the most efficient manner at any moment in time, social welfare is maximized.

Intra-industry trade, on the other hand, began as an empirical observation and led economists to wonder after the fact about its welfare prospects. At first analysts saw intra-industry trade as desirable in two respects. For one thing, it increases product variety, implying a wider consumer choice. And for another, it reduces the adjustment costs of opening an economy up to foreign trade because domestic industries can remain intact while moving to specialize in narrower product ranges. These positive aspects of intra-industry trade emerged from investigation of the European experience after the formation of the EC. Reduced adjustment cost, according to this view, explains the relative lack of a political backlash as trade barriers were removed within Europe during the 1950s.[8]

These propositions concerning the desirable properties of intra-industry trade have been challenged. First, the notion of differentiated products in an industry leads to economic theories of imperfect competition, which generate static equilibrium outcomes that are not optimal because firms can operate as monopolists or oligopolists in their niche in the market. Also, the notion of an optimal level of product variety suggests that intra-industry trade may lead to "too much" variety, or may lead to imports and exports of "inappropriate" products by developing nations. Adjustment costs may not be as low as proponents of the theory suggest because of the problem of defining an industry. Though remnants of an exporting industry may remain, individual firms within an industry may disappear when a nation opens up to trade and production becomes concentrated in a subset of firms achieving larger economies of scale in a narrower range of products. Furthermore, movement toward a world industrial organization in which a few firms scattered across nations dominate an industry may lead to international cartels, which in turn lead to inefficient allocation of resources.

While the objections to intra-industry trade as a desirable behavior should be noted, most of them seem quite thin. Concepts of optimal levels of product variety or appropriate trade patterns for developing countries are very ill-defined. Generalized arguments about the tendency of intra-industry trade to lead toward international cartel behavior are also nebulous. And while adjustment costs may be difficult to define or measure, the phenomenon of relatively low costs accompanying a rapid rise in trade is consistent with the actual experience of Europe in the 1950s and 1960s. On balance, intra-industry trade does appear to have desirable welfare properties, and its prevalence as a trade pattern strongly suggests that some efficient market process brings about such trade.

If intra-industry trade does enhance economic welfare, then Japan's low level of such trade implies that its behavior is inefficient or "unfair." Desirable welfare properties for intra-industry trade are not the crux of this analysis, though. Instead, two questions are paramount here: does Japan have a distinctively low level of intra-industry trade, and does this pattern of trade have a detrimental effect on the leading exports of other countries? This chapter answers both questions in the affirmative.

A political argument may also be relevant here. When intra-industry trade is extensive, firms in a domestic industry that exports heavily may hesitate to seek protection for fear of retaliation against their own exports to other countries. Japan cannot count too heavily on such a sense of interdependency. Foreign firms and industries have little to lose in pursuing protection from Japanese exports because so few of them have any sizable sales to Japan.[9] Throughout the earlier postwar period, much of Japanese external economic policy concerned the need to expand exports and ward off potential or real protectionism in other countries. Had domestic markets been more open to foreign firms, protectionist pressure directed against Japan would be far less. In this respect, Japanese policies that have limited access for imports have worked against the desire to expand exports.

Some Hypotheses about Japan

The theory of intra-industry trade yields several results that can be used to form hypotheses about Japan's behavior. The following propositions have found general support in empirical research:[10]

—Intra-industry trade increases as a nation's economy develops. For one thing, developed nations have more complete and complex manufacturing sectors, able to engage in specialized production across a wide array of industries. By contrast, developing countries tend to have incomplete manufacturing sectors, able to specialize in some industries, but essentially missing others. Korea in 1970, for example, had no exports at all in quite a few three-digit Standard International Trade Classification (SITC) industry categories, but with rapid industrialization had eliminated most of these blanks by 1985. Furthermore, industrial nations are engaged in more advanced industries, where economies of scale and possibilities for product differentiation may be more prevalent than in the more basic industries of developing countries.

—Intra-industry trade is higher between countries with similar market sizes. Such countries are more likely to have developed similar industries. Nations with large, affluent markets are also more likely to have a broader range of consumer tastes that can be met by intra-industry trade with similarly large nations. The United States, for example, should have more intra-industry trade with large, affluent Japan than with small, developing Korea.

—Intra-industry trade rises when market barriers fall. More international competition as barriers fall at home drives industries toward specialization and differentiation in order to survive. More opportunities to export as barriers fall abroad leads industries to expand in those product areas where they can export and take advantage of economies of scale. This is what economists have found in the case of Europe beginning in the 1950s.

—Different industries have characteristics that affect intra-industry trade regardless of national location. The possibilities for competition based on differentiated products is simply much greater in some industries (such as chemicals, a category that includes many inorganic and organic compounds) than in others (such as copper pipes, in which there are only a few standard diameters, thicknesses, and lengths). Thus nations may exhibit some differences in the average level of intra-industry trade because their industrial structures differ.

These general results lead to several more specific hypotheses about the level of Japan's intra-industry trade and how it should have changed over time:

—Japan's intra-industry trade should have expanded from the 1960s to the present as its economy developed, its market size and influence increased, its formal trade barriers were dismantled, and its opportunities for product differentiation in advanced industries multiplied. The low level of Japanese intra-industry trade found in the 1960s could be attributed to its status as a developing country at the time (albeit an advanced developing country). Today, however, Japan's per capita income is prodigious, its GNP is the second largest in the world, and its formal tariff and quota barriers are largely gone.

—A continuing low level of intra-industry trade could be due to a Japanese pattern that is skewed toward trade with developing countries in Asia, since these relationships are characterized by wide disparities in income level and market size. To find out if this explanation holds, one must look at Japan's bilateral level of intra-industry trade with other industrial countries rather than at its global level.

—Studies of intra-industry trade that focus on all traded goods may show skewed results for Japan because it has few raw materials and no common land borders that might induce intra-industry trade through transportation cost differentials. Thus the relevant comparison for Japan should be intra-industry trade in manufactured goods.

—Japan's level of intra-industry trade may be affected by an eccentric industrial pattern, skewed toward industries such as forest products (lumber and plywood) that exhibit less intra-industry trade in all nations. Through historical accident or peculiar conditions in factor availability, Japan's industrial structure may differ from that of the United States or European countries.

—The dispersion of IIT levels by industry may be higher in Japan than elsewhere. Rather than being clustered around the average, some industries may have very low IIT levels, while others have high ones. Japan's contentious problems with its trading partners could come from an undue focus on the subset of industries with low IIT, even though its national average level of such trade may be much higher. (Note that no economic theory applies here; there is no concept of a normal distribution of IIT levels.)

—A strong correlation may exist between low levels of intra-industry trade and Japanese exports. If Japan's exports are concentrated in products with low IIT levels, other industrial countries would feel the effect of imports from Japan in precisely those areas where they expect to export to Japan as well. Japan would be blocking their ability to use the combination of comparative advantage, product differentiation, and economies of scale to generate exports.

—The level of intra-industry trade in Japan may be correlated to foreign direct investment. Japan may have little intra-industry trade in sectors in which it has not invested in manufacturing facilities abroad, or in which foreign firms have not invested in Japan. As Japanese outward foreign direct investment rose in the 1970s and 1980s, intra-industry trade should have risen as well.

The Evidence on Japan

To test these hypotheses on Japan, the analysis here uses a standard statistical measure of intra-industry trade, the IIT index number. Details related to its calculation are contained in appendix A. This measure varies from zero (no intra-industry trade—either imports or exports equal zero) to 100 (perfect intra-industry trade—exports exactly equal imports), and the average value reported for a nation represents a weighted average of the level of intra-industry trade in each

TABLE 3-2. AVERAGE INTRA-INDUSTRY TRADE, FIVE COUNTRIES, SELECTED YEARS, 1959–85

Intra-industry trade index points[a]

	Index basis						
	Three-digit SITC categories						Four-digit SITC categories
Country	1959	1964	1970	1975	1980	1985	1985
	All traded products						
Japan	17	21	26	19	19	23	...
United States	40	40	53	57	57	54	...
France	45	60	67	65	67	74	...
West Germany	39	42	54	52	57	63	...
	Manufactured products only						
Japan	...	...	32	26	28	26	23
United States	...	...	57	62	62	61	54
France	...	...	78	78	82	82	74
West Germany	...	...	60	58	66	67	63
South Korea	...	...	19	36	40	49	44

SOURCES: Figures for 1959 and 1964 are from Herbert G. Grubel and P. J. Lloyd, *Intra-Industry Trade: The Theory and Measurement of International Trade in Differentiated Products* (John Wiley and Sons, 1975), p. 42; figures for 1970 through 1985 are author's calculations based on data from the UN trade data tapes. Industry groupings are SITC Revision 1; more recent revisions are available, but do not permit comparison back to 1970.

a. See table 3-1, note a.

industry. Intra-industry data presented here are based mostly on three-digit SITC categories, with some use of four-digit data. For comparison over time, the years 1970, 1975, 1980, and 1985 are used. Rather than providing a broad comparison across many nations, the analysis concentrates on the United States, France, West Germany, and South Korea as a representative comparative framework of developed and developing countries.

Basic data on these countries are summarized in table 3-2. Looking at all traded products, one sees Japan's average level of intra-industry trade has been far below that of other countries. In 1985 Japan's average IIT index number was only 23, less than half that of the United States and even further below those of France and West Germany. Not only was Japan's lower, but its level of intra-industry trade failed to rise significantly over time. The level in 1985 was virtually unchanged from that reported by others for Japan as far back as 1964, and not much higher than in 1959. The United States, France, and West Germany, in contrast, all engage in much more intra-industry trade today than they did a quarter century ago. The minor movement over time for Japan pales in comparison to the enormous gap between it and other nations.

If the comparison is shifted from all products to manufactured goods only, the disparity remains. Japan's intra-industry trade has been virtually constant since the mid-1970s at a level that is actually lower than in 1970. As of 1985 Japan's IIT index number of 26 was only 43 percent the level of the United States. In all other countries in the sample, intra-industry trade levels were higher in 1985 than 1970; only in Japan had it fallen.

Using the more disaggregated four-digit industry classifications does not change the results much; Japan's level was still only 42 percent that of the United States in 1985. Even South Korea, a relatively small developing country that theoretically should exhibit low levels of intra-industry trade, carried on twice as much as Japan in 1985, and demonstrated an enormous sustained increase over time, also in strong contrast to Japan. This pattern over time for South Korea conforms to what economists expect for rapidly industrializing countries, and is all the more interesting because South Korea lacks oil and other natural resources, the scarcity of which has been used as an excuse in Japan for the low level of intra-industry trade.

The comparison with South Korea at the four-digit level is especially revealing, because at this level of disaggregation parts and finished products are generally separate categories. For a developing nation such as South Korea, one of the causes of intra-industry trade might be a pattern of importing intermediate inputs and exporting finished products. However, if one considers motor vehicles (SITC category 732) at the four-digit level, passenger motor vehicles other than buses or special vehicles (732.1) are separate from bodies, chassis, frames, and other parts of motor vehicles (732.8).[11] But the four-digit data for South Korea imply that a parts–finished product pattern fails to explain why its intra-industry trade should be higher than Japan's. In some respects the industrial development of South Korea has resembled that of Japan: an industrial policy encouraging the growth of heavy industries such as steel and shipbuilding, a lack of natural resources requiring a trade surplus in manufactured goods, long distances to major export markets (the United States), and stiff import barriers to encourage domestic industries. If that is the case, Korean intra-industry trade performance ought to resemble that of Japan in the 1960s, but it does not at all.

These data also support this study's choice to avoid any adjustment for overall trade imbalances (detailed in appendix A). The average index numbers for manufactured goods for most developed nations have remained remarkably steady over time, or have even risen (in the cases of France and West Germany). Even studies that do make adjustment for trade imbalances reach the conclusion that Japan's intra-industry trade has been consistently far below that of other countries.[12] Furthermore, if Japan's rising overall trade surplus should have made a difference in 1985, then the rising deficit of the United States should also have made a difference, especially since the absolute deviation of the United States from balanced trade has been larger than Japan's (see appendix table A-2).

If the comparison is shifted from global levels of intra-industry trade to bilateral trade, Japan still scores quite low for flows in manufactured products (see table 3-3). The United States in 1985, for example, carried on three times as much intra-industry trade with France (showing an IIT index number of 53) and twice as much with West Germany (36) than it did with Japan (19). Even U.S. trade with South Korea, a developing country with much lower income and a smaller market, generated a higher IIT index number (26) than did trade with Japan. Similarly, France's bilateral intra-industry trade with West Germany (74) and the United States (52) are much higher than with Japan (25). Only West Germany shows rough parity in the level of its trade with the United States (41) and Japan (39). Despite this exception, the general conclusion remains that Japan transacts distinctly less intra-industry trade with its partners than they do with one another.

The disparity has widened over time. In 1970, in fact, Japan's bilateral trade the United States, France, and West Germany did not appear to be unusual. Since then the degree of intra-industry trade on a bilateral basis with Japan has consistently fallen for all three of these trading partners. The IIT index number for U.S.-Japan trade dropped steadily, from 31 to 19, while that for France-Japan dipped from 44 to 25, and that for West Germany–Japan also fell, though somewhat less, from 43 to 39.

These bilateral trends contradict all expectations. As Japan reached industrial maturity in the 1970s, and as its tariff and quota trade barriers fell, intra-industry trade with other industrial countries should have expanded, not contracted. One could blame the recent fall in U.S.-Japan intra-industry trade on the increase in the overall bilateral trade imbalance in the 1980s, but a similar deterio-

TABLE 3-3. BILATERAL INTRA-INDUSTRY TRADE IN MANUFACTURED
PRODUCTS, FOUR INDUSTRIALIZED COUNTRIES, SELECTED YEARS,
1970–85

Intra-industry trade index points[a]

Year and reporting country	Bilateral trade partner				
	United States	France	West Germany	Japan	South Korea
1985					
United States	...	53	36	19	26
France	52	...	74	25	11
West Germany	41	74	...	39	23
Japan	25	31	40	...	33
1980					
United States	...	54	43	26	19
France	43	...	76	28	12
West Germany	46	78	...	39	14
Japan	31	31	40	...	36
1975					
United States	...	47	46	31	21
France	44	...	73	30	6
West Germany	48	74	...	45	16
Japan	34	37	50	...	31
1970					
United States	...	39	42	31	15
France	35	...	70	44	0
West Germany	42	70	...	43	5
Japan	31	41	49	...	18

SOURCE: Author's calculations based on UN trade data tapes. Because of differences in data collection among countries, as well as the difference between the value of f.o.b. exports and c.i.f. imports, the numbers in the upper-right half of the table differ by minor amounts from those in the lower-left half in most cases.

a. See table 3-1, note a.

ration in balances accompanied trade with other U.S. partners without much negative impact on intra-industry trade.*

For the United States, some of the deterioration in the level of bilateral intra-industry trade with Japan may be caused by the worsening American trade deficit. The data in appendix table A-2 indicate that bilateral imbalances with all the countries included here intensified between 1980 and 1985, and the IIT index numbers for trade with Germany fell somewhat as well. However, the deteriora-

*The possible impact of overall trade imbalances on the level of intra-industry trade is explored in appendix A. The calculations of intra-industry trade used here do not include statistical adjustments to compensate for these possible effects.

FIGURE 3-1. DISTRIBUTION OF MANUFACTURED EXPORTS ACROSS
IIT INDEX INTERVALS, FIVE COUNTRIES, 1985

Percent of exports in each IIT interval

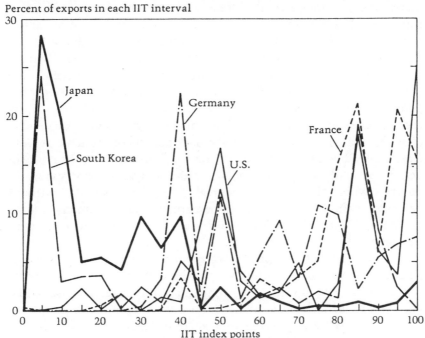

IIT index points

SOURCE: Author's calculations based on United Nations trade data tapes.

tion of the bilateral trade imbalance with Germany was much larger
than the deterioration with Japan, yet the relative drop in the IIT
index was considerably larger in the case of Japan.[13] Furthermore,
U.S. trade with France also became more unbalanced, while the IIT
index remained stable. Thus rising trade imbalances caused by macroeconomic factors fail to explain fully the drop in U.S.-Japan intra-
industry trade over time.

Japan is also strikingly different from other countries when exports are correlated with intra-industry trade. Figure 3-1 presents
this relationship graphically for five nations. The horizontal axis di-
vides the intra-industry trade index into 20 intervals, ranging from
low to high intra-industry trade. The vertical axis shows the share of
the dollar value of total manufactured exports that falls in each of
these intervals based on three-digit industry categories. Although

one might expect that the result would be a normal distribution centered on the mean for each country, figure 3-1 shows that the actual distribution is much more diffuse and uneven. Even so, Japan is astoundingly different from other industrial countries. An extraordinarily high share of its exports—53 percent—are at the low end of the intra-industry scale (the 0–15 intervals). The three Western countries have very few of their exports in this low range; the United States has only 3 percent, France 0.4 percent, and West Germany 0.2 percent. South Korea is closer to the Japanese pattern (with 31 percent of its exports in this range), but its concentration at this end is offset by a large share of exports at the upper end of the scale as well. Conversely, few of Japan's exports are in industries with heavy two-way flows. Only 5.3 percent of the value of Japan's exports is in industries where the IIT index is greater than 75, compared with 56 percent for the United States, 32 percent for West Germany, and 78 percent for France. Even South Korea has 31 percent of its exports in this range.

What do these data imply? Clearly Japan's intra-industry trade is singularly low. What's more, though, the distribution of its exports is heavily skewed toward the bottom end of the scale. In those industries where Japan has the highest share of its exports, it has (or allows) virtually no imports. This feature of Japanese trade is far beyond what one would expect from the simple comparison of the average intra-industry trade level.

Making the same cross-national comparisons for 1970 yields patterns that are basically similar to 1985. Japan's performance actually deteriorated over time; the share of exports in the IIT 36–40 interval rose between 1970 and 1985, but this jump did not come as a result of rising IIT levels for exports that had been in lower IIT ranges in 1970. It came, rather, from a falling share of exports with higher IIT levels. Rather than moving in a liberal direction as overt trade barriers fell, Japan moved in an illiberal direction.

Could these patterns reflect the exceptional influence of one industry, automobiles? Chapter 2 noted that much of the unusual concentration of Japan's exports is accounted for by motor vehicles (SITC 732). Perhaps differences in national consumer taste, road width, or other factors have led to lopsided Japanese exports. Figure 3-2 shows the pattern of exports in 1985 across IIT intervals when motor vehicles are removed from the trade figures for all four indus-

FIGURE 3-2. DISTRIBUTION OF MANUFACTURED EXPORTS
EXCLUDING MOTOR VEHICLES ACROSS IIT INDEX INTERVALS, FOUR
INDUSTRIALIZED COUNTRIES, 1985

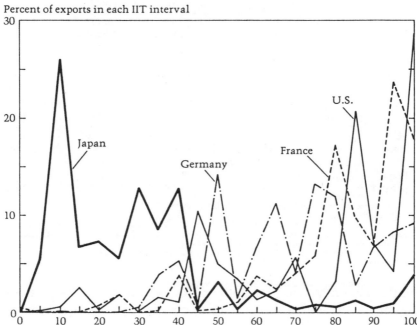

Percent of exports in each IIT interval

SOURCE: Author's calculations based on UN trade data tapes.

trial nations. The differences are slight; Japan still stands out from
the others. Hence motor vehicles are not the source of the Japanese
disparities.

The correlation of exports with intra-industry levels can be extended to a bilateral level. In this case, some similarity exists between Japan and West Germany, with a heavy concentration of their
exports to the United States at the lower end of the intra-industry
scale (because of the large share of their exports in a very unbalanced
trade in motor vehicles). But the reverse perspective, U.S. exports to
other countries, shows something quite different. American exports
to these countries do not cluster in low IIT ranges. Thus trading behavior is strongly asymmetrical; while Japan enjoys (or enforces)

TABLE 3-4. BILATERAL INTRA-INDUSTRY TRADE BETWEEN THE
UNITED STATES AND FOUR COUNTRIES, 1970 AND 1985
Intra-industry trade index points[a]

| Year and country | Total trade share | Average IIT level weighted by[b] | | Ratio A/B |
		Export share (A)	Import share (B)	
1985				
Japan	19	40	16	2.50
West Germany	36	52	30	1.73
France	51	64	47	1.36
South Korea	26	46	19	2.42
1970				
Japan	31	54	23	2.35
West Germany	43	53	37	1.43
France	39	38	41	0.90
South Korea	15	22	11	2.00

SOURCE: Author's calculations based on UN trade data tapes.
  a. See table 3-1, note a.
  b. Average intra-industry trade levels calculated with three separate weights for individual industries: the share of each industry in total manufactured trade (that is, the normal calculation of average intra-industry trade); the share of each industry in total manufactured exports; and the share of each industry in total manufactured imports. Exports are U.S. exports to the other country and imports are U.S. imports from the other country.

limited import competition for its major exports, its trading partners do not benefit from a similar lack of competition for their own exports to Japan.

At the bilateral level, the correlation between exports (or imports) and IIT levels does not lend itself as easily to the visual format used above, and the basic results are summarized in table 3-4. If the level of intra-industry trade in each industry were the same, then creating an average across all industries would be unaffected by the weights used; weighting industries by their share in exports or imports would yield the same average as the standard weighting procedure (which uses shares in exports plus imports). Because IIT levels do vary across industries, these different weighting schemes will yield different averages across all industries. In all cases, the separate weightings by exports and imports give quite different results, but for trade with Japan, the disparity is startling. For example, in 1985 the average intra-industry trade index number weighted by U.S. exports to Japan was 40, whereas the average level for U.S. imports from Japan was only 16.

In brief, the analysis shows that the United States accepts considerable imports from Japan in the same industries in which the United States exports to Japan (yielding a weighted average IIT index number of 40), but is able to export little to Japan in those industries in which Japan has heavy exports to the United States (yielding a weighted IIT index number of 16). While there is also a disparity between results from using export or import weights for U.S. trade with France and West Germany, the differences in both 1970 and 1985 were much larger for trade with Japan than for trade with other countries (shown in the final column of the table). The big distinction comes in the weighting by imports. In both 1970 and 1985, U.S. imports from West Germany and France were in industries with sizable levels of bilateral intra-industry trade (that is, in which the United States was also able to export similar products to these countries).

U.S. trade with Japan in both years most closely resembles that with South Korea, with much lower IIT index numbers generated by import share weighting than by export share weighting. However, even with South Korea the ratio of the IIT numbers generated by the two weighting procedures (2.00 in 1970 and 2.42 in 1985) are not as extreme as in the case of Japan. The implication of this comparison is that Japan is similar in its behavior to South Korea—a small, rather protectionist nation pursuing vigorous industrial policies to develop domestic manufacturing industries (much like Japan 30 years ago).

Another way of exploring the export-IIT correlation is to focus on the 10 largest U.S. export industries based on global rather than bilateral exports. As noted in chapter 2, these industries account for a large share of total U.S. exports (62 percent), and thus heavily influence the average intra-industry trade level.[14] For each of these industries, table 3-5 shows the U.S., Japanese, West German, and French IIT index numbers and arrays the differences. Most of the top 10 U.S. export industries happen to be ones in which Japan has very low levels of intra-industry trade, shown by the fact that the unweighted average difference between the U.S. and Japanese level of intraindustry trade in these industries is 56 index points. By contrast the average difference between the United States and West Germany (8 points) or France (7 points) is quite small. Furthermore, the only listed industry in which Japan has a higher level of intra-industry trade than does the United States is organic chemicals. In compari-

TABLE 3-5. INTRA-INDUSTRY TRADE IN TOP 10 U.S. EXPORT
CATEGORIES (MANUFACTURED GOODS), FOUR INDUSTRIALIZED
COUNTRIES, 1985

| | U.S. export category[a] | | | | | | Intra-industry trade index values | | | | |
| | | | | | | | | | Differences | | |
SITC	Description	Exports (millions of dollars)	U.S.	Japan	West Ger.	France	U.S.– Japan	U.S.– West Ger.	U.S.– France
732	Motor vehicles	19,274	49.5	3.7[b]	39.9	83.2	45.8	9.6	−33.7
714	Office machines	14,532	84.4	33.1[b]	94.2	79.1	51.3	−9.8	5.3
734	Aircraft	14,161	40.5	16.7	96.1	38.0	23.9	−55.6	2.5
729	Electrical machinery	11,441	98.9	38.6[b]	87.1	96.6	60.3	11.8	2.3
719	Machinery parts	10,521	98.6	26.8[b]	48.2	94.1	71.8	50.4	4.5
711	Power generating equipment	8,573	96.7	4.8[b]	64.1	99.3	91.9	32.6	−2.6
718	Special machinery	5,281	81.9	18.8[b]	38.2	80.9	63.1	43.7	1.0
512	Organic chemicals	5,189	94.2	97.9[b]	76.4	91.0	−3.7	17.8	3.2
724	Telecom equipment	3,913	47.1	6.9[b]	78.8	79.2	40.2	−31.7	−32.1
861	Instruments	3,640	81.3	23.3[b]	75.1	90.2	58.0	6.2	−8.9
Addenda									
Unweighted average		. . .	85.9	30.1	77.6	92.4	55.8	8.3	−6.5
Weighted average[c]		. . .	74.1	23.5	69.7	80.6	50.6	4.4	−6.4

SOURCE: Author's calculations based on UN data.
   a. SITC 931, "special transactions not classified according as to kind" (7th largest U.S. export) is excluded because it is not a recognizable industry and West Germany has no trade in this category.
   b. In these industries, Japanese exports are greater than imports.
   c. The weighted average is calculated using the shares of each industry category in the United States of these 10 categories.

son, while both France and West Germany have some industries in which the U.S. level of intra-industry trade is much higher than their own, the reverse is also true in a number of industries.

Not only are Japan's IIT index numbers lower, but in all but one case the low numbers reflect a large excess of exports over imports (rather than the reverse). The only exception is aircraft, Japan's entry into which has been relatively unsuccessful. These data confirm the finding that the United States has its export strength in product areas in which Japan does not have, or does not allow, significant imports. The most striking of these industries, though certainly not the only one, is road motor vehicles, the largest single U.S. export, where Japan's level of intra-industry trade was only 3.65 in 1985, so low that it might as well be zero. Whether by design or accident, the United States faces a serious problem in exporting to Japan.

Could Japan's distinctive lack of intra-industry trade reflect an ex-

TABLE 3-6. FOREIGN DIRECT INVESTMENT IN MANUFACTURING, UNITED STATES AND JAPAN, SELECTED YEARS, 1970–85

Year	United States		Japan	
	Outward	Inward	Outward	Inward
	Billions of dollars			
1970	32.2	6.1	0.9	...
1975	56.0	11.4	5.0	1.2
1980	89.1	33.0	12.6	2.3
1985	95.6	59.6	24.4	4.6
	Percentage of domestic manufacturing capital stock			
1970	10.0	1.9	0.1	...
1975	10.6	2.2	3.1	0.7
1980	8.0	3.0	2.4	0.4
1985	6.4	4.0	3.1	0.6

SOURCES: U.S. Department of Commerce, *Statistical Abstract of the United States, 1972*, pp. 767–68, *1976*, p. 828, *1981*, pp. 834–36, and *1988*, p. 759; and Ministry of Finance, *Kokusai Kin'yūkyoku Nenpō* [Almanac of International Finance], *1971*, pp. 316–17, *1977*, pp. 312–13, *1981*, pp. 356–57, 364, *1987*, pp. 380, 456–57, 464.

ceptional industrial structure? Does Japan, for example, draw a higher share of its exports from sectors that have low intra-industry trade levels in all countries? The earlier discussion suggests that this is not the case, but the analysis can be generalized. Formally, the question is whether the IIT levels by industry in Japan are from the same distribution as they are in the United States. A standard statistical calculation shows that there is wide disparity between the U.S. distribution and the Japanese one, and it is far wider than in the U.S.-French or the U.S.–West German cases.[15] Hence one cannot attribute Japan's very low intra-industry flows to a trade structure that is concentrated in products with low two-way trade in other countries as well; Japan is truly anomalous compared with the others. Only rarely does this distinctive behavior work to the advantage of countries exporting to Japan (as in the case of aircraft).

The final possible explanation for Japan's low intra-industry trade is a relative lack of foreign direct investment (FDI). Unfortunately, foreign investment data are unavailable at the same level of detail as trade data. Overall, however, table 3-6 gives some indication of the rather low level of Japanese foreign direct investment relative to the United States. In 1970 Japan's stock of cumulative foreign direct investment in manufacturing was less than $1 billion, compared with $32 billion for the United States. These amounts represented less than 1 percent of manufacturing assets in Japan, but 10 percent for the United States. A similar disparity marks inward investment, although the amounts of inward investment in both countries were much smaller than outward investment. By 1985 the picture had changed substantially. U.S. outward foreign direct investment continued to be much higher than that of Japan in dollar terms, but not by as wide a margin ($96 billion compared with $24 billion), and as a share of domestic manufacturing assets, the disparity was only two to one. A major distinction remained on inward direct investment, which rose rapidly in the United States but not in Japan (in either value or percentage terms). These data suggest that the rapid expansion of Japanese FDI over 1970–85 ought to have been a positive influence on intra-industry trade. To put it another way, if low levels of outward FDI depressed intra-industry trade in the 1970s, they had expanded enough by 1985 to be discounted as an explanatory factor. As will be discussed in chapter 5, however, the primary motivation of Japanese overseas investment until the mid-1980s was to produce for local markets or third markets, not for export back to Japan.

The one identifiable area in which direct investment may have had a positive impact in the past has been chemicals (SITC 5). Japan has carried on relatively high levels of intra-industry trade in the three-digit categories that make up the chemical industry. For Japanese direct investment abroad, chemicals were 17 percent of cumulative investment through 1985, making this sector the second-largest category in Japanese data on FDI by industry.[16]

Chemicals are also the largest single category of inward direct investment identified in Japanese data, representing 33 percent of cumulative direct investment in manufacturing by foreigners in Japan. Crude calculation indicates that foreign-owned capital in the chemical industry amounted to 3.4 percent of total industry capital as of the year ended in March 1985, and other data indicate that almost 6 percent of total chemical sales in Japan are by foreign-owned firms.[17] The sales figure is far above the 1.4 percent share for foreign-owned firms in all industries. Thus the disproportionately high levels of inward and outward investment in this industry may be a reason for the unusually high levels of intra-industry trade.

The connection between direct investment and intra-industry trade should not be pushed too far. The question remains why a rapidly rising level of inward and outward direct investment has failed to bring about an increase in Japan's intra-industry trade. There may be some relationship between direct investment and the prevalence of intra-industry trade, but the relationship varies across industries and in some cases may be relatively unconnected. Chemicals may even be something of an aberration; the level of intra-industry trade is fairly high, but neither imports nor exports are large, so the industry's significance is limited.

Conclusions

Japan is a striking anomaly. In every comparison presented here, it emerges as distinctly different from other countries. From all these perspectives, Japan engages in little intra-industry trade, and its behavior does not conform to expectations. Consider the hypotheses concerning Japan proposed earlier in the chapter:

Economic development. In the 1960s Japan was still a developing country, well along in the development process to be sure, but with per capita income levels far below those of the United States. This situation may explain a low level of intra-industry trade in the 1960s, or as late as 1970, but Japan's rapid industrialization brought it into the ranks of the advanced industrial nations by the mid- to late 1970s. In other advanced economies, development has led to a substantial increase in intra-industry trade. But Japan's level of intra-industry trade has failed to rise over time. Contrary to expectation, it has actually declined somewhat since 1970.

Trade with developing countries. The bilateral comparisons that showed Japan's intra-industry trade with other developed countries to be unusually low eliminate the possibility that Japan's global behavior is a product of high levels of trade with developing Asian countries. The bilateral comparisons are essentially as distinctive as the global comparisons, and they also move in the wrong direction over time.

A lack of raw materials. When measured over manufactured products, rather than all traded goods, Japan's intra-industry trade index number is somewhat higher. But it is still far below the level of other countries, and all the distinctive features of Japan explored in this chapter are based on manufactured goods.

A different industrial pattern. The test of whether Japan's pattern of specialization happens to emphasize sectors with low levels of intra-industry trade in all countries resoundingly rejected this hypothesis as an explanation of Japan's behavior. Industry by industry,

Japan's level of such trade is distinctly lower, and this characteristic rarely works to the benefit of those exporting to Japan because in most cases the low levels of intra-industry trade are the result of large exports and small imports.

A greater dispersion of behavior. Rather than having some industries characterized by low intra-industry trade offset by others with high levels, Japan's trade is more concentrated than that of other countries. Japan's exports are unusually concentrated in industries with exceptionally low intra-industry trade levels. When Japan chooses to engage in major exports of a product, it imports very little. Since these are often the same products that other major industrial nations export, Japan's behavior is detrimental to their preferred trade patterns. The manufactured goods Japan does import do not enjoy a similar lack of competition.

Direct investment. The relative lack of inward or outward foreign direct investment in the past may explain why intra-industry trade has been so low, but the picture is far from conclusive, since rising direct investment produced no discernible rise in the IIT index from 1970 through 1985. By that date Japan's cumulative investment position no longer appeared unusually low.

Any way the question is posed, Japan turns out to be extraordinarily different. Its pattern of behavior is seriously at odds with all the expectations generated by intra-industry trade theory. These differences are not just of academic interest; they are a critical component of current trade issues with Japan. Its behavior has been distinctive in a way that is prejudicial to the economic interests of its trading partners, and in a way that does not characterize the interaction among other industrial nations. The industrial world may have avoided some of the adjustment cost associated with expanding or shifting trade that is implied by comparative advantage theory through a move to specialization in differentiated products with economies of scale. The very fact that intra-industry trade has become a normative pattern of behavior for other countries means that Japan's failure to conform imposes adjustment costs on the industries of other countries that they do not expect to bear. Put quite simply, Japan has acted as if trade should be governed by a broad concept of comparative advantage rather than by intra-industry trade. Why it has done so is the subject of the next chapter.

CHAPTER FOUR

Japan the Outsider

WHY HAS JAPAN FAILED to participate in the extensive two-way flows of manufactured goods that characterize the trade of most other industrial nations? The patterns analyzed in chapter 3 are quite extraordinary, have changed little in the past 15 to 20 years, and are a key element in the trade disputes that have become increasingly frequent and tense. The answer involves a complex set of attitudes, institutions, and policies in Japan that have created a bias against manufactured imports—a bias that many Japanese do not understand or refuse to admit. Many of the elements of this bias are economically rational, but they are also consistent with a deep-seated Japanese view of itself as a unique culture, difficult or impossible for other cultures to understand. While the sense of superiority inherent in these beliefs undoubtedly characterizes many cultures, Japan has mobilized such beliefs to fuel its economic development process with greater success than most others.

This chapter looks at the interaction of economics, institutions, and social behavior that has produced Japan's distinctive international trade pattern. Though the explanation involves nothing sinister, nevertheless the outcome has been a trade pattern that inhibits imports and produces tension with Japan's trading partners. With the world becoming more and more interdependent, and with Japan becoming a world economic superpower, tolerance for its unorthodox trade practices appears to be more limited than in the past. Japan's behavior may have rational explanations, but other nations are increasingly unhappy with the adjustment costs associated with trading with Japan. Economic theory posits mutual benefits from international trade, but there seems to be an unequal distribution of those benefits in Japan's international trade relations. Only in the past two or three years have these patterns begun to change in a more open direction, changes discussed in the following chapter.

A Small Island Nation

Japan's present-day trade patterns are best understood by looking briefly at the history of its industrialization. The attitudes and perceptions of Japanese business and government leaders during the past century have had a profound impact on institutions and behavior patterns affecting international trade.

Japan began its modern era in the mid-19th century as the result of conscious decisions taken by a revolutionary, newly centralized government determined to make the nation strong enough to ward off the threat of domination posed by the Western imperialist powers. The image of Admiral Perry and his black ships, as well as the subsequent unequal trade treaties (limiting Japan's import tariffs and creating exclusive foreign communities with extraterritoriality in certain port cities), were powerful symbols to these leaders of Japan's weakness and peril in an era of imperialist expansionism.[1] The nation that they forged was by no means forced into industrialization, but the government certainly played a far different and more conscious role in fostering development than was the case in the United States.[2]

During the remaining years of the 19th century, the new government established a legal and regulatory framework conducive to capitalism: a commercial law, a banking law, compulsory education, and other measures that had not previously existed. With a new freedom to engage in business, and a new access to both the products and knowledge of the West, the private sector responded vigorously. The history of economic development in Japan reads very much like that of the United States and other capitalist nations, with risk-taking entrepreneurs investing in untried technologies or products, sometimes failing, sometimes succeeding spectacularly.

The sense of humiliating weakness in the face of Western competition pervaded the private sector as well as the government. The very concept of industrialization in latecomers necessarily implies a progressive substitution of domestic production for manufactured imports as development proceeds, and in Japan there was a strong sense of victory and pride whenever that substitution was achieved. From naval battleships and railroad locomotives to electric light bulbs and cotton textiles, the government and the private sector were unwilling to be daunted by the lead of foreign nations and forged ahead to produce domestically.[3]

This "catch-up" mentality reached its zenith in the first two decades following the Second World War. Devastated by war, and largely isolated from technological developments in the West since the late 1930s, Japan's eagerness to invest in new products and production processes was very strong. The power of the government to encourage domestic growth and change was also at a zenith. In the very early postwar years, government financial institutions were key lenders to assist the recovery of basic industries such as steel and electric power. Control over the allocation of foreign exchange allowed the government to decide who would have access to foreign products and technologies and who would not. The government also created stiff import barriers involving extensive quotas and high tariffs, behind which Japanese firms could make their advances without facing overwhelming competition from abroad. Barriers on inward investment by foreign firms further protected domestic firms from competition or takeover.[4]

Because of the overriding importance attached to industrialization, and the justification given to import barriers as a legitimate part of that strategy, Japan failed to embrace the concept of liberal trade that emerged in the early postwar period and was embodied in the General Agreement on Tariffs and Trade (GATT). The Western industrial nations accepted more open trade as a valid economic policy goal and endorsed a gradual pragmatic movement in that direction. For the preceding century many of these countries, including the United States, had aggressively used import barriers to foster the development of domestic industries, as Japan was doing in the postwar period. While the GATT has not brought a utopia of free trade, it has provided a basic framework for the general reduction of trade barriers that has facilitated the rapid expansion of world trade over the past 30 years.[5]

Japan stood aloof from the intellectual and policy shifts that produced this framework. With its latecomer's determination to catch up, amplified by the destruction of the war, Japan had little interest in the notion of free trade, and the main intellectual thrust was toward justifying protectionism. Japan joined the GATT in 1955 but maintained a reservation to article 12, which allowed it to continue its extensive system of quota controls on imports. As one authoritative American observer of Japanese trade put it in the early 1960s: "The total effect of habit, personal economy, conservation of foreign exchange, and protective measures in Japan has been that even in recent years little has come in from abroad that could be produced in Japan, whether manufactures, minerals, or farm products. Japanese policy has sought to reduce import dependence to the practical minimum."[6] The desire to limit foreign dependence finally reached fruition.

When Japan began liberalizing its trade barriers in the early 1960s, it did so, not because of a new-found recognition of the benefits from free trade, but because of foreign pressure. The predominant domestic intellectual rationale for liberalization from the early 1960s to the mid-1980s has been the need to meet international obligations, with an implicit belief that liberalization held no direct benefit for the Japanese economy.[7] Even those in Japan who understood and supported the basic concept of free trade often tempered their support with the argument that eventually liberalization would be in order but that the time had not yet come.[8]

A government document from the early 1970s summarizes the dominant line of thinking, arguing that the success of Japanese exports had led to a trade surplus, and, therefore, Japan needed to liberalize imports as part of its international obligations.[9] Even some recent writings continue this theme, with one analysis extolling free trade principles but only in the context of the danger of economic losses to Japan that could come from protectionism in other countries; nothing is said about the benefits of free trade for Japan.[10] Since 1985 a broader perspective has entered some other writings (discussed in chapter 5), but historically, business executives have supported liberalization only when faced with the threat of retaliation against their own exports.

Missing in much of the Japanese discussion of liberal trade has been reference to the benefits for consumers from lower prices or to the general increase in economic efficiency from the reallocation of production resources.[11] The annual white papers on trade of the Ministry of International Trade and Industry used to mention such benefits in the 1960s, when explicit protectionism was strong and in the process of being reduced, but these statements became more sparse over time, as noted in chapter 2. The overall impression given by these documents is that MITI was more interested in containing the impact of liberalization than in letting the economy receive its full benefits. In the face of a large trade surplus in the late 1970s, some commentary on benefits from imports of manufactured goods reappeared, but only briefly, and only to disappear as soon as the second oil shock eliminated the surpluses.[12]

Nor has there been any significant business interest making these arguments out of self-interest; no major group of retailers or manufacturers has had a strong enough interest in obtaining imports to bother arguing in public that their interests are being hurt by barriers. Those groups may exist, but generally they are not strong enough to speak out vigorously.

Business leaders have shared the nationalistic belief in the need to rely on domestic products, so that often the removal of formal barriers has had little impact on market outcomes. This preference pattern comes through strongly in a recent study of Japanese, American, and European manufacturing subsidiaries in Australia. Looking at the capital goods and industrial materials purchases made by these firms, this study concludes that Japanese subsidiaries exhibit an overwhelming preference for Japanese manufactured goods, whereas the subsidiaries of American and European firms demonstrate no national preference in either their purchasing procedures or their actual purchases.[13] For this important segment of the manufactured goods market, therefore, a strong and distinctive domestic preference characterizes Japanese behavior even when there are no formal restrictions.

In the absence of domestic intellectual or political support from groups interested in importing, the burden of opening Japan's markets has fallen on foreign governments, and principally on the United States. This reliance on outside pressure represents a particularly weak way to pursue more liberal trade and reflects the basic opposition to manufactured imports by the dominant economic actors. Even as recently as 1988, All Nippon Airways (ANA) was chastised by the government and others for ordering American jet engines for its planes rather than those developed by an international consortium including Japanese firms. Since participation in the consortium was heavily encouraged by the Ministry of International Trade and Industry, ANA's decision was berated as unpatriotic or detrimental to the nation.[14]

With rapid economic growth in the early postwar period causing Japan to outstrip its domestic natural resource base (a problem heightened by the postwar shift toward oil as a prime energy source), the general desire to promote industrialization gained a new ur-

TABLE 4-1. Raw Material Self-Sufficiency, Five
Industrialized Countries, 1987

Percentage of apparent domestic consumption met by imports

Raw material	Japan	United States	West Germany	France	United Kingdom
Coal	86.7	3.8	0.5	52.4	7.3
Oil	99.6	36.8	95.4	95.9	0.0
Natural gas	94.8	4.1	73.0	85.9	22.0
Iron ore	99.8	28.7	99.4	68.1	98.0
Copper	97.4	24.4	99.7	99.9	99.9
Lead	87.2	50.2	82.1	95.5	97.0
Zinc	76.2	81.0	78.1	88.1	96.6
Tin	99.7	99.7	100.0	100.0	100.0
Bauxite	100.0	93.0	100.0	44.4	100.0
Nickel	100.0	100.0	100.0	0.0	100.0
Cement[a]	1.8	18.4	5.0	2.0	4.7
Clay[a]	38.3	0.1	19.3	5.6	0.8
Gypsum[a]	10.8	38.6	28.3	2.2	4.8
Limestone[a]	0.0	n.a.	3.3	3.3	0.0

SOURCES: Keizai Koho Center, *Japan 1989: An International Comparison* (Tokyo, 1989), p. 66; and Bureau of Mines, *Minerals Yearbook*, vol. 3: *Area Reports—International* (Washington: U.S. Department of the Interior, 1987), pp. 298–304, 341–54, 501–14, 922–35, and vol. 2: *Area Reports—Domestic*, pp. 2–3, 21–27.

n.a. Not available.

a. Data for Japan, West Germany, France, and the United Kingdom are for 1986.

gency: Japan needed to export manufactured goods to pay for its raw material imports. Thus was born a new notion of Japan as a "processing nation,"[15] not possessing raw materials itself but prospering by importing raw materials, adding value to them, and exporting some of the resulting manufactured products to pay for the original materials. For income levels to rise, Japan had to move into progressively higher value-added products to enlarge the spread between the cost of the imported materials and the value of the output.

The processing-country concept involves a reality: Japan does have relatively few raw materials compared with most other nations. Table 4-1 presents import dependencies for a variety of natural resources. Japan is certainly highly dependent on imports for many of these resources. However, other countries are largely dependent on imports for some of these materials as well. Lead, zinc, copper, bauxite, and nickel are all mineral resources that most of these countries must import. The difference is a matter of degree; Japan relies on imports for a wider variety of resources than do the other nations. Still, the differences between Japan and, say, West Germany are particularly small; coal is virtually the only mineral resource that Germany possesses in abundance and Japan does not. Yet Japan's trade patterns in metal products are very different from those of West Germany and of the other industrialized countries shown in the table, as this chapter will demonstrate.

Another way in which to summarize raw material dependence is the value of mineral production per employed person. Such comparisons show Europe as a whole somewhat better endowed than Japan, but both are far below the United States.[16] The differences between Japan and Europe do not appear large enough to explain Japan's very low levels of intra-industry trade.

Furthermore, it is rising value-added that moves all nations to greater prosperity, not only Japan. The salient point here is not the truth of Japan's dependence on raw material imports but the depth of the belief in this pattern and the exaggerated sense of vulnerability that comes from it. For years the Japanese described their nation to foreigners as "four small islands with few natural resources." Even elementary school children are inculcated with this belief in Japan as a processing country: a fifth-grade text from the 1970s explained that Japan's foreign trade is characterized by processing trade, caused by the lack of raw materials and high level of Japanese technology and labor.[17]

The combination of Japan's position as a determined latecomer striving to achieve industrialization plus the postwar sense of vulnerability over imported raw materials became powerful ideologies working to spur manufactured exports and to create barriers to imports. Although policies to achieve these ends were most prominent in the early postwar years, discussion of the need for policies to promote exports and discourage imports dates back at least to the early 20th century to such major economic thinkers as Tanzan Ishibashi.[18] If successful, the catch-up process comes to a logical completion when the nation no longer lags behind other industrial nations. In Japan's case, though, the internal dynamic pushing industrialization was so strong that the process was pushed too far and for too long. The desire to produce domestically led to investment in industries that Japan had little economic reason to enter, and made such a strong imprint on Japanese thinking that it continued to dominate policy after the nation achieved advanced industrial status in the 1970s.

Distorted Institutions and Policies

For the reasons identified above, Japan's government has pursued an active role in encouraging industrialization. Playing catch up for more than a century has left a legacy: a set of interlocking institutions, policies, and behavior patterns that tend to skew resources toward the domestic manufacturing sector and away from manufactured imports, toward manufacturing and away from services, and toward manufacturers and away from consumers. Of course, Japan has not been entirely alone in having a large manufacturing sector. According to United Nations trade data, in 1960 Japan's 33.9 percent share of manufacturing in gross domestic product was exceeded by West Germany (40.3 percent) and Austria (37.0 percent), and even in 1987 by West Germany and Spain. Nevertheless, Japan certainly belongs to a select group of countries with large manufacturing sectors. Furthermore, the relative decline in the share of manufacturing in Japan over time has been less than in most other countries of the Organization for Economic Cooperation and Development; manufacturing slipped by only 5 percentage points, to 29 percent, from 1960 to 1987.

To say that the allocation of resources has been distorted sounds odd considering that the rest of the world has eagerly purchased Japanese products and per capita GNP exceeds that of the United States at current exchange rates. But the success of high-quality Japanese exports does not necessarily imply that the Japanese economy is operating as efficiently as possible. Different policies would have led to equally high or higher welfare for households; the success and productivity of manufacturing must be set against the inefficiency of other sectors and the relatively low level of social infrastructure, improvements in which would improve the quality of life in Japan. In particular, the following set of policies and characteristics in the postwar period has on balance allocated an excessively large share of production resources to the manufacturing sector and too few to consumer welfare:

Long working hours. Although the average number of hours worked has been slowly declining, Japanese workers still put in more time on the job than do their counterparts in other advanced industrial societies. In 1987 average weekly hours in manufacturing were 43.2 in Japan, compared with 38.5 in the United States, 35.9 in West Germany, and 38.7 in France. Only Great Britain comes close to Japan, with 42.2 hours a week.[19] International statistics on working hours may understate the difference between Japan and other countries because they include only hourly employees. Salaried workers in Japan put in extremely long hours, especially if one includes the time spent after hours with fellow workers (rather than at home with the family) cementing the human relationships considered important in business.[20] Longer working hours limit the time available for leisure and the consumption of services. This constraint on consumer demand implies less investment in services related to leisure (hotels, restaurants, and shops outside urban areas) and, therefore, relatively more investment in manufacturing. Even today the five-day work week is far from universal. The set of leisure services (including extended weekend travel or second homes in the countryside) that households could consume if allowed two-day weekends would be more extensive and more varied than has been the case.

Financial-sector bias. The overall allocation of funds within the financial system was skewed in the past toward large firms, especially manufacturing firms and service-sector firms related to them. Small firms, other service-sector firms, and households were allocated relatively fewer funds at higher interest rates.[21] Within the segmented financial market structure that emerged in early postwar Japan, the city banks, the long-term credit banks, and the trust banks were all oriented toward provision of funds to large firms. Manufacturing, electric power, shipbuilding, and rail transportation were all heavy borrowers from these financial sources. Consumer credit, on the other hand, was left to loan sharks.

Primacy of large business. In other ways also the interests of big business—manufacturing and finance—have been clearly favored over those of consumers. Government has worked closely and rather cooperatively with business, while the voice of consumers has been largely stifled. The advisory commissions (*shingikai, kenkyūkai,* and *chōsakai*) attached to ministries that are consulted in various aspects of policymaking have members from business and academia as well as retired government officials, but only rarely anyone from labor or consumer groups.[22] Some important changes in social policy came in the 1970s, with pollution control, social security, and health care all receiving greater attention, but in many ways the primacy of big business continues in Japan. Furthermore, use of the courts to protect consumer rights—to redress injury from unsafe products, false labeling, or toxic substances—is quite limited in Japan. Suits are expensive and lengthy, and the courts are crowded because the government severely restricts the number of lawyers and judges.[23] In this framework, business and government can work together for their priorities, including imposing obstacles to discourage foreign products.

Toleration of inefficient land use. An agricultural policy that has heavily protected inefficient domestic producers, an extremely low property tax on agricultural land, and heavy taxes on land transfer have all acted to restrict the supply of land for nonagricultural uses. Not surprisingly the restricted supply has driven residential land prices sky-high. Unable to afford larger plots of land, the Japanese live in small dwelling units, which in turn limits their demand for household durable goods. One outcome of this policy may be lower price elasticity of demand for consumer durables in Japan, since there is less price- and income-sensitive demand for second or third purchases of durables—one car but not two or three, one television set, one stereo system.[24] The combination of a need to save to purchase expensive real estate, and limited space to put durable goods after having purchased them, may also feed into the high rate of savings by households in Japan.

Skewed government spending on infrastructure. Government spending was biased toward industrially useful projects and away from social amenities in the 1950s and 1960s. Harbor facilities and highways (with high tolls to discourage nonbusiness use) were expanded to prevent transportation bottlenecks from slowing the growth of exports, while household telephone service, sewage disposal, sidewalks, and other aspects of household welfare were slighted. Many of these policies were modified in the 1970s, but even today Japan lags behind comparable economies in such measures as the percentage of homes connected to sewer systems or the amount of urban parkland.[25]

Trade barriers. An extensive set of formal and informal import barriers, coupled in some cases with collusion among domestic firms, has allowed manufacturers to maintain high retail prices in domestic markets. High domestic prices generated enough profits to attract investment, while marginal-cost pricing on exports generated sufficient volume to drive down the average unit cost of production.[26] There is a critical difference here between Japan and the United States: Japanese import barriers have been erected to protect not only inefficient, import-competing industries but also efficient, growing, export-oriented industries.

Industrial policy. Explicit packages of assistance have been directed at particular industries, including access to loans from government financial institutions, research and development funds (lent or granted), relaxation of antitrust rules or even government-coordinated industry collusion, and government procurement. The effectiveness of these policies in bringing successful industrialization to Japan is hotly debated by scholars, but at the very least, in some cases these measures have conferred a competitive advantage to Japanese firms over their foreign rivals and have obstructed the entry of foreign products into Japan.[27]

This array of policies led both to a general distortion, by feeding investment and productivity growth in manufacturing and starving investment in other sectors, and to specific distortions, by protecting and encouraging particular Japanese industries. Both the general and specific outcomes have worked in favor of manufactured exports and against imports. The impact has been strongest in any industry identified by the government as critical for the present and future development of the nation—it then becomes the lucky recipient of encouragement of the type described earlier, as well as import protection, and (in the 1950s and 1960s) easier access to funds from the financial sector. Clyde Prestowitz has aptly portrayed industrial policy as national security policy: leading industries and firms in Japan are valuable national assets to be nurtured for the sake of present and future prosperity.[28]

Rather than blaming Japan for targeting and nurturing new and growing industries, some blame the United States for not doing so.[29] However, the point here is not whether government can or should promote national growth and development through industrial policies. The point is whether the particular set of policies used in Japan to promote new industries has been pushed too far: has it encouraged a misallocation of resources between export industries and other sectors, imposing an excessive amount of protectionism in the process? Measured by the yardstick of higher living standards, the answer seems clear: Japanese national welfare would be better served by less investment in automobiles and other leading export industries and more investment in spreading the technological advances in these industries to others. Japanese national welfare would also benefit from greater investment in social amenities. A different set of industrial policies could allow Japan to have both a significant presence in important industries as well as more imports and more intra-industry trade.

A Belief in One-Sided Comparative Advantage

The industrial policies and corporate behavior aimed at catching up with the West and overcoming natural resource vulnerability rest on a belief in broad concepts of comparative advantage that, in the dominant Japanese view, seem to leave no room for intra-industry trade. Even comparative advantage may seem the wrong designation, given Japan's general lack of interest in free trade, since the efficient allocation of domestic production resources is hindered rather than helped by maintenance of trade barriers. But in Japan the view of comparative advantage is both extremely broad and very dynamic and forward looking. At the broadest level, many government officials, academics, and businessmen argue that the nation needs to build and maintain a comparative advantage in manufacturing as a whole to offset the disadvantage in natural resources. Even in less broad terms, most Japanese analysts understand the notion of comparative advantage to mean that the nation should export but not import those products in which it has an advantage.[30] There is also a notion of "future" comparative advantage: Japanese officials attend to industries in which they think the nation should have a comparative advantage in the future, and provide protection from imports as part of the strategy to guarantee that their expectation comes true.

In a recent book on U.S.-Japan relations, two Ministry of Finance officials emphasized once again the processing-trade rationale for Japan's industrial structure, and argued that this explains why the income elasticity for imports in Japan is low.[31] Their rationale is simple but flawed: Japan must be a processing nation to prosper without a large natural resource base, therefore it must import raw materials and export manufactures, and, therefore, the nation has little demand for foreign manufactured goods. But the causative connections in this logic are untrue in the extreme form generally assumed in Japan; there is no reason why the need to import raw materials means that the nation cannot import manufactures or participate in intra-industry trade to a greater extent than it has. These particular authors use the structure of exports and imports to explain why Japan so easily generates large trade surpluses, which only further invalidates the connection between Japan as a processing nation and very low manufactured imports. Japan has done far more than pay for its raw materials; it has generated large trade surpluses in the 1980s. Although they see more manufactured imports as a desirable way to reduce those surpluses and the foreign criticism resulting from them, they are silent on the notion of benefits from intra-industry trade.

Others project this belief in the dominance of broad comparative advantage on their analysis of the United States. As one economics professor comments: "There is a complementary structure of comparative advantage between the United States and Japan. U.S. exports to Japan should center on farm products and certain items of high technology; Japanese exports to the United States should center on mass-produced manufactured products."[32] Another chides the United States for industrial decline, citing as evidence American imports of steel and automobiles, industries in which the United States should have a comparative advantage. If the United States really had comparative advantage in these industries, according to this line of reasoning, then it would not import significant quantities of these products; this analysis completely ignores the possibility of both possessing comparative advantage and engaging in substantial two-way trade through product differentiation.[33] Others also speak of declining U.S. competitiveness as an across-the-board explanation of why the United States has problems exporting manufactured goods to Japan, ignoring any concept of comparative advantage at a finer level of disaggregation than the entire manufacturing sector.[34] In all these cases, the authors making these statements are not journalists or popular writers—they are well-trained officials and professional economists who represent the core of sophisticated thinking on trade issues.

In contrast to the attention given to comparative advantage, few Japanese publications in the past have considered intra-industry trade as either a concept or an empirical fact.[35] Professor Yoko Sazanami is an exception in the academic community, but even she attributes much of Japan's peculiarly low level of intra-industry trade to its lack of participation in an EC-type customs union and to the wide disparity in income levels between Japan and its nearby Asian neighbors rather than to other features of economic behavior.[36] The trade white papers mentioned earlier have made occasional reference to intra-industry trade, but until a burst of discussion in the late 1980s, the references were fleeting and underdeveloped compared with discussions of comparative advantage and justifications for why manufactured imports have been low.[37]

The two Finance Ministry officials cited earlier make no mention of intra-industry trade anywhere in their book on U.S.-Japan economic relations. Moreover, they accept Japan's low level of manufactured imports as a simple fact rather than a major peculiarity. A strong sense of Japanese superiority across a very wide range of manufactured products pervades their analysis, as when they claim that Japanese products are "built into" the U.S. economy, making it dependent on Japan for products that it cannot, or does not want to, make at home. They emphasize the non-price-competitiveness of Japanese products, and steadfastly refuse to admit that Japan's markets are not fully open.[38]

Reflecting the processing-trade rationale, most Japanese writers see their market as having "no room" for foreign manufactured goods. As one author puts it: "Because Japanese firms have relative advantage in consumer durables, there is practically no room for foreign products to enter, with very few exceptions (clothing, golf clubs, expensive pens, etc.)."[39] This notion is quite common—Japanese firms can and will provide all the differentiated products that consumers want or need, so that foreign firms can find no segment of the market to enter. While Japanese firms involved in the mass production of consumer durables are certainly well managed, aggressive, and innovative, the notion that they could or should be able to supply all possible consumer demand at a lower price than foreign products is a peculiar one, to say the least. The spark of truth involved has been magnified into a major myth.

A more sophisticated version of this argument involves a concept known as economies of scope. Kazuo Sato argues that there exists a set of industries in Japan that does not possess large economies of scale but can nevertheless compete against imports through economies of scope. This theory posits that flexible firms can achieve economies by making small quantities of a large variety of slightly differentiated goods.[40] Such economies may characterize certain industries with mid-sized firms. Sato suggests that these firms are so adept at meeting variations in product demand by consumers that "products made at home by small local firms fit Japanese tastes much better than foreign-made goods. We conjecture that it is for this reason that imports are low."[41]

While economies of scope is an intriguing concept, and one directly opposed to the conditions that bring about intra-industry trade, it is not fully convincing. All nations have some industries in which successful firms exist in the face of foreign competition through economies of scope; why should Japan stand out so much? Without import barriers, a web of ties to larger manufacturers, or dominance over the distribution sector, it is doubtful that economies of scope could account for the low level of imports.

The critical element of the economies of scope explanation may be not the superior ability of Japanese manufacturers to produce small quantities flexibly but rather peculiar consumer tastes. If Japanese consumer tastes were sufficiently different from those of all other countries, then local producers in tune with local tastes would dominate the market. But for a wide range of Japanese consumer items, close parallels exist elsewhere in the world, even if not in the United States. Indeed, many locally produced manufactured goods are deliberately patterned on foreign goods. The role of traditional, distinctive Japanese goods in consumer consumption patterns has shrunk dramatically in the postwar period. For example, in the 20 years from 1964 to 1984, ownership of traditional Japanese chests for storing kimono (*wadansu*) dropped by 14 percent (to 1,303 per 1,000 households), while ownership of Western-style chests more than doubled (to 2,179); Western-style wardrobe cabinets rose 65 percent (to 1,601); Western-style beds quadrupled (from 211 to 816 per 1,000 households); and Western-style dining room sets of tables and chairs more than tripled (to 728 per 1,000 households).[42] This shift, however, has not been accompanied by any strong increase in imported consumer goods until some very recent changes (considered in chapter 5). For some products, real differences in demand (such as shorter legs on tables and chairs) may explain the relative lack of foreign products, but this is not a convincing argument overall. If Japanese consumers were truly averse to foreign goods or designs, why have they become such avid shoppers when they travel abroad? Something more than economies of scope and comparative advantage seems to be involved.

Even if the economies of scope argument provides a partial answer to the relative lack of imported consumer products, it cannot explain the failure to import industrial goods, an area where unique national demand preferences play little role. Japan's trade in metal products provides a clear picture of the unusually strong bias toward raw material imports and processed exports that has emerged. Table 4-2 arrays data on international trade in several metal products, ranging from the basic raw materials to structural shapes manufactured from the metals. In 1985, 67 percent of copper imports in Japan came in the form of ores and concentrates, leaving 31 percent in the form of unwrought metal, and only a tiny 2 percent in the form of worked copper. Furthermore, the level of intra-industry trade was actually lower for worked copper than for unwrought copper, despite the fact that one would expect the possibilities for product differentiation and, thus, two-way trade would be much greater. The contrast between Japan and the other countries listed is striking. The United States, France, and West Germany all import more than 10 times as much worked copper as Japan, and all three of these countries import roughly equal amounts of unwrought and worked copper. These countries also conform to the expectation that intra-industry trade ought to be higher for worked copper. Even South Korea, with much smaller imports of all forms of copper, conforms to these patterns. The contrast of Japan with the United States is especially striking, since the United States is a major producer of both copper ore (14 percent of world production) and refined copper (15 percent of world production).[43] If the U.S. positions in mining and refining are indicators of comparative (or absolute) advantages, then it should be Japan, not the United States, that imports wrought copper in large quantities.

The pattern for copper is repeated for most other metals included in the table, even though in some cases the overwhelming reliance in Japan is on unwrought metal rather than on ores and concentrates. Only 4 percent of aluminum imports in Japan are in the form of worked aluminum or finished structural parts, compared with 44 percent in the United States, 46 percent in France, 43 percent in West Germany, and 30 percent in South Korea. For lead (where worked metal imports are a small share in all countries), these same ratios are 0.2 percent for Japan, 5 percent for the United States, 6 percent for France, 2 percent for West Germany, and 5 percent for South Korea. Basically similar patterns are repeated in zinc and tin. In all these cases Japan's absolute size of imports of worked metal is far below that of the other countries and represents a much smaller percentage of total imports of each metal. Moreover, Japan's level of intra-industry trade is almost always significantly lower than that of other countries. The only exception is nickel, where Japan's behavior seems consistent with the experience of other nations.

Detailed Japanese production data on aluminum further demonstrate the lack of import penetration. While the reduction in smelting capacity as a result of high energy costs since the late 1970s has been played up as a sign of flexibility and openness to imports, little penetration has taken place in manufactured aluminum products. As a share of apparent domestic consumption, imports of mill products were only 2.2 percent in 1985. For other aluminum products (castings, forgings, electric conductors, powder, and foil), imports as a share of apparent domestic consumption were a minuscule 0.5 percent. Even in the United States, with its lower energy costs and large production of aluminum ingots, imports of processed aluminum products were a higher 6.7 percent of apparent domestic consumption.[44]

Iron and steel presents a more complicated picture because the industry is so large and involves a broad set of products. The general pattern observed for other metals nevertheless holds rather well. Iron ore and concentrates make up the overwhelming share of imports (62 percent). Iron and steel scrap account for 8 percent, while crude iron and steel (pig iron, ingots, and other primary forms) account for another 21 percent, leaving only 9 percent of all imports in the form of various shapes and structures. Among all forms of manufactured iron and steel (that is, total imports minus ores, concentrates, roasted iron pyrites, and scrap), crude iron and steel imports are 69 percent of the total in Japan. For the United States, however, crude iron and steel are only 10 percent of the total, while they are 30 percent in France, 25 percent in West Germany, and 39 percent in South Korea. The only iron and steel products that Japan imports in any significant quantity are universals, plates, and sheets, and even in this category, its imports are far smaller than those of the other industrial countries. For virtually all iron and steel categories beyond pig iron and ingots, the intra-industry trade index numbers are very low, and far below those of the other countries in the table.

This pattern could hardly be solely the result of market forces operating along lines of comparative advantage. Industrial policy favoring domestic manufacture of all products beyond the simplest processing of materials has been a strong theme in Japan. In a recent

TABLE 4-2. COMPARATIVE IMPORTS OF METALS, FIVE COUNTRIES, 1985

		Japan			United States			France			West Germany			South Korea		
SITC	Description	Imports (dollars)	Share (percent)	IIT index	Imports (dollars)	Share (percent)	IIT index	Imports (dollars)	Share (percent)	IIT index	Imports (dollars)	Share (percent)	IIT index	Imports (dollars)	Share (percent)	IIT index
	Iron and steel															
2813	Iron ore and concentrates	3,044,866	61.6	0	0	0.0	0	359,502	8.5	11	1,122,891	15.9	0	0	0.0	0
2814	Roasted iron pyrites	0	0.0		0	0.0	0	528	0.0	0	0	0.0	0	0	0.0	0
2820	Iron and steel scrap	406,997	8.2	14	46,979	0.4	10	61,972	1.5	27	190,594	2.7	63	278,904	18.8	9
671	Pig iron, spiegeleisen, etc.	623,051	12.6	44	581,159	5.0	23	427,378	10.2	88	697,797	9.9	59	42,523	2.9	51
672	Ingots and other primary forms	407,023	8.2	61	546,926	4.7	10	711,855	16.9	87	731,935	10.4	66	432,653	29.2	91
673	Bars, rods, angles, sections, etc.	26,182	0.5	2	1,948,065	16.7	13	755,084	17.9	85	1,363,727	19.4	97	187,211	12.6	65
674	Universals, plates, and sheets	346,487	7.0	12	4,508,120	38.6	11	946,227	22.5	74	1,505,208	21.4	73	315,153	21.3	75
675	Hoop and strip	13,799	0.3	6	269,196	2.3	34	213,546	5.1	83	311,624	4.4	56	25,168	1.7	44
676	Rails and railway track	600	0.0	1	143,921	1.2	36	0	0.0	0	5,028	0.1	9	4,470	0.3	45
677	Wire	12,693	0.3	9	474,436	4.1	19	136,589	3.2	88	212,965	3.0	95	30,021	2.0	78
678	Tubes, pipes, and fittings	47,424	1.0	2	2,670,563	22.9	32	394,767	9.4	55	607,804	8.6	39	133,636	9.0	47
679	Unworked castings and forgings[a]	2,207	0.0	14	53,001	0.5	87	46,465	1.1	84	40,694	0.6	40	3,988	0.3	30
6911	Finished structural parts and structures	10,671	0.2	4	439,693	3.8	65	156,104	3.7	51	253,609	3.6	62	28,280	1.9	8
	TOTAL	4,941,999	100.0	...	11,680,059	100.0	...	4,210,017	100.0	...	7,043,876	100.0	...	1,482,006	100.0	...
	Copper															
2831	Ore and concentrates	1,209,723	67.2	0	3,201	0.3	4	321	0.0	42	212,358	13.5	0	163,261	56.7	0
6821	Unwrought copper and alloys	553,242	30.7	25	570,147	47.3	30	502,205	55.9	10	828,858	52.7	24	80,340	27.9	13
6822	Worked copper and alloys	38,345	2.1	14	632,896	52.5	48	395,964	44.1	89	532,583	33.8	63	44,565	15.5	87
	TOTAL	1,801,310	100.0	...	1,206,244	100.0	...	898,490	100.0	...	1,573,799	100.0	...	288,166	100.0	...

	Nickel															
2832	Ore and concentrates	0	0.0	0	94,540	13.3	0	46,576	23.7	0	0	0.0	0	4	0.0	0
6831	Unwrought nickel and alloys	129,619	74.5	3	453,631	64.0	32	103,476	52.8	46	214,546	77.0	27	18,074	66.4	0
6832	Worked nickel and alloys	44,327	25.5	96	160,333	22.6	76	46,092	23.5	94	64,196	23.0	65	9,123	33.5	1
	TOTAL	173,946	100.0	…	708,504	100.0	…	196,144	100.0	…	278,742	100.0	…	27,201	100.0	…
	Aluminum															
2833	Bauxite and concentrates of aluminum	88,566	4.5	0	300,298	12.7	4	46,034	4.1	24	152,031	8.5	9	1,613	0.6	0
6841	Unwrought aluminum and alloys	1,786,410	91.3	1	1,037,096	43.8	60	491,239	43.8	47	877,572	49.0	59	182,529	69.2	1
6842	Worked aluminum and alloys	74,879	3.8	22	1,029,350	43.5	64	505,441	45.1	89	677,578	37.8	69	70,725	26.8	85
6912	Finished structural parts and structures	6,373	0.3	24	0	0.0	0	79,041	0.7	89	84,556	4.7	63	8,725	3.3	81
	TOTAL	1,956,228	100.0	…	2,366,744	100.0	…	1,121,755	100.0	…	1,791,737	100.0	…	263,592	100.0	…
	Lead															
2834	Ore and concentrates	70,141	57.6	6	0	0.0	0	55,888	68.6	0	58,939	44.8	6	3,845	15.2	20
6851	Unwrought lead and alloys	51,292	42.1	35	55,915	95.5	45	21,082	25.9	87	70,047	53.2	96	20,373	80.4	1
6852	Worked lead and alloys	261	0.2	24	2,645	4.5	71	4,519	5.5	68	2,562	1.9	23	1,131	4.5	29
	TOTAL	121,694	100.0	…	58,560	100.0	…	81,489	100.0	…	131,548	100.0	…	25,349	100.0	…
	Zinc															
2835	Ore and concentrates	187,955	74.7	0	0	0.0	0	138,281	60.6	0	144,052	44.3	33	37,489	78.4	0
6861	Unwrought zinc and alloys	62,830	25.0	63	517,509	97.5	1	76,911	33.7	1	140,118	43.1	87	9,685	20.3	8
6862	Worked zinc and alloys	874	0.3	33	13,185	2.5	66	13,175	5.8	66	40,723	12.5	50	651	1.4	81
6913	Finished structural parts and structures	0	0.0	0	0	0.0	0	0	0.0	0	0	0.0	0	0	0.0	…
	TOTAL	251,659	100.0	…	530,694	100.0	…	228,367	100.0	…	324,893	100.0	…	47,825	100.0	…
	Tin															
2836	Ore and concentrates	0	0.0	0	0	0.0	0	0	0.0	0	0	0.0	0	0	0.0	0
6871	Unwrought tin and alloys	349,650	99.8	1	431,051	99.2	1	91,106	97.4	7	224,449	99.1	25	17,700	96.0	2
6872	Worked tin and alloys	556	0.2	31	3,435	0.8	31	2,477	2.6	53	2,127	0.9	22	740	4.0	0
	TOTAL	350,206	100.0	…	434,485	100.0	…	93,582	100.0	…	226,576	100.0	…	18,440	100.0	…

SOURCE: Author's calculations based on United Nations trade data tapes.
a. Not otherwise specified.

study of Japanese trade, Sazanami pointed out that some shift away from ores to processed metals occurred in the 1970s, but this is a shift only at the very bottom of the vertical chain of products.[45] In some cases that shift has been driven by large differences in energy costs, and in others by pressure applied by developing countries with natural resources (insisting on local processing to further their own industrialization goals). The consistent and strong avoidance of significant imports of items beyond crude metal is striking and deviates from the behavior of the other nations in the table.

A Gullible Public

While academics, government officials, and corporate businesses championed the notion of broad comparative advantage as the governing principle for Japanese trade, households acquiesced complaisantly. With little first-hand exposure to foreign countries, and limited exposure to foreign products in Japan, consumers accepted, first, the need to protect small, weak Japanese firms from international competition, and then, in the 1980s, the myth of overall Japanese superiority.

The image attached to imported consumer goods illustrates the general problem. Japanese consumers certainly express no bias against foreign goods, but traditionally have expected such goods to be exotic. The very term used for imported manufactured products, *hakuraihin*—goods that come by ship—carries an image of exotic products coming from afar.[46] In department stores, foreign goods are often prominently displayed with little flags showing the country of origin. They tend to be expensive specialty items with enormous markups over the price in other countries—hand-cut crystal glass, expensive pots and pans, expensive ball point and fountain pens, and Scandinavian furniture. In some cases, these products appear to be more for show than for sale. There are also a limited number of foreign brand names that have acquired the necessary exotic appeal in Japan—Burberry, Louis Vuitton, and Pierre Cardin among them.

Some foreign products fit into such niches in other countries as well. Skippy peanut butter sells in specialty food shops in London, Parker Pen has specifically targeted the upper end of its market in all countries, and Japanese handsaws are advertised in U.S. catalogs of high-priced woodworking tools. But what has been generally missing in Japan in the past has been the availability of a range of foreign products in the broader marketplace. One looks largely in vain for everyday foreign products in local supermarkets or appliance stores, for example.

Products at the upper end of the scale in their own markets (including Burberry raincoats or Louis Vuitton bags) end up at the top of the Japanese market as well. These are the products that supply most of the success stories of market penetration in Japan. But many foreign products are pushed into a high-priced fringe even when they do not belong there. A fifth of Johnny Walker Black Label scotch whiskey, for example, cost ¥4,200 ($32.30) in Toyko in the fall of 1988, compared with about $18 in the United States. Not only are prices high; many Japanese retailers choose to import and display inappropriate product models. To illustrate, Seibu department store in Tokyo recently had four foreign (all American) refrigerators on display, General Electric models in the 16-, 20-, and 22-cubic-foot range, and one Sears 22-cubic-foot model. The 22-cubic-foot GE model (with water and ice dispensers on the front door) retailed for ¥708,000 ($5,446), more than four times the retail price of $1,340 in the United States.[47] Note that the very choice of displaying the largest, top-of-the-line refrigerators in a market dominated by much smaller refrigerators relegates the foreign product to a minor niche. These facts have nothing to do with quality or design; at such high prices few Americans would buy GE refrigerators or Johnny Walker whiskey either.

The reason consumers have been largely unaware of the variety and prices of foreign goods is that such products do not often get into mass-distribution channels. Foreign firms are often advised to aim for the small-scale, high-price, high-quality niche in the market rather than for the average price and quality (but large volume) center of the market. Although the Japanese custom of extensive gift-giving (*omiyage*) makes the upscale niche for some products a bit larger in Japan than in other countries, the fact remains that demand is limited. However, the belief that high prices are an effective sales strategy persists among Japanese and foreigners alike: "Because the Japanese view imports as high-class, if the price is lowered, often sales drop."[48] Economists call this a backward-bending demand curve, and while the phenomenon is not unknown, it is certainly not a common one. But for those products for which this peculiar condition is true in Japan, it comes as a result of the *hakuraihin* imagery attached to the product. If products entered the mainstream of the Japanese market without enormous markups in price, the shape of the demand curve would probably be quite normal. Deliberately pushing foreign products into this niche, and creating the appropriate imagery, condemns them to staying there. Japanese manufacturers are often willing to concede the very top of the market because they know it is limited in size, and because granting the foreigners a minor market share may keep down criticism from abroad.

The government participates in this pattern. A recent government publication counseling foreigners on how to sell manufactured goods to Japan advised them to head either for the low-price end of the consumer market (where Japan has lost comparative advantage in labor-intensive goods), or to the high end with distinctive, brand name goods carrying high prices.[49] Japanese firms certainly do not follow this strategy when marketing abroad; in the past they often entered a market at the bottom end, then moved quickly into the mainstream, competing with a range of differentiated products and building brand name recognition. Why should foreign firms not be advised to do the same in Japan?

The implication is that foreign firms attempting to enter the main market will be vigorously attacked and kept out or pushed out by all possible means—economic and political, legal and illegal. Because the Japanese market is not as open or pluralistic as the U.S. market, this threat is more viable in Japan. For products with brand name images, the control is often reinforced through use of sole distributorships even though "parallel imports" (that is, imports by companies other than the designated Japanese distributor) are now legal.

A common response by the Japanese is that foreign firms simply do not try hard enough to enter the market. Akira Ueno, a senior specialist on corporate management at Nomura Research Institute, argued in a recent book that the failure of American firms to try harder was the reason that yen appreciation was having no effect on the bilateral trade imbalance, and he urged the Japanese government to speak up more forcefully on this and other American failures when accused of protectionism.[50] Certainly foreign firms have made errors in attempting to break into the Japanese market: some have not spent enough time cultivating personal relationships; others have been impatient when faced with detailed questions and demands from potential corporate buyers. But this accusation presumes that if foreigners only tried harder, they would be successful—a presumption that is not always true. In some problem industries, foreign firms cannot enter or expand their market share no matter how hard they try. This was the case with autos and steel from 1950 to 1985, with textiles in the 1960s, and today for Monsanto with silicon wafers and for others with semiconductor chips, beer, rice, orange juice, gasoline, and other products. If determined efforts yield no results, why should foreign firms try? Put another way, the cost to the firm of attempting to enter the Japanese market is high and the expected payoff very uncertain, so many foreign firms perceive that their financial resources can be better allocated to other projects or countries.

More broadly, the very fact that foreigners are told they must make exceptionally determined efforts indicates the market is hostile and resistant to newcomers. Foreign firms have generally lacked powerful economic allies in Japan to further their cause, in contrast to the basic receptivity of large American distributors and manufacturers to foreign products. In many respects, large foreign firms are relegated to the same status as small domestic firms attempting to enter a market. It is one thing for large Japanese firms to use their market power, sense of social hierarchy, and political and bureaucratic influence to restrict smaller domestic firms to insignificant market shares, but this behavior has been projected on imports from large, efficient foreign firms that ought to do well in open competition. Even Robert Christopher, who emphasizes the need for American firms to adapt to the tough quality, delivery, and service expectations in the Japanese market, recognizes and discusses the ability of powerful Japanese manufacturers to shut out foreign competition. He cites, for example, Wacoal's retaliation against Playtex when it attempted to enter the Japanese lingerie market. Wacoal simply threatened to pull out its entire line from any retailer willing to buy from Playtex.[51]

Some exceptions exist, and Japanese officials quickly point to them in trying to convince foreigners that the market is open. Coca-Cola, Schick safety razors, and Pampers have all done very well, occupying large shares in their respective markets. In some cases, however, success came by getting in before a viable Japanese industry existed (as with Coca-Cola's successful entry right after the war, when the U.S. Occupation officials demanded that Coca-Cola be allowed to establish local bottling plants to serve the Occupation forces), or by attacking a minor market to begin with (as with

Schick's success in a market where most men use electric razors). Success also depends on the definition of the industry or market: Coca-Cola dominates the carbonated cola drink market in Japan, but it is only one of a great variety of bottled and canned nonalcoholic drinks available. All in all, success stories mostly reinforce the conclusion that they are exceptions. Most foreign products have been excluded from mainstream markets.

Why do Japanese consumers tolerate such behavior? For one thing, until recently they have had no basis for comparison. In 1960 only 119,000 Japanese traveled abroad (a figure that includes double counting because of multiple journeys by government officials and businessmen). In that same year official data record 1.6 million Americans traveled abroad, an understated figure that excludes travel to Canada and Mexico, as well as military personnel, governments officials, and other U.S. citizens living abroad.[52] Even as recently as 1970, fewer than 1 million Japanese nationals left their shores, less than a fifth the number of Americans. Not until the 1980s did Japanese foreign travel begin to approximate the U.S. level on a per capita basis, and the rapid growth after yen appreciation began in 1985 led Japanese officials to predict that the number of travelers would reach 10 million in 1989, not far from the current U.S. level in absolute terms.[53] Hence until rather recently Japanese individuals have had relatively little exposure to different product varieties and prices.

Consumers have also enjoyed an improvement in general living standards in the postwar period that has been so swift it has swamped concerns over prices. Prices might be high, but incomes rose so fast that all products became more affordable over time. Consumers have also been rather disorganized and complaisant as a group, which is probably no different from the situation in the United States. Consumers are most effective when they can express their opinion through their purchases, but in Japan the obstacles to getting foreign manufactured products into mainstream markets preclude them from exercising their voice. Furthermore, some of the organized consumer groups are not independent of producer interests. Co-operative supermarkets (seikyō), for example, have close ties to the Japanese farm organizations, which explains why they have opposed liberalization of rice imports despite the obvious benefit to the consumer.[54] Another group, the Consumers' Union of Japan, has also opposed agricultural liberalization and adjustment of standards on manufactured products; it is, in fact, headed by a former official of the Ministry of Agriculture, Forestry, and Fisheries.[55]

Japanese consumers have also been quite gullible, willing to accept without much complaint the myth that most (perhaps all) Japanese products are superior and the various excuses put forth by government and business about why foreign products are unsuitable or unavailable. Indeed, consumers may not think of their purchases as heavily oriented toward domestic items. Lifestyles have shifted away from what could be identified as traditionally Japanese and toward what is assumed to be Western—away from tatami mats and toward rooms made for tables, chairs, and beds; away from the *kimono* and toward Western clothing; away from rice and toward bread. Japanese consumers buy blue jeans, eat hamburgers and fried chicken at fast-food restaurants, and listen to Western classical music. In most cases, though, what they consume is produced domestically and may have little or no foreign content; a Western lifestyle is not synonymous with imported products. Because most mainstream products have no country-of-origin label, consumers may even be largely unaware whether a product is domestic or foreign. Whereas one might expect that the lack of such labeling would help foreign products rather than hinder them, in Japan it has left consumers unaware of the lack of foreign goods.

Consumers have also transferred certain functions to the government bureaucracy that belong to the courts in the United States, as discussed earlier. The result has been that consumers find their interests subordinated to those of domestic manufacturers. There is nothing necessarily wrong with this, since one could argue that the United States represents an extreme in which consumer interests have been overrepresented by the courts, imposing a financial burden on the corporate sector that may be unhealthy in the long run. But the Japanese alternative to a vigorous use of the court system— namely, government administrative protection of consumer health and safety—may lead to simple overreaction by officials charged with setting standards, or unreasonable suspicion about foreign products made under conditions over which inspectors can have no control. Because of the limited recourse to the courts, officials feel an obligation to devise regulations tightly enough that no one would have a need to use the courts and thereby challenge their competence or integrity. Consumers hold the same expectation, and often blame the government as much as the manufacturer when injury occurs.

The more important implication of this delegation of power to the government is that it opens the way for government-business collusion to set standards and testing procedures in such a way as to block the entry of foreign products deliberately (for example, U.S. aluminum baseball bats, skis, tire chains, infant clothing, and other items noted in table 2-1). Since consumers expect the government to protect them, they are willing to believe official claims that foreign products fail to meet fair and unbiased standards, whereas the truth is often that restraint of trade rather than consumer welfare guides formation of these rules. This intent was especially true in the cases of aluminum baseball bats and skis, where safety concerns became the excuse to establish new standards deliberately designed to exclude foreign products that have not had safety problems.

The notion of Japanese uniqueness, popularized in numerous books on *Nihonjinron* (Japaneseness), predisposes consumers to accept some of the rather ridiculous arguments put forth by government and business, such as a major politician's recent assertion that imported beef is unsuitable to the Japanese market because Japanese intestines are longer than those of Westerners. Government and corporate officials have similarly argued that Japanese snow is different from that of other countries, making imported skis or tire chains unsuitable. The public seems largely unaware that their feelings of cultural singularity have been exaggerated and manipulated by government and business to further the anticompetitive commercial interests of Japanese manufacturers.

As noted earlier not all Japanese consumers are parochial in their tastes—far from it. The Japanese produce and consume many products that are similar to those produced and consumed in other countries as income levels rise and lifestyles become less traditionally Japanese. The similarity of production and consumption patterns that have emerged as Japan has achieved advanced industrial status ought, therefore, to have led to an increase in intra-industry trade. As shown in chapter 3, this did not happen.

Japanese consumers traveling abroad are well aware now of the wide differences in price between domestic and foreign markets. In New York, Hong Kong, Singapore, and other major foreign cities, businessmen and tourists stock up on products—including those with Japanese brand names—that are much more expensive at home. Part of the buying frenzy can be attributed to the gift-giving aspect of Japanese society, but that can hardly explain the totality. A recent publication noted that Japanese consumers stand out overseas because of their heavy buying activities.[56] In 1988, in fact, Japanese travelers abroad spent an average of $2,218 each, with overseas spending accounting for more than 2 percent of domestic consumption spending.[57]

Balance-of-payments data provide eloquent testimony on the rising awareness of Japanese consumers of lower prices abroad. Payments for passenger transportation and travel have experienced explosive growth since 1985, after being virtually flat in the first half of the 1980s. From $6.7 billion in 1985, these expenditures climbed to $23.5 billion in 1988, a $17 billion increase in only three years. A considerable portion of this increase represents purchases of merchandise abroad.[58]

Bias in Business Relationships

Consumer products and consumer behavior are only part of the story of low imports of manufactured goods, since a large portion of trade involves machinery or intermediate products that are sold to other manufacturers. Here, too, institutions and behavior patterns that evolved in Japan have worked against imported products. The huge trading companies that handle a large share of both imports and exports, as well as the traditional long-term cooperative relationships between firms, have been biased against manufactured imports.

General trading companies such as Mitsui are a distinctive Japanese institution, although some industrializing countries have recently developed similar organizations. These vast firms handle everything from petroleum to machinery as well as dealing in imports, exports, and domestic trade.[59] Besides buying and selling commodities, they perform other trade-related functions: market research, financing, transportation, warehousing, and investment in manufacturers. The nine largest of these firms handle 45 percent of total Japanese exports and 77 percent of imports.[60]

The long history of these large general trading companies is one reason to doubt the importance of geographical distance as a factor in Japan's peculiar trade patterns. Such firms evolved specifically to overcome the economic obstacles presented by distant, culturally different markets. They maintain a large number of overseas offices that gather and process information about products, markets, and consumer preferences. Economies of scale apply to these operations; having established a network of offices and the communications network to connect them, the firm's marginal cost of investigating an additional product or market is quite low. The nine largest trading companies had 682 overseas offices in 1980, with the largest four each maintaining 100 or more.[61] These corporations have also had a specialized work force knowledgeable in foreign languages and cultures, which was especially important when such expertise was scarce in Japan.

On the export side, these firms have reduced the cost of entry into foreign markets for Japanese firms by providing the market research, foreign business contacts, and other services that manufacturers may have been reluctant or unable to get on their own. Theoretically the same should have worked in reverse, with the trading companies acting as a cultural and business bridge for foreign firms interested in Japan, since the trading companies also maintain a network of domestic offices and engage in extensive domestic trading.

In fact, though, trading companies have never been an effective route for selling sophisticated manufactured goods that require intensive sales efforts or after-sales service networks. Their main business has been and continues to be raw materials and basic manufactures (steel, chemicals, and textiles). As a direct actor in international trade, therefore, they are not particularly well suited as a vehicle for increasing manufactured imports from the United States and other industrial countries. Since much of the international trade function in Japan was relegated to these companies in the earlier postwar years, one could argue that this is a reason for the low penetration of foreign manufactured goods. However, because these firms also play a facilitating role, they could do much to open doors for foreign manufacturers.

Overall, the performance of the trading companies has been asymmetrical and matches that of the general pattern of Japanese trade: assisting the export of manufactured goods, but on the import side concentrating on raw materials. They have been available to assist foreign firms desiring to export to Japan, but often these relationships do not work out well. The very fact that a small number of general trading companies dominates imports means that the government must deal with only a few firms if it desires to apply informal restraints on imports, as has happened in the past on textiles and steel. Furthermore, the large general trading companies all have important and extensive business relationships with leading Japanese manufacturers that constrain the eagerness with which they can promote competing foreign manufactured goods or assist foreign firms in finding domestic allies.

Restrictive business relationships between firms are a general market-access problem. Ties between buyers and suppliers are much tighter in Japan than in the United States. Although large manufacturers purchase parts from many suppliers and often have no equity position in them, nevertheless a web of ties acts to make these relationships unusually close. First, businesses invest an extraordinary amount of time and money building personal relationships. Once built, these relationships involve a strong sense of commitment and hierarchy. Small suppliers know that they are economically and socially inferior to large well-known manufacturing firms and are willing to accept demands on price, quality, and delivery that more independent and equal firms sometimes would reject. Second, even though equity is not involved, trade financing is extensive, whereby large manufacturing firms finance the investment and production of their suppliers.[62] Finally, the "lifetime employment" system of large manufacturers and the paternalistic attitude of these firms toward their workers implies an obligation for firms to find postretirement jobs for their employees (since retirement is relatively early). Subcontractors are a favorite dumping ground for retirees, who in turn constitute another link. This web of mutual dependency and obligation is quite unlike business relationships in the United States or other industrial countries, where such behavior is often seen as harmful to economic efficiency because it unduly restricts competitive forces and yields higher prices.

How tightly woven is this web? Is it possible to have interfirm relationships consistent with Japanese social values but allowing greater freedom to switch among competing foreign and domestic suppliers? This is a difficult question to answer, but an affirmative response is certainly plausible. The first thing to note is that the current system is not the product of centuries of unchanging tradition; tight relations between buyer and seller in the auto industry, for example, date mainly to the 1960s and were actively encouraged at that time by the government.[63] Note also that whereas the Japanese argue that close relations between buyer and seller are a fact of life foreign firms must accept (and can even benefit from if they are lucky enough to become the favored supplier), the causality may be the opposite: close business and social ties exclusively among Japanese firms evolved because foreign firms were kept out of the market. Had foreign products and foreign firms been more heavily involved in Japan in the 1950s and 1960s when many of the features of current business relations matured, interfirm ties, obligations, and expectations might have evolved somewhat differently and in a less exclusive manner. The system has been a luxury, not a necessity. Allowed to develop in a protected market, the existence of this social web then becomes yet another element in asserting that Japan is unique and that foreigners cannot understand or participate. The reasoning becomes circular: the relationships developed when foreigners were kept out, and now their absence is taken to imply that they cannot adequately understand or participate.

Horizontal ties among firms have also worked against imports. At one level, many large Japanese manufacturers belong to loose conglomerate business groupings known as *keiretsu*. Brought together through modest levels of interfirm equity ties, lending ties through the group bank, and periodic meetings of the presidents of participating firms, these groups evolved out of the prewar *zaibatsu*, tight family-controlled conglomerates that were broken up during the Occupation.[64] The impact of these particular organizations on import behavior can be exaggerated, but it is true that when no overwhelming reason exists to buy a foreign product, a group member will accede to pressure from other group members to buy their products. Clyde Prestowitz cites the example of Nissan choosing to buy a Hitachi supercomputer (rather than a Cray) because they both belong to the Fuyo group.[65]

Perhaps more important than the *keiretsu* are the industry associations and other, more informal means of coordinating interests within particular industries. Japan has an antitrust law, and various forms of collusive behavior within industries are illegal. Each year several price-fixing cartels and other illegal actions are prosecuted by the Japan Fair Trade Commission (JFTC).[66]

The Fair Trade Commission is charged with enforcement of the Antimonopoly Law, which was enacted in 1947 as part of the Occupation reforms imposed by the United States. Unlike the U.S. procedures, however, virtually all Japanese antitrust cases are handled administratively by this agency rather than through private suits.[67] The Fair Trade Commission is hampered in its enforcement work by its small size; as of the mid-1980s, it had just over 500 employees, not many to cope with the entire burden of antitrust enforcement.[68] Furthermore, the letter of the law and the mandate of the JFTC are often seriously at odds with the industrial policy aims and plans of MITI and other government ministries. One Japanese legal scholar, Kenji Sanekata, admits that "in general, antitrust enforcement in Japan can only develop to the extent that it does not conflict seriously with industrial or overall economic policy."[69] The JFTC appeared to be gaining power vis-à-vis MITI in the 1970s as the number of cases it prosecuted increased, and as it specifically confronted MITI in challenging its use of administrative guidance toward the oil refining industry.[70] The general increase in public interest regarding antitrust enforcement during the high-inflation years of the 1970s actually led to an amendment of the Antimonopoly Law in 1977 that strengthened the law and increased the punishments for cartel activities.[71]

The strengthening of the Antimonopoly Law and the decision in the oil cartel case were assumed at the time to undermine MITI's ability to use administrative guidance to carry out industrial policy, but that does not appear to be the case. In fact, the 1980s show strong evidence of a substantial drop in the influence and power of the Fair Trade Commission. During the 1980s the number of antitrust cases actually decided by the JFTC has fallen dramatically: from a peak of 69 cases in 1973, the number of decisions fell to a range of 16 to 20 at the beginning of the 1980s, and was only 6 in 1987.[72] Even the more informal actions by the commission have dropped: keikoku (warnings) dropped from 118 in 1983 to 84 by 1987, and chūi (cautions) dropped from 60 in 1983 to 28 by 1987.[73]

Thus many collusive actions within Japanese industry either go undetected or unprosecuted. For example, imports of soda ash, a product used in the manufacture of glass and steel, have been carefully controlled by the domestic industry, the firms of which jointly own the only specialized unloading facility in Japan in conjunction with a few specialized trading companies. This collusive, anticompetitive activity, which limited American producers to a 6 percent share of the market despite a 20 percent price advantage in the early 1980s, was not investigated by the Fair Trade Commission until brought to its attention by the U.S. government.[74]

Because formal import barriers have been greatly reduced, and because the government is eager to portray Japan as generally open to imports, entry problems are often very subtle and deniable. A recently filed antitrust suit in polycrystalline silicon, an intermediate product used for making the silicon wafers for integrated circuits, exemplifies this dilemma. Despite foreign polysilicon's advantage in production cost (the process is energy-intensive), its market share in Japan has behaved oddly indeed. When the yen was weak in the first half of the 1980s (which should have made imports less attractive), the share of imports rose, reaching a peak of 59 percent in 1984. However, once the yen began to strengthen (which should have made imported polysilicon more attractive), its market share fell quickly, down to 33 percent by 1986, and recovered only slightly, to 38 percent, in 1987.[75] What was happening? The key event was a Japanese government-business study group that met from 1983 to 1985 and produced a report on problems in the industry. The main problem identified in the report was Japan's high dependence on imports, and among the solutions, the report endorsed the notion of new Japanese entrants into the industry.[76] Within six months of the release of the report, a Japanese entrant appeared, with heavy financing for its new facility provided by the Japan Development Bank. All these events could be attributed to coincidence, but that possibility is unlikely enough that a major American firm in the industry has now filed an antitrust suit.[77]

These examples underscore a broad problem of collusive behavior within Japanese industries when faced with foreign competition. Vertical ties—between parts suppliers and major manufacturers, or between manufacturers and distributors—involve unequal, hierarchical social relationships used to exclude foreign (and domestic) outsiders from markets in ways that are illegal in the United States. Horizontal ties among members of manufacturing industries also involve collusion to exclude or limit the role of foreigners, often with the informal approval of the government. The Japanese Fair Trade Commission has opposed some of these activities, but as a small agency it often loses in competition with the Ministry of International Trade and Industry or other powerful government ministries.

Conclusions

The general bias against imports and the lack of intra-industry trade in Japan are the results of factors that run far deeper and are more complex than traditional, identifiable import barriers. Some of these factors are cultural, but that term is not completely accurate. Japan has exhibited a strongly held dominant intellectual belief in creating a comparative advantage for domestic manufacturing that has permeated most of academic, government, business, and (in a more amorphous way) consumer thinking and behavior. Although the discussion in this chapter has focused on recent statements, these attitudes and behavior patterns are rooted in the ethos of a struggling developing country dating back to Japan's position in the late 19th century. A broad consensus of government, business, and academia has favored producing virtually all manufactured goods at home. Substituting domestic production for imports is an important part of industrialization, but these policies have been carried too far, or were too successful, and have distorted the Japanese economy. Too many resources have been allocated to manufacturing in general, and the pattern of trade in individual industries shows an excessive bias toward raw materials and away from specialized trade in manufactured goods. Support for this pattern has been strong, with imports relegated to those product areas in which Japan has an absolute disadvantage (such as petroleum), or in which there exists some unalterable technological or institutional disadvantage (such as large commercial aircraft).

Once this dominant ideology took root, alternative concepts and behavior patterns were submerged or suppressed. Government reinforced the pattern by imposing stiff formal import barriers in the 1950s; business nurtured ties with other domestic firms fraught with heavy social obligations; manufacturers established dominance over distribution routes; trading companies were structured to handle manufactured exports and raw material imports; and even consumers wondered why Japan would want to buy manufactured goods from abroad since domestic firms could produce what consumers wanted. Notions of benefits from free trade and from a greater degree of intra-industry trade have not been part of mainstream writing on trade in Japan. As a theory, free trade may be a standard part of the economics curriculum in Japan, but it has remained a theory without conscious application to real-world Japanese policy—except when decrying the deleterious effects of protectionism in other countries on Japanese exporters. The belief that Japan must be a processing nation that imports only raw materials and exports manufactured goods has thoroughly dominated the thinking, and the idea that a more finely divided concept of comparative advantage could guide trade has been conspicuously absent.

These overlapping and mutually reinforcing patterns of thinking and behavior in different sectors of Japanese society have made Japan a discouraging prospect for foreign firms with competitive products and for government officials charged with negotiating on their behalf. The basic opposition to foreign products implies that removal of formal barriers does not always solve problems of access; an array of other, informal obstacles, from standards to toleration of industry collusion, has remained to impede access.

This bleak assessment of the status of foreign manufactured products in Japan should be tempered a bit. Some manufactured products have entered Japan; all the differences considered here are ones of degree. Japan has less intra-industry trade and imports fewer manufactured goods, but they are not entirely absent in most industries. Second, Japan is now undergoing important changes in attitude and behavior that could lead to substantial increases in the role of imports. These changes are considered in the next chapter.

CHAPTER FIVE

A Changing Japan

THAT JAPAN HAS behaved very differently from other industrial countries because of intertwined economic, political, and social factors should now be clear. The explanations in chapter 4 involve deeply rooted attitudes, policies, and organizational structures that have been biased against imported manufactured goods in general and against intra-industry trade in particular. Years of bilateral and multilateral trade negotiations appear to have influenced Japan's actual trade behavior very little.

Since 1985, however, important changes have begun to take place in Japan. The impetus for change comes from a dramatic rise in the exchange rate of the yen against the dollar—from ¥260 per dollar in February of 1985 to a range of ¥140 to ¥145 by late 1989, an enormous currency adjustment (roughly 100 percent) over a short period. This chapter explores the real impact of the currency movement on trade behavior, as well as evidence of shifting attitudes and policies in the media, government, and corporate sector.

The impact of the currency adjustment on Japan's trade patterns is still in an early phase. Just how far or how fast these patterns will shift remains to be seen. But the evidence to date signals the beginning of policy and attitudinal changes that could, over several years, significantly alter some of the protectionist characteristics identified in earlier chapters. The sense of rapid change is now very strong in Japan; some would even see the shifts as revolutionary.[1] The reality to date is far from revolutionary; attitudes have shifted further than market outcomes. Nevertheless, there is reason to believe that at least a moderate pace of change in behavior will continue for some time and may, in fact, be accelerating. Government officials, journalists, and business executives have all begun to speak quite openly about some of the problems identified in the preceding chapter. If the talk is translated into action, the results could be quite striking.

95

Why Should Japan Change?

The fact that manufactured imports are rising rapidly in Japan is not surprising. The appreciation of the yen has substantially lowered the landed cost of imported goods in Japan and, depending on the price elasticity of demand for imports, ought to lead to expanded purchases. But the validity of these standard economic responses is not so obvious in Japan. The combination of a strong belief in comparative advantage, an industrial policy that has limited imports, lack of exposure to foreign products or prices, and a belief in Japanese uniqueness could be maintained in the face of an appreciating currency. Furthermore, a moderate expansion of imports in response to yen appreciation could be consistent with maintaining previous patterns of import behavior—Japan does import manufactured goods, and there is no reason to suspect that the price elasticity of demand is zero.*

One recent Japanese estimate put the price elasticity of demand for manufactured imports at just under 1.1.[2] Robert Lawrence confirms these results, finding a price elasticity for manufactured imports of 1.01 and, at a disaggregated level, price elasticities on some manufactured products that are higher than those for the same products in the United States.[3] These results are not surprising; rarely does Japan behave in completely economically irrational ways. (The example in chapter 4 of polycrystalline silicon, where the volume of imports actually fell as the yen rose, is unusual, and indicative of the high degree of policy intervention in the market.) The system is flexible enough to respond to price signals in most cases, while still maintaining a pattern of behavior that can be described as implicitly protectionist—exchange-rate gains can be passed on to the consumer without altering the fact that prices may have been very high compared with those in other countries both before and after the currency movement. For structural change to occur, price reductions on many imported goods will have to be much greater than a simple

---

*If the price elasticity of demand for imported manufactured goods is greater than 1, the yen value of purchases will rise as the yen-denominated price falls, and the dollar-denominated value of purchases will rise even more. If the price elasticity is between 0 and 1, then the yen-denominated value of imports will fall (with the rise in volume insufficient fully to offset the drop in unit prices), but the dollar-denominated value will rise (because dollar-denominated prices are unchanged and the quantity increases).

pass-through of exchange-rate gains because the original markups are so high.

Some of the changes analyzed in this chapter do go beyond a response limited by or consistent with past patterns of behavior. But neither are the shifts as easy or obvious as one would expect in a more open economy. Japan is in the throes of a fundamental multidimensional reassessment of its role in the world, and a somewhat more liberal or favorable position toward imports is part of that process.

Chapter 4 debunked the lack of manufactured imports as mainly a cultural phenomenon, although the belief in Japanese uniqueness has certainly contributed to, or been manipulated to, produce this result. Cultural values may change slowly, but many of the factors in import behavior have been a conscious, deliberate response to specific economic conditions: Japan's position as a developing nation with a strong determination to industrialize, the willingness of other nations to tolerate Japan's import barriers during the first two decades of the postwar period, and constraints on travel or investment abroad imposed by low income levels and government policy.

By the 1970s Japan had achieved the position of an advanced industrial nation, yet the changes in import behavior usually associated with this shift had failed to occur. Incipient moves in the direction of greater openness toward manufactured imports occurred in 1971–73 and 1977–79 under the impact of yen appreciation but were truncated by the two oil shocks that pushed Japan back toward an introspective stance.[4] The rise in oil prices and the short-term trade deficits these higher prices imposed caused the yen to depreciate and returned government and business to a strategy of promoting exports and restricting imports. Formal import barriers continued to fall, but little progressive change took place in the distribution sector or other institutions affecting import behavior, and the strong depreciation of the yen following each of the two oil shocks kept unit labor costs on many manufactured goods below foreign costs.[5] Only since 1985, with the sustained increase in the value of the yen, has real change begun.

A strong currency should not have been a necessary condition to bring a reappraisal of trade behavior in Japan: even at earlier exchange rates the nation imported an unusually low amount and actively avoided intra-industry trade. Prices of many imported manufactured products were artificially high. Had liberal trade ideals had a broader following in Japan, trade patterns could have been very different. That such an enormous movement in exchange rates has been a necessary catalyst is clear testimony to the strength of previous attitudes and policies.

A growing body of political science and sociology writing emphasizes the inability of Japan to respond quickly to new international or domestic conditions or to endorse new policy directions.[6] The essence of these studies is that groups and group dynamics are the key variables in understanding Japanese behavior. Observers have long noted that Japanese society is far more group-oriented than is American society. Although this observation is commonplace, academics have begun exploring the implications of a group orientation for economic policymaking and political behavior. In the dynamics of group-centered decisionmaking, identifiable leadership is often lacking, and a complex and intense process takes place when disagreement, outside challenge, or shifting conditions require new responses. This process involves partial accommodation or compensation to reduce the threat posed by the challenge. Sharp discontinuities in policy or behavior are rare in this dynamic, although change can and does take place. Overarching principles or ethics are not the primary determinants of behavior or policy formation; group dynamics dominate the process, something Ruth Benedict pointed out about Japanese society long ago.[7] Those in power may alter their behavior in the face of new conditions or challenges, but the accommodation will be slow and partial, especially if the challenges involve the government as an arbiter. As Thomas Rohlen notes: "It is in the art of compromise, consensus building, and lateral linkage that the government plays an indispensable role. The key term is always balance."[8] Those in opposition will moderate or drop their opposition in the face of compensation or accommodation rather than continue to press their own position. In determining the outcome, the hierarchy among or within groups is an important element.[9]

These values and behavior patterns are deeply embedded in Japanese society and are instilled from an early age through the educational system.[10] While small units such as the family or school represent groups where many of these dynamics might be most visible, these patterns have a large role in a broader setting as well. As Kent Calder notes so well in his study of a variety of important policy challenges in the postwar period, a system of material compensation and mutual obligation has become highly developed and institutionalized at a broad political level as part of the group dynamic of balance that Rohlen identifies. The pattern of Japanese political behavior Calder analyzes, in which challenges or crises are met through material compensation of opposing groups, is in many respects the same pattern that sociologists describe for small groups in general in Japanese society. Karel van Wolferen, in a less academic work, identifies virtually the same pattern in Japanese policymaking and politics as does Calder, though he labels it (somewhat less charitably) an "inescapable embrace" by the "system" in which opponents are bought off or otherwise defused.[11] For this process to work, those in opposition must be willing to accept the embrace, to be bought off, and to drop their opposition. As Rohlen notes, conflict resolution in Japanese society "works only if the opposition is willing ultimately to compromise and be reintegrated. . . . [R]e-attachment must be at least somewhat a voluntary act."[12]

These characterizations of Japanese society have an important bearing on economic behavior. The same principles that govern social groups also affect the interaction within and among firms, and between firms and government. Rodney Clark, for example, has written of a "society of industry" in Japan, within which such social concepts as groups and hierarchy are important determinants of economic behavior. Yasusuke Murakami has also explicitly coupled the social concepts of group behavior with Japanese economic behavior.[13] The typical behavior of Japanese businessmen endorses the concept of social behavior patterns shaping economic actions—for example, the intense training to build corporate loyalty, the endless meetings, an open work environment with desks crowded in large rooms, the deference corporations show toward government officials (and the frequency with which they consult with the government before making major decisions), and the extraordinary amount of time spent maintaining personal contact with buyers. These aspects of corporate behavior all attest to the different context in which corporate decisions are made in Japan, and it is one in which decision-making is not motivated purely by a calculation of short-term economic gain or loss.

Japanese behavior patterns provide good reason to be discouraged about how fast and how far Japanese trade behavior will change. The close social bonds between established buyers and sellers, the strong sense of hierarchy (in which foreign products and firms are relegated to low priorities), explicit or implicit cartels (often with informal government approval or encouragement), and the sense that at the broadest level Japan is a group to be protected from foreign products are daunting obstacles to be overcome.[14]

Economic behavior, though, is somewhat different from other forms of social interaction. Corporations must earn some profit or they go out of business. That hard reality somewhat constrains the priority they attach to their social bonds with other economic and political actors; economic survival of the primary group (the corporation) must be more important than conforming to the expectations for behavior in wider groups. If existing relationships are economically unviable—if the price of domestic products is much higher than imports, for example—then firms can and must react at some point.

These economic necessities imply that even in a basically protectionist society such as Japan, there must exist some exchange rate at which the comparison between domestic and foreign prices becomes so stark that the aversion to imports diminishes. As the number of yen per dollar moves toward zero, dollar-denominated products come closer to being free goods, and at some point import prices must become overwhelmingly attractive. In the case of intermediate goods, an industry in Japan can hold the line against imports only as long as all industry members collude tacitly by agreeing to stick with higher-price domestic suppliers; as soon as one firm decides to purchase from abroad, all others must follow suit or face a production-cost disadvantage.

Western economists, though, assume far too much economic rationality on the part of Japanese individuals and corporations. Economic necessity will bring changes in behavior, but these responses are always modified and limited by norms of Japanese social behavior. As far as possible, corporations will make decisions within the context of the groups within which they operate—the web of their supplier-buyer network, other firms in their industry, and the industry-government connection. This context and the group dynamic that it implies mean that economic rationality will be modified and moderated as it is bent to conform to social reality. In the case of imports, yen appreciation will lead to more imports, but pressure from import-competing manufacturers and established distributors of domestic products must be listened to, accommodated, and compensated. These social necessities mean that the inroads of imports into the Japanese economy will be blunted. Rising imports are certainly possible—as the numbers discussed later amply demonstrate—but the rise may have a lower ceiling than the one that would occur under similar circumstances in the United States or other societies with less group-oriented social and political dynamics. Historically the price and income elasticity of demand for manufactured imports in Japan has been roughly 1, as noted earlier. If that structural relationship continues to hold, the response to yen appreciation will be quite visible because of the large size of the exchange-rate shift, but will leave the ratio of manufactured imports to GDP unchanged. Japan would still be distinctly low compared with other industrial nations.

Many of the changes needed to push Japan toward a more meaningful openness in economic terms involve decisions that must be filtered through the group-oriented decisionmaking process, and changes that would be desirable in promoting greater openness have an explicitly political dimension as well: less administrative guidance by the government, less tacit approval of business collusion, and less control by manufacturers over the distribution system (or greater freedom for innovative entrepreneurship in distribution). Such changes, carried to extreme, would be a fundamental threat to many of the group values and processes around which Japanese economic behavior has been centered. Hence this chapter takes a very cautious view of change in Japan.

On the other hand, economic necessity will compel room for change. Japanese society and behavior patterns have not been static, and there should be room for modification in a direction that will result in greater access for foreign products to the Japanese market.[15] The data presented later suggest that such a process has begun and the economic forces propelling it are likely to continue. This is unlikely to amount to a "revolution" because group dynamics will co-opt the process and will limit the benefit of greater openness for foreign firms. But the direction of change looks positive.

An equally important corollary to the leaderless-group model of Japanese society is that when faced with a need for major change, outside pressure is often necessary to bring it about because the group dynamics of compensation or co-optation are ill-suited for decisiveness. T. J. Pempel argues, in fact, that because Japanese politics are more splintered than was the case 20 years ago, coalitions between foreign groups and groups in Japan that desire a policy change are more important than before.[16] Yen appreciation provides a powerful reason for change, but foreign pressure on Japan will almost certainly be a necessary ingredient in ensuring that moves in the direction of greater openness continue.

Japanese history has been punctuated with episodes of radical change, such as the Meiji Restoration of 1868, which established a modern nation-state and initiated sustained industrialization, and the Occupation after the Second World War, which altered many social and economic institutions. Each of those episodes, however, took place in a revolutionary, crisis atmosphere that does not characterize Japan today. Furthermore, even these two extreme examples involved outside pressure—fear of Western imperialism in the 19th century, and the overt domination of the Occupation after the war. Internal pressures today are moving toward change but are far from revolutionary. This fact strongly suggests that foreign pressure will be a necessary ingredient to strengthen the hand of those in Japan desiring change.

Rising Imports

Measured in dollars, manufactured imports in Japan have been rising rapidly since 1985—up at an average annual rate of 33 percent between 1985 and 1988 (table 5-1). This rapid increase has been interpreted by the Japanese government as evidence that major structural adjustment is taking place. The development most widely cited by Japanese observers is the rising share of manufactures in total imports. Japan used to be criticized for its low ratio of manufactured imports to total imports, although as noted earlier Japanese government officials justified this outcome on the grounds of high import dependency on raw materials. But since 1985 this ratio has shot up, reaching 43 percent in 1988 (and likely to exceed 50 percent in 1989)—a share no longer conspicuously below that of other nations. The change, though, is only partly due to rising manufactured imports, with the dramatic drop in raw material prices providing an equally important explanation. Moreover, the rising dollar value of manufactured imports does not necessarily translate into larger yen amounts because the dollar has depreciated against the yen. In fact, the yen value of manufactured imports actually dropped in 1986, and did not exceed the 1985 value until 1988. Because the yen value has

TABLE 5-1. JAPAN'S TRADE IN MANUFACTURED GOODS, 1980–88[a]

| | Denominated in dollars (millions of dollars) | | | Denominated in yen (billions of yen) | | | Imports as a share of[b] | |
| | | | | | | | GDP (percent) | GDP in manufacturing (percent) |
Year	Exports	Imports	Balance	Exports	Imports	Balance		
1980	124,651	30,566	94,085	28,213	6,961	21,252	2.9	11.4
1981	146,875	31,271	115,604	32,337	6,880	25,457	2.7	10.6
1982	134,256	30,251	104,005	33,291	7,506	25,785	2.8	11.1
1983	142,247	31,943	110,304	33,798	7,591	26,207	2.7	10.8
1984	165,097	37,175	127,922	39,135	8,807	30,328	3.0	11.5
1985	170,673	36,414	134,259	40,769	8,744	32,025	2.8	10.8
1986	203,535	44,038	159,497	34,341	7,427	26,914	2.2	9.0
1987	222,950	60,560	162,390	32,403	8,794	23,609	2.5	10.4
1988	257,116	85,598	171,518	32,940	10,072	22,868	2.7	n.a.

SOURCES: Japan Tariff Association, *The Summary Report: Trade of Japan* (Tokyo), December 1980, pp. 90–131, and similar pages in the December issue of each year through 1988; GDP data are from Economic Planning Agency, *Annual Report on National Accounts*, 1988/9 ed. (Tokyo: Ministry of Finance Printing Office, 1989), pp. 108–09; GNP for 1988 is from Bank of Japan, *Economic Statistics Monthly*, May 1988, p. 178; and GDP in manufacturing is from Economic Planning Agency, *Annual Report on National Accounts*, 1987 ed., pp. 178–89, and 1989 ed., pp. 186–96.

n.a. Not available.

a. Manufactured goods are SITC categories 5–8. For 1988 GNP rather than GDP is the denominator for calculating the share of exports in the economy.

b. These figures differ from those in chapter 2, table 2-2 (in which manufactured imports as a share of GDP in 1985 was reported as 2.6 percent) because different sources report slightly different data.

not risen significantly, manufactured imports as a share of gross domestic product (GDP) have actually fallen—from 3.0 percent in 1984 to 2.7 percent in 1988 (although this level represents a recovery from a temporary low of 2.2 percent in 1986). How can a structural adjustment in which imports play a more important role be taking place if imports actually represent less of economic activity in Japan now than they did in the early and mid-1980s?

To some extent, change has been taking place despite these figures. Because of the exchange-rate movement, the Japanese can buy more foreign goods with a given amount of yen. The physical volume of manufactured goods, therefore, is up sharply even though yen expenditures are not. From 1985 through 1988 the quantity index of manufactured imports rose 80 percent.[17] This corresponds with casual visual evidence; foreign goods are more visible in Japan than they were several years ago. Structural change that does not produce a rise in the share of the yen value of manufactured imports in total GNP, however, will still leave a Japan that has far less import penetration than other industrial countries.

Some Japanese econometric estimates support the contention that import behavior is changing. The Bank of Japan reports that the income elasticity of manufactured imports has been rising and would exceed 1 by the end of 1988. From a level of 0.60 to 0.70 in the 1970s, the income elasticity of manufactured imports rose to 0.84 in 1986, 0.88 in 1987, and 0.96 in the first quarter of 1988.[18] The 1988 trade white paper issued by the Ministry of International Trade and Industry reached similar conclusions with a slightly different model, although it shows the income elasticity of demand rising from 1.40 in the 1970s to 1.70 by the second half of the 1980s, and the price elasticity of demand rising from less than 1 to just over 1.[19] For consumer goods, the Economic Planning Agency reports a similar rise in both price and income elasticity of demand for imports over the last several years.[20] Even without a rise, the studies mentioned above found price elasticities for manufactures of approximately 1 over a longer period. However, estimates of income and price elasticities greater than unity appear to be inconsistent with the data presented earlier on the share of manufactured imports in the economy. Price and income elasticities greater than 1 should have caused the share of manufactured imports in GDP to rise after 1985 as incomes grew and yen-denominated import prices fell. The only way to defend the econometric results is to note that what happened in 1986 and 1987 was a short-term phenomenon, in which exchange-rate movements were so rapid that import behavior lagged behind. Manufactured imports as a share of GDP dropped dramatically in 1986 as a result of this effect and have been returning to levels closer to earlier years since that time, suggesting that a long-run price elasticity of unity remains.

What about intra-industry trade? Has the increase in imports brought about a shift? The rapid increase in imports does not necessarily bring about a corresponding rise in intra-industry trade, and chapter 3 and appendix A demonstrate that in the past Japan's average level of such trade has been rather invariant to changes in the overall trade balance. If Japan continues to be a nation dominated by the concept of broad comparative advantage, yen appreciation will simply lead to abandoning certain products or industries in favor of imports from other nations, switching from a predominance of exports to a predominance of imports. Intra-industry trade will rise only temporarily as this transition takes place. Yen appreciation, however, could produce a new approach to trade in which Japan embraces the concept of two-way trade in more finely demarcated industry classifications that produce the high levels of intra-industry trade characterizing other industrial nations.

The international comparative statistical data bases used in chapter 3 are available only through 1985, but detailed Japanese data are available through 1988. These data, unfortunately, are not compatible with those used earlier. The United Nations trade data are denominated in dollars and use an industry classification scheme known as the Standard International Trade Classification (SITC). The trade data published by Japan are denominated in yen and use a classification scheme known as Customs Co-operation Council Nomenclature (CCCN). Therefore, an international comparison for 1988 of the sort presented earlier is impossible. Nevertheless, it is possible to compare Japan in 1988 to Japan in 1985.

The fact that Japan's trade data are calculated in yen interjects another disparity. Because of lags in adjustment in prices and volumes of traded goods, currency movements cause the dollar-denominated and yen-denominated trade balances to behave differently. Between 1985 and 1988 the dollar-denominated overall trade surplus rose by more than 70 percent (from $46.7 billion to $77.3 billion), while the yen-denominated surplus dropped (from ¥10.9 trillion to ¥9.9 trillion). Much of the rise was due to falling raw material prices. When the focus is shifted to manufactured goods, the dollar-denominated surplus also continued to rise after 1985, up 28 percent by 1988, while the yen-denominated surplus showed a rapid decline—a 29 percent drop over the same period. If shifts in the overall trade balance affect the calculation of intra-industry trade, the use of yen-denominated data here would tend to overstate any improvement.

During 1988 the Japanese government revised the CCCN industry classification scheme, adopting a new version, known as the Harmonized Commodity Description and Coding System (HS), which is being adopted by most other nations as well.[21] This change means that the industrial classifications in 1985 and 1988 are not completely uniform. Still, most of the changes are relatively minor. At the four-digit level the change led to a large expansion of the number of categories, from 372 to 972, resulting from further subdividing categories in the previous CCCN classification.* The resulting av-

*For example, motor vehicles (CCCN 8702) was divided into passenger vehicles (HS 8703) and goods vehicles (HS 8704); televisions and radios and

erage intra-industry trade (IIT) index number calculated for Japan in 1988 using the new HS classification, therefore, must be equal to or less than what would have resulted using the old CCCN classifications.

With these caveats in mind, calculation of the average IIT index number for manufactured products at a four-digit level using the Japanese data yields a 27 percent increase in the index, from 19.5 in 1985 to 24.8 in 1988. This rise is encouraging, but not particularly large yet, especially given the substantial reduction in the yen-denominated manufactured trade surplus that occurred over the same time.

Figure 5-1 shows the shares of Japan's manufactured exports that fall into each of 20 IIT intervals, similar to the figures in chapter 3. Some change has occurred in the skewed pattern, with the extremely heavy concentration of Japan's exports in very low IIT intervals diminishing somewhat. The share of exports in the IIT interval 0–5, for example, dropped from 38 percent to 15 percent, while that in the somewhat higher interval of 10–15 rose from 9 percent to 25 percent. The share of exports in the intervals 20–35 also rose somewhat. These are encouraging developments, to the extent that they represent a real phenomenon and are not just the result of the changing industrial classification in 1988.[22] However, no improvement has taken place in IIT levels of 40 or above, and Japan's extremely low share of exports in that range was a major contrast with the other countries considered in chapter 3.

Table 5-2 shows the IIT index numbers for the 12 largest export categories under the CCCN classification in 1987 and their corresponding categories under the new HS classification in 1988 (consolidating those that had been further subdivided in the change). These data suggest that the rise in IIT levels for the four largest exports is real, but is insignificant or negative for the rest of the list.

How should these data be interpreted? That the average IIT level for Japan has risen is encouraging and may be a sign that Japan's behavior is beginning to converge with that of other industrial nations. But the shift to date still leaves Japan far below the levels of other

---

related products (CCCN 8515) was divided into four groups (HS 8525 to 8528); and vacuum tubes and semiconductors (CCCN 8521) was split into three categories (HS 8540 to 8542).

FIGURE 5-1. DISTRIBUTION OF JAPAN'S MANUFACTURED EXPORTS ACROSS INTRA-INDUSTRY TRADE LEVELS, 1985 AND 1988

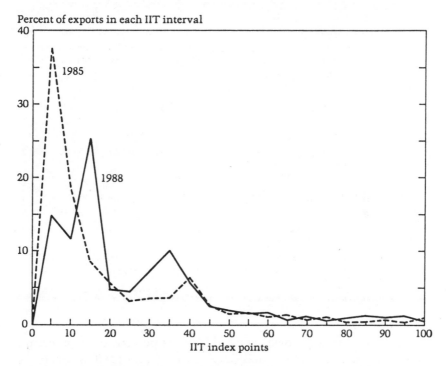

Percent of exports in each IIT interval

SOURCE: Author's calculations based on United Nations trade data tapes.

nations and may be attributable in large part to the drop in yen-denominated prices for large export items like automobiles. In and of itself, the rise in the IIT level for automobiles should not be belittled, but a broadly based increase in intra-industry trade remains elusive. In particular, the lack of any measurable change in the upper tail of the distribution in figure 5-1 is discouraging. Japan still has far to go.

In some other respects, moderate change is beginning in Japan's import structure. One of the problems identified in chapter 4 was Japan's unusual preference for raw materials over processed goods. An area where this preference has been a point of contention between the United States and Japan has been forest products. Appendix table B-1 shows Japanese imports (denominated in yen) for a variety of forest products. According to recent data, the share of

TABLE 5-2. JAPAN'S INTRA-INDUSTRY TRADE IN MAJOR EXPORT
PRODUCTS, 1987 AND 1988

CCCN category	Harmonized Standard classification[a]	Description	1987		1988		Change in IIT index number, 1987–88
			Exports (billions of yen)	IIT index number	Exports (billions of yen)	IIT index number	
8702	8703, 8704	Motor vehicles	6,463	8.9	6,085	12.2	3.3
8706	8708	Auto parts	1,556	6.2	1,168	8.9	2.7
8515	8525–28	TV, radio	1,527	10.7	1,241	12.5	1.8
8453	8471	Computers	1,360	25.8	1,461	30.5	4.7
9211	8521	TV, sound recorders	1,249	2.1	796	2.2	0.1
8521	8540–42	Tubes and semi-conductors	1,206	31.1	1,579	31.3	0.2
8406	8407–08	Internal combustion engines	699	7.2	528	2.1	−5.1
9010	9009	Copiers	601	3.1	529	2.3	−0.8
8901	8901	Ships	596	10.1	461	6.4	−3.7
8455	8473	Computer parts	507	34.2	702	32.2	−2.0
8513	8517	Telephones, fax, etc.	485	13.5	643	13.5	0.0
7318	7304	Iron and steel tubes and pipe	371	7.5	359	1.1	−6.4

SOURCES: Japan Tariff Association, *Japan Exports and Imports: Commodity by Country* (Tokyo), December 1985, December 1988.
   a. Harmonized Commodity Description and Coding System (HS) classification numbers correspond to the CCCN classification categories used by Japan in 1985. In most cases, there is a one-to-one correspondence, but for some industries, the new HS classification has subdivided industries into more than one category.

"wood in the rough" (logs) declined from 71 percent to 46 percent of total imports of forest products between 1980 and 1988. Much of the change is attributable to a switch from logs to the simplest manufactured product—sawn lumber—the share of which went up from 13 percent in 1980 to 27 percent in 1988. Plywood, however, also rose, from 0.3 percent in 1980 to 6 percent in 1988. Part of this rising (though still small) share in dollar values of wood imports for processed items comes from relative price changes; between 1980 and 1988 the yen-denominated unit price of logs dropped precipitously, while that of processed items fell less (so that unchanged physical volumes of imports would show a smaller value share for logs and a higher share for processed products). Nevertheless, the quantity figures show that the cubic meters of imported logs have moved erratically and remain below the level of 1970. In stark contrast, square meters of imported plywood quintupled between 1985 (44 million) and 1988 (262 million). Forest products are a particularly interesting product chain to observe, since Japan's import barriers in this area have been on the bilateral agenda for many years—and some easing of those barriers has taken place, although forest products remain one of the areas named for further talks under the Super 301 provision of the Trade Act of 1988. The rising share of processed imports is encouraging, although the continued predominance of log imports in a nation with high-cost timber resources and an inefficient forest products manufacturing industry indicates that these changes could or should proceed much further.

Appendix tables B-2 through B-5 provide similar detail for a number of metals: iron and steel, copper, nickel, and aluminum. Chapter 4 discussed the sharp contrast between Japanese trading patterns and those of other countries, with an overwhelming pattern of raw material and basic metal imports in the case of Japan. Has this pattern changed over time? The data in these tables indicate that for most metals, relatively little change has taken place.

Iron and steel (appendix table B-2) show the most change. In 1970 virtually all imports (97 percent) were in the form of ore, concentrates, and scrap. Since that time the share of these raw materials has dropped to 71 percent. Most of the shift comes from a rising share of basic iron and steel products (ingots, blooms, billets, slag, and coils) that must be processed further. The share of this category rose from less than 1 percent in 1970 to 9 percent in 1985, then accelerated to almost 19 percent in 1988. This pattern—shifting from raw materials to crude metal inputs—characterizes all the metals considered here. For iron and steel, however, imports of some other processed forms have also risen—especially iron and steel sheets and plates (from virtually zero in the 1970s to 14 percent of imports by 1988). This category, however, represents the low-technology, low-value-added end of iron and steel products. Nevertheless, smaller but noticeable increases have occurred in higher value-added products such as tubes, pipes, and fittings (up from less than 1 percent of imports in 1980 to almost 4 percent by 1988). These shifts may be relatively modest, but they do represent a real change reflected in the volume figures and are not just a result of relative unit-price shifts.

For copper (appendix table B-3) the share of ores and concentrates in total copper imports has also fallen somewhat—from 73 percent in 1975 to 61 percent by 1988, but the shift was mainly to a basic refined copper product (electrolytic cathode copper) and to waste and scrap. The total share of ores and concentrates plus these basic unwrought products was 99 percent in 1970, dipping only to 97 percent in 1985 and falling somewhat more, to 95 percent, by 1988. Thus imports of manufactured copper products remain negligible, even though some individual items have increased (with imports of copper foil doubling between 1985 and 1988).

Imports of nickel ores and concentrates (appendix table B-4) have dropped precipitously over time; they too have been replaced largely by intermediate products and unwrought metal, so that the subtotal of these basic forms drops only moderately, from 93 percent in 1970 to 90 percent by 1985, and actually rises a bit, to 92 percent, by 1988. A few processed nickel products do show substantial increases, with foil, flakes, and powders up from 1 percent of imports in 1970 to 7 percent by 1985, but with a decline to 5 percent since 1985. Only part of this rise can be attributed to differential price movements.[23]

Aluminum is an especially interesting case because the Japanese government made much of its willingness to let the aluminum-refining industry contract as energy prices soared in the 1970s. Aluminum refining is energy-intensive, and the rapid rise in oil prices in the 1970s put the Japanese industry in an uncompetitive position relative to foreign producers. Aluminum-refining capacity in Japan declined rapidly in response, with some coordination through the Ministry of International Trade and Industry (MITI) to ease the process. This disinvestment and acceptance of imports is supposed to be an example of the greater openness of the Japanese market, since the government did not protect the domestic industry from foreign competition as energy prices rose.

The data in appendix table B-5 give a different picture of what has happened to aluminum imports. Raw material imports, bauxite and aluminum concentrates, have declined sharply, from ¥35 billion in 1980 to only ¥10 billion in 1988, or only 1.3 percent of all aluminum imports. This drop in raw material imports, however, has been replaced entirely by a rise in unwrought aluminum and scrap, so that the subtotal for raw materials plus unwrought aluminum as a share of all aluminum imports was virtually the same in 1988 as in 1975 (91 percent). Imports of some manufactured aluminum products, especially wrought bars and wire, plus wrought plates, sheets, and strip have actually dropped in value (although not always in volume).

These four examples indicate that changes in Japan's heavy preference for raw materials or for the simplest refined form of a metal

continues virtually unabated. Except for iron and steel, little increase in the share of higher value-added products has taken place.
Even in the case of iron and steel, the increase is confined largely to
a small subset of rather low value-added products.

Besides the rise in the yen that might have been expected to bring
a change in metal imports, tariff levels have fallen. Japan has had a
graduated tariff structure on metals—no tariff on raw materials, with
rising rates on processed metals. Table 5-3 shows these rates for the
metal products considered here for 1970 and 1989. The graduated
structure remains, although the range of rates has been compressed
considerably. This structure was especially important in the past because of what is known as effective tariff protection, in which the
real protection afforded a domestic manufactured product depends
on the import duty for the manufactured good relative to value added
in the domestic product.* By levying a tariff on processed products
but not raw materials, the effective rate of tariff protection can be
much higher than indicated simply by the nominal tariff level. Thus
a fall in the nominal rates on processed materials should have reduced the effective rate of production by a proportionately larger
amount. But the general reduction on tariffs seems to have had relatively little impact on the import structure for these metals.

Other evidence published by the government shows rising import
penetration of some Japanese domestic markets, shown in table 5-4.
These are real changes that cannot be ignored, but the list is selective and the conclusions that can be drawn from it are ambiguous.
Twenty-two of the 33 products show double-digit penetration of Japanese markets in 1987 (of which 13 already had double-digit penetration in 1980), and some (such as electric fans) show rapidly rising
market shares, but the rest are single-digit, and some of the increases
are quite small (such as automobiles from 1 percent to 3 percent of
the domestic market).[24] This particular government document also
sticks to the more traditional reason that the market share of imports should rise to higher levels: "Japan must become a leading importer of manufactured goods in order *to fulfill its obligations toward the international community*" (emphasis added).[25]

---

*The formula for calculation of effective tariff rates is: effective tariff =
$e_j = (t_j - \Sigma_i a_{ij}t_i)/(1 - \Sigma_i a_{ij})$, where t = nominal tariffs, a = shares of the
costs of the various inputs to product j.

TABLE 5-3. JAPAN'S TARIFFS ON METALS, 1970 AND 1989

Percentages unless otherwise specified

Item	1970	1989
Iron and Steel		
Ores and concentrates	0	0
Roasted iron pyrites	0	0
Iron and steel scrap	0	0
Pig iron	6.0–7.0	3.0 (2.0–7.7)
Ingots	8.75 (6–13)	3.4–4.6
Shapes	10.5 (12–22)	3.4–4.6
		(3.9–6.6)
Castings, forgings	14.0	3.9
Structures and parts	7.0–10.5	3.9
Copper		
Ores and concentrates	0	0
Unwrought	8.8–9.1 (17)	¥15/kg (0–4.8)
Worked	14.0–22.0	4.6–6.6
Nickel		
Ores and concentrates	0	0
Unwrought	¥210/kg (31.5)	11.7 (0–8.1)
Worked	15.0 (15.0–31.5)	4.6–5.8
Aluminum		
Bauxite and concentrates	0	0
Unwrought	10.6	1.0
Worked	12.0–20.8	4.1–6.3
Lead		
Ores and concentrates	0	0
Unwrought	8.5 (9.0–15.2)	¥8/kg (0–4.6)
Worked	15.0–20.0	4.6–6.6
Zinc		
Ores and concentrates	0	0
Unwrought	¥10–12/kg	0–3.3
Worked	10.5–17.0	3.8–5.8
Structural parts	10.5–14.0	3.9
Tin		
Ores and concentrates	0	0
Unwrought	0 (7.0)	0 (2.6)
Worked	7.0–14.0	3.0–4.6

SOURCES: Japan Tariff Association, *Customs Tariff Schedules of Japan* (Tokyo), 1970 ed., pp. 91–94, 313–64; 1989 ed., pp. 185–86, 702–72. Tariff rates for alloyed products are shown separately in parentheses when these rates are higher than those for unalloyed metal products.

TABLE 5-4. IMPORT PENETRATION IN SELECTED JAPANESE MARKETS, 1980, 1985, 1987[a]

Item	1980	1985	1987
Iron and steel			
Hot-rolled sheets and coils	2.1	23.9	31.0
Cold-rolled sheets and coils	0.0	3.1	6.8
Surface-treated sheets	0.1	0.2	1.1
Steel pipe	0.6	3.8	5.2
Shapes (rails, bars, etc.)	0.0	0.4	1.4
Wire rod	0.9	2.8	7.5
Heavy or medium plates	4.9	14.5	16.3
Chemicals			
Ethylene dichloride[b]	8.9	23.7	28.4
Ethylene glycol	16.3	44.7	48.2
Acrylonitrile	12.3	19.0	19.3
Phenol aldehide resin	0.7	2.7	3.5
Interfacial active agents	2.0	4.2	5.3
Industrial goods			
Milling machines[b]	15.4	20.1	41.9
Lathes	20.5	30.4	40.2
Integrated circuits	22.2	21.2	25.3
Consumer products			
Photographic film	29.4	36.8	39.5
Sewing machines	8.8	22.6	30.5
Calculators	12.9	44.7	49.0
Black and white TVs[b]	1.5	14.3	54.4
Portable radios	38.8	39.9	55.7
Radio cassette recorders[b]	4.6	15.3	47.5
Electric fans	21.6	30.1	54.8
Automobiles[c]	1.6	2.2	3.0
Bicycles	0.0	2.6	7.7
35mm cameras	7.7	19.4	46.6
Cotton fabrics	10.6	24.9	28.8
Knit fabric	1.2	2.1	4.0
Outerwear	20.8	34.8	46.3
Underwear	12.2	25.4	36.2
Knitted socks	n.a.	18.9	25.1
Pianos	0.8	2.0	3.8
Plastic toys	29.8	31.8	37.7
Fountain pens, ball point pens	4.6	7.9	13.0

SOURCE: *News from MITI*, NR-354 (88-02), May 1988, pp. 14–15.

n.a. Not available.

a. All calculations are based on quantity volumes rather than yen or dollar values. Import penetration is calculated as: (import volume)/(production volume − export volume + import volume).

b. Calculations based on imports divided by production volume rather than on apparent domestic consumption.

c. Calculation based on registrations of imported cars divided by registrations of all new cars.

Changing Government Attitudes

Japan is a capitalist nation in which market forces underlie most production, price, and investment decisions. Nevertheless, the government plays a role quite unlike that of the federal government in the United States. Long the subject of debate among economists and political scientists, it is at least accepted by most that the relationship between government and the private sector in economic matters is closer, more organized or clearly articulated, and less confrontational than is the case in the United States.[26]

In such an environment, realization of the expected economic shifts stemming from yen appreciation or a restructuring of import patterns requires that the central government intervene. Market changes stemming from yen appreciation imply a redistribution of economic benefits in society—away from export-oriented manufacturers or import-competing manufacturers and toward distributors of imports. A greater role for imports also involves a shift away from the domestic manufacturing sector as a whole and toward services and households. In the social context discussed earlier in this chapter, such a redistribution is difficult to achieve; the web of existing relationships among buyers and sellers is not so easily broken, and both the gainers and losers feel bound to conform to group dynamics involving compensation and balance. The government is often a necessary and important informal mediator in this process. Through both explicit policy changes and moral suasion or administrative guidance, the government can buttress or hinder the increase of imports in Japan. If the government chooses to play a positive role, then the emerging shifts gain broader acceptance and the changes can take place more quickly.

Until recently, government reports have often justified (rather than lamented) the low level of imports and the low income and price elasticities for imports. That behavior pattern was described as rational and efficient.[27]

As noted earlier, the international trade white papers of the 1960s and 1970s occasionally discussed but did not emphasize direct benefits from manufactured imports and gave only minor attention to the possibility of intra-industry trade. Over time the tendency became stronger to justify low levels of manufactured imports rather than to promote further reductions in access barriers. Even as recently as 1985 and 1986, the trade white papers issued annually by

MITI displayed little enthusiasm in their discussion of manufactured imports. In both years the emphasis was on the special demands of the Japanese market for quality and service, as well as price, as features that foreign manufacturers would have to address better in order to become more successful in Japan; little was said about the benefits of imports to the Japanese economy. The 1985 report also downplayed the seriousness of the high markups on foreign goods, showing for a quite selective list of imported products that retail prices in Japan were no higher than in other markets. The overall message from these reports was clear: if market penetration by foreign manufactured products in Japan was low, the blame lay with foreign manufacturers for failing to produce competitive products. At no point did these reports admit to any peculiarity in Japan's import behavior; if changes were needed, they were needed abroad, not in Japan.[28] These reports provide at least a partial guide to government attitudes. The trade white paper is a product of MITI as a whole, and the discussion represents the dominant or consensus view, although it varies from year to year depending on the personnel assigned to do the actual writing. The analysis in the white papers often resurfaces in international meetings or negotiations, especially the plethora of reasons for why imports are low.

Since the mid-1980s, though, the government has exhibited a new attitude favoring imports, and the changes appear to go beyond the short discussions of intra-industry trade in earlier years or the routine pro forma comments on the benefits of free trade. This trend is clearly visible in an outpouring of materials mainly from MITI, the Economic Planning Agency (EPA), and the Japan Fair Trade Commission, written in 1988 about Japan's role in the world and about structural change in the Japanese economy. Replacing the previous emphasis on comparative advantage (and the assumed comparative advantage in all manufactures except labor-intensive products), the government is now promoting *suihei bungyō* (the horizontal division of industry) as a dominant catch-phrase or concept, one that encompasses the notion that imported manufactured goods and intra-industry trade are beneficial to Japan.

In the past many government comments about the openness of the Japanese market were directed at a foreign audience, with little real policy change behind them. A long series of "market-opening packages" in the first half of the 1980s did little truly to increase market access.[29] In 1985 an advisory commission headed by Saburo

Okita issued a report endorsing greater imports,[30] as did a follow-up report outlining an "Action Program" on easing the way for imports. But these reports stuck to the old view of why Japan should change. The Action Program announced that "in the light of its present status in the international community, Japan is asked to fully utilize its strength, even at its own sacrifice to a considerable extent, so as to help the world attain a medium- and long-term development." At least this report goes on to say that "efforts in this direction, through increased imports, especially imports of manufactured goods, . . . will bring about price stabilization and expansion of selection, [and] will contribute to the further upgrading of the lives of the people."[31] The following year, yet another advisory commission, headed by former Bank of Japan president Haruo Maekawa, issued another general report in the same vein, calling for broad structural change in Japan. But it, too, put its primary emphasis on international obligations rather than on direct benefits to Japan, stating that "Japan should undertake responsibilities commensurate with its economic position and strive for harmonious co-existence within the world economy."[32] Since that time, however, continued yen appreciation has created a new environment in which the government has become more interested in the domestic benefits from increased manufactured imports.

Now the government is engaged in a domestic dialogue with the private sector in Japan, extolling the virtues of imports and thereby giving moral encouragement to those businesses interested in importing, and signaling those who oppose imports that the government will be less willing to support their cause. In 1985, when this process began with the Okita Report and Prime Minister Nakasone's ostentatious purchase of $100 worth of foreign merchandise in Tokyo department stores (and a televised address exhorting his fellow citizens to do likewise), it was soundly ridiculed by the press as a ludicrous public relations ploy. But more serious discussions favoring imports come through clearly and strongly in a number of recent government reports.[33]

For example, looking at the long-term future, the Economic Planning Agency published a book in 1987 emphasizing continued structural change: greater reliance on domestic demand rather than exports to drive the economy, greater market openness, a rapid rise in foreign direct investment by Japanese manufacturers, and a need for smooth industrial adjustment with government cooperation. The report anticipates that the horizontal division of industry will proceed rapidly and bring about a substantial rise in intra-industry trade— without admitting that the past was distorted by barriers to entry of foreign goods.[34]

A somewhat shorter-term vision of the future was produced by the EPA in 1988—the new long-term economic "plan," which is a forecast or set of desired economic outcomes for the five years from 1988 to 1992. This document stresses the need for further reduction or elimination of formal tariff and quota barriers, as well as further action on standards and approval procedures to make them more efficient, fast, and simple. The need for greater openness is put in strong terms: "We must do *much more* to promote access to the market and *more positively* offer a 'business chance' [to foreign products]" (emphasis added).[35] One might reasonably wonder how Japan could have been as open to imports as the government had been claiming for years if such strong language was justified in 1988.

The most detailed document from the EPA, though, is the 1988 economic white paper, an annual survey of the economy and analysis of topical issues. This report provides a lengthy analysis of structural changes in Japan and of the rise in manufactured imports, and reinforces again the need for greater openness. Moreover, the white paper even discusses intra-industry trade in the context of analyzing the progress in the international horizontal division of industry. The appearance of any analysis of intra-industry trade in a government document is a welcome development, though the purpose of the discussion in the white paper is to highlight the rise in intra-industry trade since 1985 rather than to acknowledge the low level of such trade relative to other countries. The conclusion that the EPA draws from the data may not be warranted in any case, since the most striking development portrayed in its figures is the sustained drop in IIT levels in trade in nonelectric and electric machinery with the Asian newly industrializing countries, the European Community, and the United States from 1975 to 1985. In fact the level of intra-industry trade in these industries since 1985 has risen very modestly, falling far short of reversing this prolonged drop.[36]

The 1988 trade white paper published by MITI makes essentially similar points in a long section on manufactured imports, with extensive discussion of how manufactured imports benefit Japan by lowering inflation, widening consumer choice, and enabling a more efficient allocation of domestic economic resources.[37] MITI has also published its own long-term view of Japan's position in the world, in which the ministry pushes the concept of more open markets, stating that Japan must thoroughly open its markets and "work hard" at increasing imports. It clearly lays out the need to restructure industry as part of the solution to the earlier excessive dependence on exports and restrictions on imports.[38]

The Japan Fair Trade Commission (JFTC), the antitrust enforcement agency, has also joined the crowd in calling for greater openness. Its annual report for 1987 devoted a chapter to an antitrust perspective on market access, based on the premise that a greater presence of foreign products means competitive benefits for Japan. The discussion is mainly technical, clarifying the antitrust rules that apply to legalized cartels, importer associations, and distribution sector behavior (including advertising rules and parallel imports). Even though the JFTC is a relatively weak agency with a limited staff, its focus on market-access questions is an encouraging development.[39]

During 1989 the government took another positive and unusual step in admitting and emphasizing price disparities on consumer goods between Japan and other countries. A study by MITI, released in the spring of 1989 and covered in the press, found the average price for a basket of 11 brand name products to be 38 percent cheaper in New York and 29 percent cheaper in Paris. Given the ease with which such surveys can be manipulated through selective choice of goods, cities, and retail outlets, MITI demonstrated a surprising openness in admitting such large differentials.[40] In September of 1989 the Economic Planning Agency released its own survey of prices, which was also given considerable play in the press. Its conclusions are consistent with the MITI survey, finding that Tokyo prices for 397 items were 28 percent higher than New York prices.[41] Yet a third survey, jointly conducted by MITI and the U.S. Department of Commerce, was released late in the year. Covering 122 products priced in Japan, the United States, and third markets, it found that prices for these products averaged 42 percent higher in Japan, a result quite similar to the findings of the other surveys.[42]

These various reports from the government demonstrate the new set of attitudes gaining currency in Japan. Most of them are not very specific in terms of what policy actions are necessary or appropriate, and dissension within MITI and the EPA, not to mention between these agencies and others within the government, remains strong.

Nevertheless, the fact that the documents are the products of the EPA or MITI as a whole means that others within the agency gave tacit approval to the final versions. This alone represents a significant shift of the dominant or majority attitude within these ministries.

But advocating greater openness is not synonymous with actually undertaking new policies to achieve that end. Given the short period since yen appreciation began in 1985, it is still too early to see much movement, but some changes are under way. MITI, for example, has two advisory commissions studying the distribution sector to prepare for changes in regulations that currently restrict the expansion of new, more efficient distribution channels.* The combined group has issued an interim report that endorses moderate changes in the administration of the Large-Scale Retail Store Law that would make it easier to open large chain store outlets.[43] Keidanren (Japan Federation of Economic Organizations), the association of big business, also endorses such changes, as did the follow-up group to the advisory commission on administrative reform (in which Keidanren was a principal player).[44] By late 1989 the fate of these proposals was less certain because of the loss of the Liberal Democratic party in elections for the upper house of the Diet during the previous summer, but some forward movement seemed likely.

The Japan External Trade Organization (JETRO), a government-owned group established in the 1950s to promote exports, is also playing a more vigorous role on the import side. In conjunction with MITI and the Manufactured Import Promotion Organization (MIPRO), another government-owned organization, JETRO has been involved in import seminars within Japan. Although the small size of the program suggests that it is largely a public relations gesture, the seminars are addressed to a domestic audience and thus do not have any direct public relations value abroad.[45] JETRO has also established an on-line import information data base to match domestic firms interested in importing with foreign firms interested in ex-

---

*Called *shingikai*. In many cases, ministries are required by law to submit proposals to these advisory commissions before drawing up legislation for the national Diet. While the ministries supply the draft reports and other data that the commissions discuss, this format does allow some nongovernmental opinions into the process. The commissions generally fulfill the role provided by open hearings in the United States, although their membership is very selective.

porting. Most of the inquiries to the system have been from the medium-sized and small firms that were JETRO's main constituency when it was actively promoting exports in the 1950s and 1960s. As with the import seminars, the number of inquiries is not large, so that the service could be dismissed as a public relations move, but it also is addressed to a Japanese audience, and news about its activities is being published in the Japanese media, which would be a puzzling choice if the intent were mainly to improve Japan's image abroad.[46]

To date, actual changes in policy toward imports have lagged behind the rhetoric of greater openness. But the shift in rhetoric is a necessary part of change and signals the direction in which Japan is moving; the words can no longer be dismissed as empty public relations ploys designed to placate foreigners. Real shifts in government policy—toward imports directly and indirectly through shifts in such areas as distribution sector policy—should continue.

The Private Sector

Nevertheless, the real change in behavior must come from private sector manufacturing and distribution firms. For years specialists on Japan have argued over the motivation of Japanese firms—whether they are concerned with profits, market share, or some other corporate goal such as employee welfare. In the long run, however, all Japanese firms must make a profit, even if they fail to pursue profit-maximizing strategies. They must respond in an economically rational way to changing price signals from markets. As noted at the beginning of this chapter, that response may be slowed or partially blocked by strong social constraints and collusive behavior, but at some set of relative prices, behavior must begin to change in order to preserve profitability. Those changes include imports from foreign direct investment operations, internal organizational shifts, and new attitudes and policies toward imports in general.

The most noticeable shift is the stepped up pace of foreign direct investment by Japanese manufacturing firms. This trend is also the easiest response of firms to yen appreciation. More foreign direct investment will affect Japanese trade in two ways: as a substitute for manufactured exports from Japan, and as a source of imports to Japan. The predominant pattern of Japanese manufacturing investment in the past was as a substitute for exports; factories produced

TABLE 5-5. JAPANESE FOREIGN DIRECT INVESTMENT,
1980, 1985, 1989

Millions of dollars, percentage growth

Area	December 31, 1980	December 31, 1985	March 31, 1989	Annual growth rate	
				1981–85	1986–89
Total	12,179	23,819	49,843	14.4	25.5
North America	2,332	7,440	23,944	26.1	43.3
Asia	4,444	7,434	12,371	10.8	17.0

SOURCES: Ministry of Finance, *Kokusai Kin'yūkyoku Nenpō* [International Finance Bureau Annual Report] (Tokyo), 1986 ed., pp. 458–59; 1981 ed., pp. 352–53; and *JEI Report*, no. 31A (March 11, 1989).

goods for local markets or third markets (largely to circumvent import barriers in those countries). As a source of imports, the only significant past investments were for the processing of raw materials unavailable in Japan, or in textiles (an industry that had lost comparative advantage in Japan by the late 1960s).

Table 5-5 provides summary data on Japan's recent foreign direct investment in manufacturing. Since 1985 direct investment in the manufacturing sector has accelerated moderately, from an average annual growth of 14 percent in 1981–85 to 26 percent in 1986–89. The biggest recipient of this investment has been North America, with investment jumping to a 43 percent annual growth (from 26 percent in the earlier period). But investment in Asia is also growing somewhat more quickly—from 11 percent in the earlier period to 17 percent in 1986–89.

These data show that yen appreciation has led to an acceleration of foreign direct investment, and some of that investment is probably motivated by an intention to export back to Japan. Little of the investment in the United States will produce such exports,* but it could be a significant motive for investing in Asia. This distinction lends a note of caution to judgments about the impact of the current wave of Japanese foreign direct investment on intra-industry trade.

*In 1988 Honda began shipments of automobiles from its U.S. factory back to Japan, but such examples will remain an exception. ("Self-Reliant U.S. Car Company to Be Developed by Honda," press release, Honda of America, Marysville, Ohio, September 17, 1987.) One should not overestimate the impact of foreign direct investment on Japanese imports, since even after the yen began appreciating, North America has remained the dominant location for Japanese investment ($24 billion in accumulated investment as of the end of March 1989, compared with $12 billion in Asia). *JEI Report*, no. 31A (March 31, 1989), p. 4.

Internal statistical data compiled by MITI indicate that in fiscal 1980, 9.8 percent of sales by Japanese-owned firms in Asia were exports back to Japan, with that share rising marginally to 10.8 percent in fiscal 1983, and then more sharply to 16.7 percent by fiscal 1987. The ratio ought to continue rising, as more firms make the decision to move production overseas in response to yen appreciation. Overall, however, the share of output from overseas Japanese manufacturing operations destined for Japan has actually fallen (from 10.9 percent to 9.1 percent over the same period) because of the shift in the location of investment toward North America.[47]

This statistical evidence that additional overseas investment in Asia is driven by an intention to export back to Japan has echoes in the Japanese business press. By 1986 articles appeared stressing the cost advantages of moves overseas, rather than the need to circumvent protectionism in foreign markets. Nevertheless, the belief that production in Japan is the efficient choice because of higher labor quality, easier management conditions, and tighter inventory control has meant that even with yen appreciation, caution has been the watchword on producing abroad for the Japanese market.[48] Furthermore, any move by a Japanese firm to relocate production abroad implies a change in its existing relationships with its workers and domestic suppliers. The social dynamics discussed earlier in this chapter lead to the conclusion that such changes cannot be carried out as easily or quickly as in the United States and may cause some firms to shy away from making any such move. These constraints make the rapid acceleration of foreign direct investments since 1985 quite impressive.[49]

A large increase in manufactured imports and any change in intraindustry trade patterns requires more than a turnabout in corporate attitudes toward foreign investment. The pattern of corporate organization has been geared to production in Japan and export to the rest of the world. The changes at one major Japanese general trading company will demonstrate how much internal restructuring is necessary to deal with increased imports of manufactures. Traditionally, the firm had separate export, import, and domestic trading groups. The export specialists understood manufactured goods but not importing procedures; import specialists understood raw materials but not manufactured goods; and domestic traders understood domestic distribution channels but not foreign manufactured goods. In order to respond to the greater demand for imported manufactured goods, this firm is collapsing the distinction between export, import, and domestic trading, forcing employees with these separate various specialties to work with one another to fill in the gaps in expertise necessary to handle imported manufactured products. Another trading company, Mitsui, has given directors responsibility for expanding manufactured imports through efforts that similarly cut across the traditional operating groups within the firm.[50] The hand of the government is visible in some of these moves, since it had "requested" 60 leading firms involved in distribution to enlarge imports as part of the 1985 Action Program.[51] Once again, the government is playing an informal role of mediator, lending some legitimacy to change and also guiding or coordinating the kinds of activities undertaken by private sector firms.

Some large manufacturing firms are also creating new subsidiaries to import manufactured goods. Nippon Steel, for example, has established a subsidiary to import superminicomputers with CAD/CAM (computer-aided design/computer-aided manufacturing) capability, while Ishikawajima-Harima Heavy Industries and Nippon Kokan have established subsidiaries to import California wine. Matsushita, on the other hand, has transferred responsibility for promoting manufactured imports out of its trading subsidiary and placed its own vice chairman in charge.[52] None of these examples will bring a major shift in Japan's import patterns; a steel company turning to wine imports will not create revolutionary change in Japan. Nevertheless, the idea that these large export-oriented manufacturing firms are interested in importing finished manufactured products (albeit, far removed from their own product areas) is a visible change for Japan. So too is the fact that at Matsushita imports are being assigned a higher priority. And once corporations make organizational changes, the new structures tend to take on a life of their own.

The Distribution Sector

Foreign direct investment by the manufacturing sector, or the creation of new subsidiaries by these firms, is only part of the needed change, since the distribution sector can make independent choices about sourcing—when independence from manufacturers exists. Here, too, trends are surfacing that should ease access for imports.

The preceding chapter discussed the role of restrictive relationships in producing Japan's peculiar trading patterns. The traditional distribution network in Japan for consumer products, criticized by foreigners as inefficient and difficult to penetrate, has lengthy and convoluted channels with multiple layers of wholesalers.[53] The inefficiency or convoluted nature of the system is not the problem, though; the real difficulty lies in the tight relationships between distributors and manufacturers. The usual web of social dynamics in Japan—group loyalty, close personal relationships, the movement of retirees into distribution firms handling the manufacturer's products, and a sense of hierarchy (with large manufacturers outranking wholesalers)—all conspire to limit the ability of any newcomer, domestic or foreign, to enter a market in Japan. Some manufacturers have complete control over segments of their distribution networks through franchised outlets (such as the stores specializing in Matsushita products),[54] but the influence over distribution is much broader. Resale price maintenance is legally authorized for some consumer products under the antimonopoly law, although the range of products covered by this provision has declined somewhat over time.[55] Retailers are also tied by informal links to particular wholesalers, who depend on other wholesalers, who are, in turn, beholden to particular manufacturers. The chain of dependency can provide effective control over the line of products carried by the retailer and the prices charged.

In this context, new forms of retail distribution become an important element in promoting a more open and receptive system. They also represent a typically Japanese approach to a problem, in which a major alteration of policy toward existing organizations or practices is eschewed in favor of creating new, alternative structures that will exist parallel to older ones.[56] In particular, the expansion of the superstore chains—a type of retail outlet that combines the features of an American supermarket and a discount store—is a key element in opening up traditional distribution. These chains are large enough to be relatively free of dominance or control by wholesalers and manufacturers. Dealing in low- and mid-price items, they are more concerned with price than are traditional department stores, which compete with one another in terms of service.

Because of the obstacles imposed by the traditional distribution system, any effort to increase manufactured consumer goods must involve a reform of distribution, through a rising market share for the superstore chains and other innovative, independent retailing networks. The government, however, passed the Large-Scale Retail Store Law in 1974 to regulate the expansion of superstore chains.[57] This law illustrates some of the important mediating and political functions of government policy. Small wholesale and retail businesses have acted as an employment buffer in Japan, helping to keep unemployment low. In the 1970s, when Japan faced a real recession in the wake of the first oil shock and manufacturing employment fell, the number of very small retail outlets increased.[58] Calder notes that this employment function has an explicit political dimension, since low unemployment deprives opposition parties of a political issue that they could otherwise use against the conservative ruling Liberal Democratic party.[59] Furthermore, small shop keepers became an increasingly important support base for the LDP in the 1970s.[60] That importance took a dramatic jump in 1989, when farmers deserted the LDP for the Socialist party in the election for the upper house of Diet, causing the LDP to be far more dependent on its urban support base. These political factors militate against any rapid change that would adversely affect small wholesalers and retailers.

The Large-Scale Retail Store Law appears to have been a serious constraining factor, slowing the growth of large discount chains. The law's continued existence, and the glacial pace of restructuring of the distribution sector over the past decade and a half, are yet another example of how the Japanese economy avoided important structural changes that usually come with economic maturity. Now, however, three types of movement have become visible in the distribution sector: the government may ease the regulation of the superstores; alternative distribution systems that favor imported goods are expanding rather freely (and even with some official encouragement); and some change favoring imports is occurring within existing distribution networks. As with other changes in Japan, though, these developments are still in an early stage, and the social and political constraints on rapid shifts are particularly strong.

The status of changes to the Large-Scale Retail Store Law was considered earlier; within the existing legal framework, some easing of regulations may take place by 1990, although opposition to these changes is strong. For example, fewer than 9 percent of the superstores have been able to acquire liquor licenses because of objections raised by small liquor retailers.[61] This fact may be constraining wine imports, a product that was not consumed much in Japan until the 1970s and 1980s. Other aspects of these stores have also been controlled—floor space, opening and closing hours, number of days open per year, parking space, and other features that have all served to diminish the competitive advantage of these stores over small local shops.

Alternative distribution networks represent an intriguing development. The latest fad is foreign mail-order catalogs. In the past most Japanese had little knowledge of such catalogs, had little experience in obtaining acceptable forms of foreign currency payment, and would have found the postal authorities responsible for customs inspection uncooperative.[62] Now individuals can purchase books that explain all the mysteries of ordering from abroad and provide pictures, descriptions, and addresses for foreign catalogs.[63] The postal system is reported to have changed its procedures in handling individually imported packages, although those procedures are still unnecessarily complex, expensive, and arbitrary, involving customs handling fees in addition to import duties, and complications if the authorities do not believe the goods are for personal use. At least the government has given some encouragement: JETRO has its own book on how to order from foreign catalogs.[64]

From the government's viewpoint, mail-order sales are an ideal way to permit some change. Japanese who want access to a wider variety of foreign products can obtain them (albeit with shipping charges, import duties, and handling fees attached) without directly challenging broader issues of access to foreign products in domestic retail outlets. Because of economies of scale in international transportation, these small shipments will never be a cost-effective way to import from abroad, so such sales are unlikely to be a major competitive challenge to existing distributors. In this way pressure for change can be defused and the sense of balance maintained, preserving the standards of Japanese social dynamics.

Over the past decade another form of distribution has grown quickly: franchise chains of small convenience stores, pioneered in Japan by Southland Corporation's 7-Eleven chain. While these stores are not much bigger than traditional small shops, they are under the strict control of the parent corporation, which makes purchasing decisions, monitors inventory, and supervises financial accounts. Their recent popularity may stem as much from the fact that they represent a way for large superstore chains to expand unrestricted by the Large-Scale Retail Store Law (because individual store size is below the law's purview) as from the convenience to consumers of long

TABLE 5-6. STRUCTURE OF RETAILING IN JAPAN, 1982, 1985, 1988

	1982		1985		1988		Average annual growth rate	
Outlet	Sales (trillion yen)	Share (percent)	Sales (trillion yen)	Share (percent)	Sales (trillion yen)	Share (percent)	1982–85 (percent)	1985–88 (percent)
Department stores	7.2	7.3	8.0	7.8	9.6	8.3	3.7	6.2
Superstores	9.2	9.8	11.1	10.9	12.1[a]	...	6.5	4.4[a]
Shopping centers	9.1	9.7	10.6	10.4	11.9[a]	...	5.4	5.8[a]
Voluntary chains	7.9[b]	8.4	10.3	10.2	12.9	11.2	7.0	7.5
Franchise chains	3.9	4.2	4.5	4.4	5.9[a]	...	4.9	14.7[a]
Convenience stores	2.2	2.3	3.4	3.3	n.a.	...	15.8	...
Food supermarkets	4.1	4.4	4.8	4.7	n.a.	...	5.1	...
Consumer electronics shops	0.7	0.8	1.1	1.0	1.6	1.4	12.5	14.9
Door-to-door sales	1.6	1.7	2.2	2.1	2.3[a]	...	10.8	5.6[a]
Mail-order sales	0.6	0.7	0.8	0.8	1.2[a]	...	9.1	17.7[a]

SOURCE: Sangyō Kōzō Shingikai Ryūtsū Bukai [Distribution Subcommittee, Industrial Structure Council] and Chūshō Kigyō Seisaku Shingikai Ryūtsū Shōiinkai [Distribution Subcommittee, Medium and Small Industry Policy Council], 90 Nendai ni Okeru Ryūtsū no Kihon Hōkō ni Tsuite (Chūkan Tōshin) [On Fundamental Directions of Distribution in the 1990s (Interim Report)] (Tokyo: Ministry of International Trade and Industry, June 1989), p. 8, table 1-10. Figures are rounded.
n.a. Not available
a. Data for 1987; growth rate for 1985 to 1987.
b. Data for 1981.

hours of operation. Because these are large chain operations, they, too, represent a way of circumventing traditional distribution networks and providing countervailing power against that of manufacturers.

Another new distribution channel is the specialty shop carrying goods imported from Asian developing countries. The principal entrant is a new firm called Inbix, running a chain called "NICs Super Shop." These stores are small (to remain below the threshold of the Large-Scale Retail Store Law) and will never be a major distribution route for imported products, but their existence is at least a symbolic change. Japanese manufacturers and distributors in the past would have actively and successfully sought the suppression of such outlets. Today they exist, although they avoid advertising and have suffered a variety of threats.[65] The rise of these stores exemplifies both the hope and the caution involved in evaluating change in the distribution system: their presence is a hopeful sign, but the informal constraints on them indicate the caution that any new, innovative distributor must exercise to avoid being crushed by the power and vested interest of older firms.

Table 5-6 summarizes the structure of the retailing industry in

Japan. Some of the newer forms of distribution have had above-average growth rates in recent years. Mail-order sales, for example, rose from 9.1 percent average annual growth in the period 1982–85 to 17.7 percent in 1985–88. Franchise stores also accelerated, from 4.9 percent annual growth to 14.7 percent, and stores specializing in consumer electronics grew rapidly throughout. However, despite the encouraging growth, mail-order sales are only 1 percent of all retail sales, discount electronic goods stores are also 1 percent, convenience stores are just over 3 percent, and the growth of sales by superstores actually slowed; major structural reform of distribution still has far to go.

Perhaps the most important development is expanded import activity by existing distributors. There are even reports that a few automobile distributors, which have traditionally been confined to handling the products of a single Japanese manufacturer, are beginning to add imported cars to their existing sales lines.[66] However, the dominant example is the superstore, a distribution format more receptive to imported products. Many of these chains have been participating in a MITI-sponsored import promotion campaign, in which stores have come up with a series of plans to "actualize yen appreciation."[67] The very notion of a government plan to get retail chains to take advantage of the lower cost of imports may seem incongruous but exemplifies the role of government in Japan. A main feature of this program has been a series of import fairs at participating stores. During roughly a one-year period, some 35,600 department stores, superstores, and other self-service stores held import promotions.

Fairs are short-lived phenomena and tend to emphasize exotic items rather than mainstream manufactured products. They provide a means for both the stores and the government to demonstrate activity (of a sort that can be easily tabulated and released to the press) without effecting much real change in distribution. The official government report on the progress of the plans, though, speaks rather ebulliently of the role of these events in introducing the "history, culture, and life-styles of foreign countries in addition to imported goods" and "familiarizing consumers with new imported products."[68] Perhaps this form of government involvement helped make the concept of imported goods at major retail outlets more acceptable in the context of a manufacturing and wholesale distribution system that has had a record of opposing imports. Import fairs featuring exotic, noncompeting goods provide an innocuous way in which to begin the process of opening the distribution network to other imported goods. But the real test will be whether these goods move out of the temporary promotion sections of the stores and into the mainstream.

A more concrete and longer-term development is the fact that many of these large retail chains are increasing their overseas purchasing offices at a fairly significant pace: a 21 percent jump in the number of offices among surveyed stores in 1987 and a further 12 percent rise anticipated in 1988.[69] This gives them more points of contact for seeking and obtaining foreign merchandise.

More significant than the number of overseas offices is the emergence of a new concept among distributors in Japan: *kaihatsu yu'nyū* (development imports). This term encompasses the import both of products from overseas subsidiaries of Japanese manufacturers and those manufactured abroad by independent local firms to the specifications of Japanese purchasers. The importance of this new bit of jargon and the concepts that it embodies cannot be overemphasized, despite how ordinary it may seem in an American context. Large American distributors have been purchasing manufactured goods designed and made to their own specifications and bearing their brand names for many years under what are known as original equipment manufactures (OEM) contracts. This concept has been virtually unknown in Japan; most foreign manufactured products available in Japan in the past have been unmodified and carried their foreign brand labels. Now retailers and the media have discovered a "new" concept that could make a big difference in import penetration.[70] Little of the discussion in Japan of this concept makes any reference to the long history of OEM contracts in the United States.

According to one government report, *kaihatsu yu'nyū* rose from 13 percent of the total imports of a sample of large retail chains in 1984 to 21 percent by 1987. Most of these imports were from Asia (90 percent) and were dominated by food and clothing (84 percent).[71] If this survey has any accuracy, such imports have experienced a sizable jump over a short period. If retail chains become more involved in developing products to their own specifications rather than simply evaluating existing foreign products, this form of imports should expand rapidly.

All the developments in the distribution sector considered above provide more flexibility and adaptability to imports than in the past. While these changes are a rational economic response to yen appreciation, they come in the context of a system that has blocked or impeded new entrants. Even now, change would not be proceeding so rapidly were it not for the fact that the economy is performing well. As noted earlier, the distribution sector served as a shock absorber for people who would otherwise have been unemployed in the 1970s as the economy experienced recession and slower growth. Today, however, unemployment is falling, and Japan may be ready to accept a somewhat faster pace for labor-saving change in the distribution sector, although the political restraints imposed by small shop keepers remain strong.

Discovering Asia's Newly Industrializing Countries

The notion that only Japanese-made products could meet Japanese design and performance standards has been deeply ingrained, embodied in the comment frequently heard in the past that the United States produced nothing Japan would want to buy. This attitude toward the manufactured goods of the United States and other nations had to change for yen appreciation to lead to a sustained increase in imports. Judging from the Japanese news media, 1987 was the year in which Japan discovered the Asian newly industrializing countries, while 1988 saw the discovery of the ASEAN nations.

Japanese attitudes toward the products of its nearest Asian neighbors bears some resemblance to American attitudes toward Japanese goods in the 1950s: prices might be low, but quality is poor. Americans were often willing to buy Japanese products on the basis of price despite low quality, but this same set of attitudes in Japan became a reason to impede the entry of Asian goods into the Japanese market. Consumers had little chance to make their own decision on price versus quality because the manufacturers and distributors made the decision on their behalf, spreading the myth of low quality and blocking distribution channels.

In 1987 this set of attitudes underwent a startling and abrupt change, marked by a flood of upbeat articles on the Asian NICs. A major Japanese business publication put it this way: "As the United States and Soviet superpowers decline, Europe stagnates, and Central and South America become debt ridden, the Asian NICs and China show vigor. The NICs especially are catching up fast, based on the strong yen and the oil price decline."[72] In short, other Asian countries were now worthy of increased economic involvement with Japan. This same magazine chose to emphasize Asia in its year-end wrap-up, downplaying Taiwan and South Korea as economic threats and speaking positively of the horizontal division of business that was featured in the government reports cited earlier.[73]

At the annual industrial nation summit meeting in 1988, held in Toronto, Prime Minister Takeshita chose to raise the issues and concerns of the Asian NICs. This self-assumed mantle of Asian leadership prompted the government-owned broadcasting system (NHK) to run a three-part series on the Asian Pacific (the NICs plus the other members of ASEAN) just before the summit. A magazine-format publication issued in conjunction with the series emphasized the theme of Asia as a dynamic area worthy of stronger economic interaction with Japan, and took a positive attitude toward manufactured imports from other Asian countries. Because the broadcasting network is owned by the government, it cannot stray too far from broad consensus positions within the bureaucracy.[74]

Among the four Asian NICs (South Korea, Taiwan, Hong Kong, and Singapore), most of Japanese attention has focused on South Korea and Taiwan. Relatively ignored in the past, and with Japanese-Korean relations never particularly good during the postwar period, the NICs have enjoyed a burst of positive and optimistic coverage that is truly astounding. One principal business magazine recently devoted an entire issue to South Korea, emphasizing the changes occurring in bilateral trade due to yen appreciation and promoting the concept of a horizontal division of industry.[75] Even the English-language public relations magazine from MITI devoted a cover story to an upbeat assessment of the Korean economy.[76] This surge of interest in and coverage of Japan's nearest neighbor represents a great shift, especially since it is combined with a redefinition of Korean manufacturing capabilities. The willingness to engage in this sort of redefinition is closely related to the rise in Japanese direct investment in Korea and the other Asian NICs; if Japanese manufacturers wished to export products from their own factories in these countries back to Japan, they needed to overcome the image of poor import quality.

Just as 1987 appeared to bring a discovery of the NICs, 1988 appeared to bring a discovery of other Asian countries. Almost as soon as businesses justified the idea of outsourcing to the NICs, they discovered that these rapidly industrializing nations have rapidly rising wages. Today the ASEAN nations, Thailand in particular, are the focus of a new Japanese interest because of their lower wages and rapidly improving manufacturing capabilities.[77] The only Far Eastern nation that does not figure prominently in the Japanese press is China, where investors were rather cautious even before the Tiananmen Square incident, and references generally place it in the category of a possibility for the future.

Assessment

The Japanese media tend to exaggerate the size and significance of the changes in import behavior that have occurred. The statistical evidence presented earlier suggests moderate progress in increasing the role of imports in Japan, with at least some rise in intra-industry trade. But all the emphasis in Japan is on extolling the rapid pace of change rather than pointing to the continued disparity between Japan and other nations. One article in 1987 trumpeted the swift increase in imported cars in Japan, only to admit later in the article that import penetration at that time remained 1 percent, far below that in the United States, Britain, and West Germany.[78] The small base from which many imports are expanding makes such inflated comparisons easy to generate. Another article, emphasizing the competitive impact of imported cement from Korea and Taiwan in some parts of Japan, includes a table showing that Japan imported no cement whatsoever in 1979, and that imports are still a tiny 4 percent of apparent domestic consumption.[79] In 1987 a local building supply firm tried to import South Korean cement and created a local uproar because it was "upsetting order" in the domestic cement industry.[80] This sort of social pressure against imports continues because the underlying pattern of behavior is so deeply embedded in Japanese society. The cement industry may be particularly difficult to penetrate, since it has been cartelized for years and was included in the 1983 depressed-industries law, which allowed it to form joint sales companies. Clearly, it is significant that an industry that has traditionally suppressed competition is no longer able to block lower-cost imports completely, but the step is a small one. Similar complaints and protest were voiced by the chocolate industry in 1989, where the import share was also a tiny 4 percent.[81]

One of the more progressive marketing channels can be found in the Akihabara section of Tokyo, where a vast collection of electric and electronic appliance discount stores compete for the consumer's business. Because this retailing district led a moderate increase in retail price competition in the 1970s, it would logically be on the frontier of accepting imports at the present time. Import penetration in these stores, however, is mostly limited to OEM products; virtually no foreign brand names are visible.

Japan was in need of a price and market share revolution on imported goods prior to yen appreciation, and still is. The prices mentioned in chapter 4 for whiskey and refrigerators applied in the fall of 1988; they remain extremely high despite the considerable shrinkage in yen-denominated prices. A government survey of specific price changes for imported products contains many similar examples.[82] A range of imported consumer products remains overpriced in the few Japanese stores in which they are available, attributable to marketing behavior patterns discussed in chapter 4. At least one media source has criticized government public relations efforts to showcase the changes by pointing out the continuation of large price discrepancies, and notes that the pass-through of exchange-rate gains has been incomplete in many cases, so that the margin of difference between prices in Japan and abroad has risen rather than fallen.[83] Government agencies are not exempt from involvement in the incomplete pass-through of exchange-rate gains. Wheat and other grains are imported through the government's foodstuff control account (Shokuryō Kanri Tokubetsu Kaikei) and then resold to the private sector at much higher prices. Published accounting data show that from fiscal 1984 to fiscal 1988 the expenditures for imports dropped 44 percent, while the revenue from resale to the private sector fell only 16 percent (causing gross profit on these transactions to jump from ¥149 billion to ¥183 billion).[84] Some improvement has taken place since fiscal 1986, when profits peaked at ¥227 billion ($1.35 billion at average 1986 exchange rates). Note also that the markup over purchase price in that year was 294 percent, almost three times the purchase cost.

Another government survey measuring the pass-through of exchange-rate gains for a variety of products shows a mixed picture. The retail prices of many items in the sample list declined more than the drop in the landed import price over the period from September 1985 to April 1988. Indeed, out of a list of 36 products, 29 fell into this category. This survey suggests some progress toward reducing excessive markups on foreign products may be taking place. But whiskey, automobiles, neckties, and compact discs are all on this list, and despite the progress they still stand out in the market as overpriced relative to comparable products elsewhere.

Indicators on the penetration of imports are also mixed. A survey of sales of imported consumer products at a sample of 18 department and superstore chains showed that imports rose only marginally as a share of total sales between fiscal 1985 and fiscal 1987—from 9.3 percent to 10.5 percent.[85] If a revolution is occurring, most of it is yet to come.

How can this conflicting evidence be assessed? At least mild optimism seems justified. A nation that had developed sophisticated arguments to explain why it imported so few manufactured goods from the rest of the world is now building a new consensus around a more open and favorable attitude toward imports. Whereas many of the government policy measures taken in the past have been justly criticized as public relations gestures to defuse criticism from abroad, there are now more substantial forces of change at work in Japan, driven less by foreign pressure and more by domestic dialogue. The evidence in this chapter implies that these forces of change are gathering momentum as corporations take steps, such as foreign direct investment, establishment of subsidiaries in the import business, or internal organizational changes, that will have long-term effects on the nation's propensity to import manufactured goods.

The continuing need for Japan to shed its panoply of biases against imports cannot be overemphasized. The upturn in the index for intra-industry trade has been minor, many prices remain far too high, and import penetration in many areas remains far below what a truly open market ought to yield. Social and political pressures that impede change remain as strong as ever, and the 1989 upper house election for the Diet has made bureaucrats and politicians even more cautious about regulatory changes in the distribution sector. Radical change bringing Japan's import behavior in line with that of other countries would be applauded by Americans. Since 1985 important changes have taken place in a progressive direction, but radical they are not.

CHAPTER SIX

An American Policy Agenda

WHAT SHOULD THE United States do about its trade relationship with Japan? Should the federal government stop pushing Japan and let the changes identified in chapter 5 proceed without interference in anticipation that better access to the Japanese market will result? Or should the government keep up the pressure and risk damaging the close strategic relationship between the two countries? Should the concept of free trade be abandoned and replaced with a generalized system of managed trade, in the belief that Japan's peculiar trade behavior can be handled in no other way? These are serious policy questions, and each position has its advocates.

According to the rationale of "uniqueness" put forth by many Japanese, their country's trade behavior should be accepted as grounded in a mysteriously different culture. Other Japanese agree that their past behavior was protectionist, but that recently attitudes and behavior have changed, so the United States should simply wait for the results to manifest themselves. Such views have been expressed for the past two decades and elicit increasingly skeptical and cynical responses in Washington. As demonstrated in chapters 3, 4, and 5, Japan may be changing, but its current behavior remains at odds with the pattern of other major industrial nations. Some American policy response seems justified.

At the same time the basic concept of free trade retains its appeal as a system that generates mutual benefits for participating nations by allocating production resources most efficiently. Those gains do not depend on every nation having the same consumer preferences or the same set of production patterns. Japan's behavior could be passed off as representing such differences, with industrial policy or the restrictive impact of intercorporate ties embodied in these functions. Thus economists can argue that both the United States and Japan have gained from their bilateral trade. Such a justification notwithstanding, the validity of free trade as a principle also implies that the United States and other countries should continue to pressure Japan to reduce its import barriers. More open trade will benefit both Japan and its partners.

Free trade remains, however, a theory of static efficiency: how to allocate resources most efficiently at any given time. Japan's trade policies assume that certain industries will be in the nation's interest in the future, so that they deserve protection from imports (as well as other industrial policy benefits) in the present. Comparative advantage, according to this view, is a dynamic process and must be treated as such; as nations grow and develop, the set of industries in which the nation should or must possess comparative advantage changes, moving toward higher value-added, more capital-intensive, and more technology-intensive products. For these changes to be realized, the government should provide incentives to encourage the continuous reallocation of resources, including the use of import barriers. If this argument is correct, Japan should feel justified in protecting both its emerging industries and its sunset industries.[1]

The challenge that Japan poses to economic theory and to economic policy in the United States is unprecedented in the postwar era. Japan's success combined with the evidence of an overt, articulated industrial policy has led to a useful questioning of American policies.[2] If a dynamic view of comparative advantage and a set of industrial policies have worked well for Japan, why should Americans criticize Japanese trade behavior? In fact, though, several strong objections can be raised to this laudatory view of Japanese policy. First, Japan is no longer a developing nation, and market forces should be able adequately to guide the economy toward further development in most cases. Much of the need and conditions for success of Japan's industrial policy during the past 40 years came from its position as a latecomer catching up with industrialized countries, conditions that no longer apply to Japan (and certainly do not apply to the United States).

Second, rather than mapping out the most efficient path of development, industrial policy in Japan has distorted the economic structure in favor of manufacturing at the expense of services and social infrastructure. Is Japan really better off with a highly efficient and productive manufacturing sector but a lower standard of living than other industrial countries? Reallocating resources would improve living standards (through lower prices for services and agricultural products and more government-funded social infrastructure) without seriously affecting future growth and prosperity. These distortions also impose costs on Japan's trading partners, limiting their manufactured exports to Japan, particularly in industries in which they, too, possess comparative advantage.

Third, even if governments pursue industrial policies to promote industrial growth, import protection need not and should not be a central part of the policy package. Perhaps the United States should consider a more cohesive industrial policy for itself, involving support for research and development, government financing, changes in antitrust policy, investment incentives, and job-training programs. But protectionism, explicit or implicit, has been a key feature of industrial policy in Japan and, for some industries, may have been the most important element in the policy package.

If Japan's trade behavior cannot be accepted as a natural outcome of successful and benign industrial policies, then is its behavior sufficiently at odds with international norms to require some sort of special response from the United States? This chapter argues that Japan does require more focused attention by the U.S. government, but that a general abandonment of free trade as a governing principle is unjustified. Our trade policy toward Japan must be one of continual pressure, backed by carefully calculated, realistic retaliation when faced with intransigence, and grounded in a recognition that free trade is desirable but sometimes impossible. Conditions now favor the United States: because of the high yen and the accompanying shift in attitudes, calculated pressure on Japan is more likely to achieve the desired results now than in the first half of the 1980s.

Assessing Japan's Posture

To lay the groundwork for the recommendations that follow, it is useful to summarize Japan's position on trade. As shown in chapters 2, 3, and 4, Japan's import pattern has differed greatly from that of other nations in the past, despite the effort of some American and Japanese economists to prove otherwise. Even though its overall trade patterns roughly conform to comparative advantage, Japan has engaged in much less intra-industry trade than other nations. Once attributed to Japan's position as a developing nation, these trade patterns have hardly changed since 1970. Other measures of openness to trade, such as the ratio of manufactured imports to gross domestic product in manufacturing, have actually dropped over time. This distinctive and de facto protectionist pattern has caused more and more resentment among Japan's trading partners, leading to heavy pressure to achieve change.

Since 1985, however, Japan has begun fundamental shifts in attitudes, corporate behavior, and government policy toward imports of manufactured products. As discussed in chapter 5, these shifts show up increasingly in the media and in government policy statements, and are embodied in modest real changes in corporate structure, in choices about overseas investments, and in a gradual opening up of distribution channels. Measured in dollars, total imports of manufactures have risen rapidly since 1985, both as a share of total imports and, in some cases, as a share of the domestic market. And imports seem to be continuing to grow at a fairly rapid pace.

Certainly Japan's partners have found these changes encouraging, but the trend should be interpreted with caution in at least two ways. First, the general trend does not mean that trade problems are over. Imports in some industries will remain obstructed despite an overall improvement in access, especially if pressure from abroad lessens. While obviously true in agriculture, where Japan would probably not have made any progress on opening the market for beef and citrus, or now for rice, without heavy foreign pressure, this is also the case for any high-technology area singled out as important to the nation's future. The overall growth of imports will become part of a public relations effort to divert attention from the fact that problems in these other areas continue unabated.

Absent foreign pressure, the dynamics of industrial interaction or government-business cooperation will probably fail to produce a satisfactory outcome. Japanese opponents of imports will be compensated in ways that obstruct the interests of American exporters, and foreign interests will always be placed outside the circle of concerned groups whose interests must be coordinated or compensated. The rise of an internal debate with strong voices arguing in favor of manufactured imports is encouraging, but these voices will participate in and accept the outcome of the domestic group dynamic; they will accept outcomes that are less open than foreign manufacturers desire.

Furthermore, the purely domestic process of change will be biased toward imports from Japanese-owned overseas manufacturers. What easier way to compensate domestic manufacturers than to make them the importers of their own products? The discovery of the

Asian newly industrializing countries (Taiwan, Singapore, Hong Kong, and South Korea) discussed in chapter 5 appears to be part of this process—an improved image for the NICs was necessary when Japanese manufacturers themselves wanted to expand investment and increase shipments of their products back to Japan. Trade among the worldwide plants of multinational companies is an important element in the trade of other industrial countries, but the danger is that the benefits of more open trade will be biased in this case toward Japanese multinationals only. If liberalization and internationalization are skewed heavily toward Japanese-owned manufacturers, the United States and other trading partners of Japan will not be satisfied, and friction will continue.

The second reason for being cautious over the evidence of change is Japan's relationship with Asia. While Japan's discovery of the NICs has been a welcome sign of its greater openness to manufactured imports, this newfound interest could also foreshadow a regionalism that seeks to exclude the United States. Though none of the rhetoric specifically points this way, the possibility must be recognized. What the Japanese find so encouraging about the rest of Asia (and especially the four NICs plus Thailand) are similarities to Japan's own past economic development. Japanese business analysts, for example, have described the spread of Japanese department store and superstore offices in Asia as part of a new, large regional distribution network being built throughout the Far East, led by these Japanese firms. Because they maintain both buying and sales outlets, these Japanese distributors are described as having superior information-gathering abilities and "greater trustworthiness" than American or European distributors, though the latter have had purchasing offices in these countries for years.[3] Others have referred to Asia as a large high-quality market in which Japanese firms will plan their procurement from the "most appropriate" production base.[4]

The keynote of these Japanese commentaries on Asia is exclusivity. The United States or other industrial nations are rarely mentioned, or if they are, they are portrayed as being unfair to the rest of Asia, in explicit or implicit contrast to a more benevolent Japan. Consider, for example, the title of a recent cover story in a major business publication: "No More Japans! Japan and the U.S. Policy of Beating Up South Korea and Taiwan."[5]

Some have gone so far as to see evolving regionalism in the western Pacific proceeding as far as it has in Europe, driven by both the high yen and the continuing economic development of others in Asia. Last year in a roundtable discussion a specialist on Asian economic development, Professor Toshio Watanabe, surmised that "Japan and other Asian countries will increasingly draw away from the United States," a trend that he views with favor because Asia has been "overly dependent" on the United States.[6] An economic forecast to the year 2000 issued by the Japanese Research Institute on the National Economy (a private group) adopts a similar position, predicting that the continued rapid growth and development of the Asian NICs will make closer ties more likely. This report predicts a greater horizontal division of industry and a rise of intra-industry trade, bringing about a de facto yen bloc as the proportion of regional trade denominated in yen rises naturally.[7]

More conservative organizations avoid endorsing any exclusive regional grouping but highlight the same trends in trade and investment that imply much closer ties between Japan and the rest of Asia.[8] An advisory committee to MITI with a heavy representation of "internationalists" foresees a different posture for Japan toward Asia and makes a main point of Japan's continued generalized system of preferences (GSP) treatment of the Asian NICs, in contrast to the undesirable decision of the United States and European countries to "graduate" these countries out of GSP. This same report speaks of Japan becoming a major market for the exports of these countries and, although it generally casts its discussion in a multilateral framework that explicitly includes the United States, sees Japan's Asia policy as a coherent package that will draw the Japanese and Asian economies closer together. The elements of this coordinated package include importing more from Asia, using foreign direct investment to bring about industrial specialization, carrying out the new foreign aid plan (including monies granted specifically to service Japan's private sector direct investment activities), cooperating on energy policy, and increasing regional dialogue.[9]

Other Asians have generally viewed such attitudes on the part of Japan with alarm and suspicion, uncomfortable reminders of the 1930s and 1940s. Even those too young to remember that era react negatively to Japanese attitudes of superiority. But the new wave of Japanese trade and investment ties has failed to raise as much protest as the initial postwar wave of Japanese trade and investment in the region at the beginning of the 1970s.

One Korean economist, interviewed for a Japanese business magazine, even speaks favorably of the rising interconnections between Japan and Asia, driven by American protectionism and the high yen, and sees a stronger horizontal division of industry bringing deepening interdependence and creation of a "stable regional export market." Although he fails to endorse the concept of a free trade area within Asia and does note that Japan still has far to go in opening its markets, the significant point is that he believes Japan will continue to open up and that Japanese investment in the region will (and should) continue to expand rapidly.[10]

These views may be in a minority in Korea and other countries, but the benefits from exporting more to Japan and from higher employment through Japanese direct investment could do much to submerge Asian opposition to Japanese dominance in the region. Japan already dominates bilateral foreign aid given to Asian countries, and the disparity will only increase as Japan continues to expand its aid program rapidly. The prospect of a neatly wrapped package coordinating aid, trade, and private sector investment markedly contrasts with the looser, more liberal structure of U.S. involvement in the region during the postwar era. Asia could become closely tied to Japan in a relationship that is clearly hierarchical, despite the rhetoric of a horizontal division of industry.

An Asia tied in such a fashion to Japan presents two problems for the United States. First, if the U.S. trade deficit is to shrink, exports must expand, and Asia must be part of that expansion. Open markets are important for this expansion to occur, and an Asia tied to Japan could be far less open or receptive to U.S. exports. Second, the United States continues to play the major military role in Asia, a role that can be credited with doing much to maintain the peace and stability that has enabled Asian market-oriented economic expansion and industrialization to take place.[11] An Asia strategically coupled to the United States but centered economically on Japan presents an anomaly. How can the United States maintain the necessary political commitment to a strategic role if it no longer derives economic and other benefits? If the United States reduces its military role, will the region remain stable? These are troubling issues.

For years Americans have been urging Japan to play a larger international role, one more commensurate with its economic strength. Now Japan is beginning to do so, and the result is a new set of problems and issues. While these issues should be manageable, there is no reason to expect that Japan's interests will be entirely congruent with those of the United States.

The Reagan Legacy

During the eight years of the Reagan presidency, bilateral tension seemed to flare up with increased frequency on a wide range of specific trade issues. Congress contributed to the heated atmosphere both through pugnacious public statements by individual senators and representatives and through a series of resolutions and pieces of legislation aimed at retaliating against a variety of perceived unfair trade practices. At times during these years overall U.S.-Japan relations appeared in some danger, with the anger over trade matters potentially spilling over into other areas. The actual record, though, is less dismal than the public posturing, and a review of the Reagan administration's trade policies holds salutary lessons for future policy.

When the Reagan administration came into office in 1981, it faced continued protectionist behavior in Japanese markets. As portrayed in chapters 2 and 3, penetration of the Japanese market by foreign manufactured goods was no deeper in 1980 than it had been in 1970 or earlier, despite two decades of negotiations to lower overt import barriers. In the meantime, though, Japan had become the second-largest economy in the world, and its corporations were competing with American firms head on all over the globe. This combination of facts meant that American government officials could ignore trade issues only at the risk of incurring the wrath of business and Congress. The postwar bilateral framework, in which maintenance of Japan's position as a close strategic ally was the primary goal, was beginning to break down. Quiet diplomacy and compromise solutions were no longer satisfying the American business community.

Complicating the Reagan administration's task was the emergence of a very strong dollar. The result of macroeconomic developments beyond the scope of this book, the strong dollar provided a discouraging backdrop outside the control of trade negotiators. American exporters found sales to Japan more difficult because their products were handicapped by a price disadvantage, and all American firms felt intensified price competition from Japan at home and in third markets. At times the macroeconomic and microeconomic issues were confused by the administration and Congress, with allegations that trade barriers in Japan caused the trade imbalance. Such allegations served only to obfuscate the market-access issue, allowing the Japanese to shift the locus of discussion away from microeconomic trade problems and berate Americans for their profligate macroeconomic policies. Microeconomic trade barriers are a legitimate problem in their own right, but the strong dollar meant that progress in reducing overt trade barriers could be negated.

Further complicating the task of the Reagan administration was the continued defensive posture of Japan analyzed in chapter 4. The legacy of a heavily protectionist past, a belief in the superiority of all domestic manufacturing, the lack of much recognition of intra-industry trade as a desirable paradigm, and the lack of an active domestic lobby in favor of reducing import barriers all worked against the success of trade negotiations. Progress would require heavy foreign pressure, and reducing or eliminating overt barriers might make little difference in the face of the basic hostility of the dominant actors in Japanese markets to new entrants from abroad. Indeed, having stripped away some of the more obvious import barriers, officials now had to identify and negotiate the more subtle obstacles against American products.

To these problems the Reagan administration brought a bedrock ideological commitment to the concept of free trade. This commitment was so strong that it became a stumbling block in the tactical approach to Japan. Economists in the administration opposed any measures at home that could be construed as protectionist, and assumed that Japan (as another market-oriented capitalist country) behaved according to the same principles. In reality, the administration made a number of protectionist moves, including explicit or implicit restrictions on imports of autos, motorcycles, machine tools, and semiconductors. But even in these cases free trade principles lost only after a struggle.

The basic approach to Japan, the administration decided, was to be one of pressing for greater market access (despite making restrictions on auto imports the very first trade policy action toward Japan). In doing so the administration adopted the same laundry-list strategy used by past administrations. The list of issues to be negotiated was assembled from the collection of complaints received from

American business. This list, initially put together in the fall of 1981, included most of the problems that were to occupy the next seven years.

To deal with these problems, the Reagan administration formed several new bilateral consultative organizations—the High-Technology Working Group, the Industrial Policy Dialogue, and the Trade Committee. These were intended to discuss issues rather than negotiate specific problems and thus act as educational forums for both American and Japanese officials. They also served to regularize trade meetings and to alert the Japanese government to problems that could become significant issues if no preemptive voluntary actions were taken. In addition, one standing organization left over from the Carter administration, the Trade Facilitation Committee, was continued. This group was designed to be a clearinghouse with working-level meetings between the Department of Commerce and MITI to handle specific complaints received from American businesses.

Over the next seven years the Reagan administration tackled a large number of specific trade problems (see table 6-1). Each had multiple aspects, many of them detailed and technical, and the negotiations took convoluted paths. Trade policy is hard to analyze without entering into the details of each problem, and each one has generally involved overlapping sets of restrictions and protracted talks. Rather than focusing on the details of each, this study will emphasize the patterns that emerged, with aluminum baseball bats, tobacco products, and the Market-Oriented Sector Selective (MOSS) negotiations as illustrative cases.[12]

Early in the administration, U.S. strategy tried to bypass detailed, technical discussions, hoping that simply alerting the Japanese government to a problem area would suffice. Recognizing the existence of a problem and the need to take action, the Japanese government could then devise its own solutions. This approach puzzled the Japanese. Given their defensive posture, they saw no reason to respond to general complaints and tended to deny that any problem existed unless specific obstacles were pointed out to them. The Trade Committee was established in September 1981 as part of this process, as was the High-Technology Working Group in 1982, and the Industrial Policy Dialogue (1983–84).

Having failed to procure much action on problem issues through general discussions, U.S. officials focused increasingly on intensive,

TABLE 6-1. REAGAN ADMINISTRATION TRADE NEGOTIATIONS WITH
JAPAN, 1981–88

Commodity	Problem
Beef	Stringent quotas (to be ended and replaced with a tariff in 1992)
Citrus (oranges and orange juice)	Stringent quotas (to be ended in 1992)
12 other agricultural products	Quotas and tariffs (most to be ended)
Telecommunications equipment and services	Government procurement practices, standards, testing procedures and limits on foreign investment in domestic telecommunications companies
Medical equipment	Standards, customs procedures, manipulation of reimbursements for hospitals through national health insurance scheme to favor domestic equipment
Pharmaceuticals	Testing issues
Software	Attempt to place software under patent law, with extensive disclosure and mandatory licensing requirements (defeated)
Forest products	Tariffs on manufactured forest products, standards on plywood limiting sales of products more sophisticated than logs and roughly sawn timber
Semiconductors	Collusive market practices
Metal baseball bats	Standards
Supercomputers	Government procurement, budgetary pressure on government-funded organizations to prevent purchase of foreign computers
Leather products	Quotas
Auto parts	Inspection standards, and collusive market practices to limit use in either new cars or as replacement parts

detailed negotiations. Aluminum baseball bats are the preeminent example of this process. This issue actually predated the Reagan administration and may have stemmed partly from the effort of the Japanese government to protect its aluminum manufacturers in the late 1970s as rapidly rising energy costs made Japan an uncompetitive producer of aluminum ingots. The bats, originally introduced in Japan in the early 1970s, were largely imported at first. After several incidents of injury from broken bats (especially a highly publicized case in 1974), Japanese officials brought them under the consumer product safety law, which required conformance to a standard and a government safety symbol ("S-mark") after lot inspection or factory inspection. Simultaneously the Japan rubberized baseball league set its own standards and granted approval to six Japanese manufacturers.[13] These standards were set cooperatively by the Japanese industry in consultation with the government and the baseball league in a manner that excluded foreign products.

Beginning in 1980 the U.S. industry approached the league for approval but met with no success, hardly surprising since relations between the league and the six approved Japanese firms were now well established. Among the reasons cited for not granting approval to foreign products were the arguments that conditions in Japan were unique, and that Japanese players and spectators disliked the sound made by American bats when they hit the ball—transforming the issue into one of "cultural" misunderstanding.[14] In 1981, after a year of fruitless effort, the issue was raised to a higher priority (mainly through the extensive efforts of Herbert Cochran, a commercial officer at the American consulate in Osaka at the time) and included in one of the market-opening packages announced by the Japanese government. In this announcement the league promised to modify its procedures so that any bat that met its standards could receive approval. The Japanese government, however, refused to grant factory approval (so that each lot would not have to be inspected individually on arrival in Japan). The U.S. government filed a complaint with GATT because of this refusal; the Japanese government responded by eliminating its formal standard. But then the industry adopted a voluntary, private standard ("SG" mark) identical to the discarded government standard, so the need for additional approval from the baseball league remained. While the government-to-government issue was supposedly closed, the foreign market share of bats remained at less than 1 percent in the late 1980s.[15]

Aluminum baseball bats are a minute market, and one may wonder why so much energy was expended on such an insignificant product. The answer is that broader concerns were at stake. Pressure on baseball bats plus other standard problems fed into a political process in Japan that led to a substantial revision of 16 laws establishing the framework for standards and testing procedures. The U.S. government specifically raised these broader concerns when the GATT case on baseball bats was opened.[16] The changes in these laws, passed by the Diet in the spring of 1983, by no means solved or eliminated problems related to standards and testing, but did represent an important first step in a progressive direction.

The long-running issue of tobacco products also illustrates how Japan defends its markets through delaying tactics. Until 1985 all cigarettes in Japan were sold by a state monopoly—the Japan Tobacco and Salt Corporation (JTS). This company, which was required to buy the domestic tobacco crop, manufactured cigarettes (with a blend of domestic and imported tobacco) in inefficiently small factories and also distributed all imported cigarettes. Imports were discouraged through a variety of means: a high tariff (35 percent in the early 1980s), an excise tax based on the landed cost including the import duty (resulting in double taxation), limits on the number of retail outlets licensed to sell imports, an advertising ban, and fixed retail prices for imported cigarettes set well above domestic brands.[17]

Negotiations in 1978–79 produced a minor reduction in the retail price differential in 1980, a minor expansion in the number of outlets handling imports, and limited permission to advertise. A market-opening package announced by the Japanese government in May 1982 promised to increase the number of retail outlets selling imports in a series of steps lasting until 1986 (at which time all outlets would be allowed to handle imports). The Reagan administration then requested formation of a special bilateral tobacco products study group (which had been mandated two years earlier in the 1980 concessions) to consider all remaining issues. No progress came until 1984, when the Japanese government announced that JTS would be privatized as part of its administrative reform movement. Imports could then be handled outside the control of the new private company. Other issues—tariffs and double taxation among them—remained, and the administration self-initiated an unfair trade practices case under U.S. trade law in 1985. Final agreement came in 1986 with complete elimination of tariffs, simplification of pricing approval, and better access to domestic distribution.

Tobacco products represent one of the areas of success in negotiations. From just over 2 percent in 1985, foreign cigarettes exceeded 10 percent of the Japanese market by late 1987.[18] The process, however, took nine years with multiple agreements, each of which involved obstinate resistance by Japanese negotiators. Success in this case came partly because of private sector pressure for administrative reform in government, an initiative that included privatization, not just of JTS, but also of the Nippon Telegraph and Telephone Company (NTT) and the Japanese National Railways (JNR). Had the Japanese market for tobacco products been dominated by a small number of private sector manufacturers from the beginning, rather than a single inefficient government-owned operation, this degree of progress would have been less likely. Privatization and rooting out inefficiency in government became a theme that was largely congruent with American interests in opening the tobacco products market and provided a domestic force for change that reinforced pressure from the outside.

A perception of a lack of progress was surfacing among Reagan administration officials by 1984 as issues such as tobacco products and baseball bats each proved to be an uphill struggle, and these feelings were fed further by the Japanese predilection for offering "market-access packages" on the occasion of major international meetings and bilateral summits. Intended to impress the United States with the Japanese government's commitment to opening its markets, these packages tended to have precisely the opposite effect. In an effort to generate large numbers of actions, individual items on the lists were often of trivial value, represented only minuscule changes, or even repeated changes supposedly made earlier but which had never been implemented. Five of these packages were issued between 1981 and 1984.[19]

Concerned over the lack of progress behind the facade of action, the administration adopted a new approach in late 1984. Rejecting the proposal by some to move to a general system of managed trade outcomes, the administration decided to choose a limited number of product categories and subject them to a burst of intensive negotiations. Labeled the Market-Oriented Sector Selective (MOSS) approach, it was endorsed at a bilateral summit meeting in January 1985. Over the next year negotiations proceeded in four areas: forest products, medical equipment and pharmaceuticals, electronic products (including software but largely excluding semiconductors), and telecommunications equipment and services. Some issues in all of these areas had been negotiated earlier with unsatisfactory results. This approach recognized the existence of multiple obstacles and aimed at dealing with them all simultaneously.

The four industries were chosen because they were areas of American competitive strength, represented large markets, and involved serious access problems in Japan. Negotiations were completed by January 1985, while a fifth area, auto parts, was officially considered to be the next round of the MOSS process (but was never given the same level of attention as the first four) beginning in 1986. In all four sectors involved in the initial MOSS round, the Japanese government made concessions on at least some of the problems identified by the Reagan administration, although progress varied widely.

Telecommunications equipment and services talks focused on obstacles in value-added telecommunications services (such as on-line data banks), problems in testing and certification (including requests for type approval based on a company's own test data), transparency in rule making and standard setting, and concerns that the privatized NTT would cross-subsidize different kinds of services to keep competitors out (that is, would charge high prices on services with no competition and use the profits to subsidize low rates and losses on those facing competition).[20] Improvements came in most of these areas, although negotiations were often bitter, and at one point stalled progress prompted the Senate to pass a resolution calling for retaliation against Japanese exports to the United States. By the end of the yearlong process, however, self-certification became possible; technical standards and requirements for terminal equipment were reduced in number (and restricted in principle to those necessary for protection of the telecommunications network); testing and approval was placed in the hands of an independent agency (without direct participation by Japanese manufacturers); paperwork for approvals was simplified; some easing of conditions for participation of foreign firms in new telecommunications businesses was announced; channels for satellite communications were expanded (allowing two private firms using American satellites to enter satellite communications); agreement was reached to begin consideration of deregulation of cellular telephones; and foreign firms were allowed to gain membership on an advisory committee to the government as well as on an independent private sector standards-setting body.[21] Even this lengthy list is only a partial tally of the detailed outcomes announced at the end of the MOSS negotiations, but it gives the flavor of the range of market-restricting behavior that foreign firms faced in this field. Few of these problems were completely eliminated, though. Restrictions on foreign participation in

new international telecommunications businesses became a sore
point in 1987, and cellular telephones were subject to a bitter dispute in 1989.[22]

Medical equipment and pharmaceutical talks focused on testing
and test data (an issue that supposedly had been resolved in earlier
market-opening packages and the 1983 revision of standards and
testing laws), approval and licensing procedures, linkages between
approval and pricing mechanisms, the National Health Insurance
reimbursement system (which had discriminated against imports),
and transparency in decisionmaking. Although the Japanese government never admitted that the regulatory system was overtly or co-
vertly discriminatory,[23] several concessions resulted from the negotiations: acceptance of foreign clinical test data; streamlining of
approval of reagents; clarification of modifications in medical equipment not requiring product reapproval; other actions designed to
ease approval of both pharmaceuticals and medical equipment (including easing complications due to a change of local vendor or business location); and increased transparency in setting health insurance reimbursement rates.[24] These and other minor changes
addressed procedures that American firms felt were being used per-
niciously to obstruct their products.

Electronics negotiations under the MOSS framework produced
fewer results. Semiconductor trade was not part of this initiative,
and a key issue of software protection (in which MITI attempted to
use patent law to undermine software protection for foreign ven-
dors)[25] had been largely settled before the MOSS talks began. Another issue, protection of semiconductor chip design, was also already under negotiation.[26] The MOSS process was left with ensuring
that the software and chip design protection settlements did not unravel. In addition, negotiations led to the lowering or elimination of
some tariffs, better access to government-owned patents, and an invitation to foreign companies to participate in a government-sponsored software development project.[27]

Forest product talks involved tariffs and standards, negotiations
on which dated back at least to 1981. Because of opposition from the
domestic industry, final agreement was not reached until just before
the end of the one-year MOSS time frame, and the final settlement
was short of what the U.S. government had requested.[28] The full list
of items in the eventual settlement is very detailed and long, but
besides some moderate tariff reductions, it included revision of

building codes to allow more wood and wood panels, a restructuring plan for the domestic industry, participation of foreign firms in standards setting, promises to set standards for American products not previously used in Japan (such as structural laminated lumber of lodgepole pine and ponderosa, plus oriented stand board and waferboard), action on designating foreign testing organizations to provide certification on exports to Japan, completion of capacity reduction in the domestic corrugated containerboard industry under the depressed-industries law, and review of the competitive impact of joint containerboard industry actions under the same law.[29]

This brief review of the MOSS negotiations and their results spotlights how detailed and complex some trade issues have been. Though settlements in all four areas included lengthy lists of major and minor items affecting imports, none were comprehensive enough to preclude future problems and negotiations on many of the same issues. Some American officials involved have expressed dissatisfaction with the outcomes.[30] In another sense the MOSS talks represented no change in Japanese bargaining tactics: issues were pushed to the smallest level of detail, defensive attitudes persisted, and relatively little support came from domestic Japanese forces (except perhaps for certain forms of foreign participation in the newly liberalized telecommunications market in Japan). Many of the settlements involved promises for future action, such as standards revisions or foreign data acceptance, that could still be twisted or ignored at the implementation stage. By the end of the process, U.S. negotiators were literally exhausted by the intensity of the schedule.

An objective measure of success ought to be increased sales of the affected products. As part of the follow-up on the MOSS talks, the Department of Commerce has compiled statistics on the sales of these product categories. Table 6-2 presents the results through 1987. Most American exports to Japan of manufactured goods have been expanding because of the sharp depreciation of the dollar after 1985. However, from 1985 through 1987 exports to Japan in the MOSS categories rose at annual rates of −0.3 to 25 percent, for an average growth of 14 percent, well above the annual 6 percent increase in total U.S. exports to Japan over the same period. This suggests that the removal of trade barriers in the MOSS talks may have made a difference in U.S. sales to Japan, although the evidence is far from conclusive. More rapid growth in sales of these products could simply be a result of faster expansion of the overall markets for them

TABLE 6-2. EXPORTS TO JAPAN IN THE MARKET-ORIENTED SECTOR
SELECTIVE (MOSS) CATEGORIES, 1984–87
Millions of dollars, percentage growth

Commodity	1983	1984	1985	1986	1987	Annualized growth, 1985–1987
Telecommunications equipment	196	185	203	269	358	24.6
Electronics products	1,091	1,420	1,485	1,593	2,093	13.8
Medical devices and pharmaceuticals	785	832	871	1,009	1,154	11.5
Forest products	642	641	643	810	1,039	17.5
Auto parts and equipment	89	201	191	203	199	−0.3
Subtotal of MOSS categories	2,803	3,279	3,393	3,884	4,843	14.5
Total U.S. exports to Japan	21,894	23,575	22,631	26,882	28,249	6.2

SOURCES: National Security and International Affairs Division, *U.S.–Japan Trade: Evaluation of the Market-Oriented Sector-Selective Talks* (Washington: U.S. General Accounting Office, July 1988); statistics supplied by the U.S. Department of Commerce.

in Japan rather than a structural change favoring imports. For wood products the data in chapter 5 and appendix table B-1 suggest the structure of Japanese imports has shifted modestly, with a rise in the share of processed wood products. But without detailed data on the domestic markets for the other products involved, the question of improved access cannot be answered conclusively.

While the MOSS talks were under way, the Reagan administration made a conscious decision to intensify the pressure on foreign trade practices, announcing in the fall of 1985 that it would establish a "strike force" on trade issues and self-initiate trade cases.[31] Among the cases brought under this policy were a dumping case on semiconductors, an interagency fact-finding investigation of supercomputers (under section 305 of the Trade Act), and the unfair trade practices case on access to the Japanese cigarette market mentioned earlier. At the same time, a decision to take a dispute to the GATT over continued Japanese quotas on 12 agricultural products finally produced a resolution of that problem, and a similar decision on leather products led to a GATT finding against Japan. Initiation of GATT proceedings on beef and citrus in 1988 were instrumental in the subsequent Japanese agreement to a phased removal of its quotas.

Reagan administration policy toward Japan generally became more coercive over time once U.S. negotiators realized that broad discussions and gentle persuasion were ineffective in many cases.

Virtually all major issues involved multiple layers, so that success in resolving one particular problem rarely represented a final resolution of an issue. As discouraging as the record of eight years of sustained and rather intensive trade negotiations may seem, real progress did occur. Some problems have been resolved, and at the very least, the removal of these obstacles means that access will be easier if and when the Japanese are more interested in importing.

Other problems remain. The 1989 annual report on foreign trade barriers issued by the Office of the U.S. Trade Representative still devoted more pages to Japan than to any other country.[32] A summary of the long list of items included in the report is presented in table 6-3, and it contains many areas previously negotiated—including all four of the MOSS categories. Bilateral trade problems have hardly been solved.

A Bargaining Strategy

A liberal world trading environment in which barriers to imports in all countries are lowered remains the fundamental tenet of international trade. These basic principles are embodied in the GATT. American trade policy has supported and fostered this international system since the late 1940s. No good reason exists to break with the liberal trade principles that have governed the international system. These principles do not constitute a rigid free trade ideology; free trade does not characterize the international system today nor is it likely to do so in the foreseeable future. All nations face domestic pressures for protection or pursue industrial policies that limit imports in some industries. Political reality makes the complete elimination of barriers difficult at best. What the postwar international system does endorse is reducing such barriers to the extent that is politically feasible on the basis that the widest scope for international competition is good for all participants, whether on traditional economic grounds of static efficiency gains or on dynamic considerations of pushing industries toward greater efficiency and specialization.

These modest goals and the benefits that flow from them remain valid today as an approach to international trade in general. Furthermore, American national interest lies in the continuation of open trading systems in the 1990s because of needed macroeconomic adjustments. Reducing the U.S. trade and current-account deficits

TABLE 6-3. UNRESOLVED MARKET-ACCESS PROBLEMS IDENTIFIED BY
THE OFFICE OF THE U.S. TRADE REPRESENTATIVE, 1989

Commodity or area	Problem
Cigarettes	Tax collection system
Leather	Tariff quota system
Wood and paper products	Tariffs, misclassification, standards
Aluminum	Tariffs
Agricultural products	Quotas, state trading, tariffs
Feedgrains	Regulations and collusion
Telecommunications equipment	Standards and testing procedures
Pharmaceuticals	Regulatory and testing issues
Medical equipment	Regulatory and testing issues
Food additives	Restrictive policies
Supercomputers	Government and university procurement
Satellites	NTT procurement
Government procurement	Single tendering, prequalification, other
Patents	Delay, pernicious administration
Trademarks	Delay
Copyrights	Inadequate protection of sound recordings
Construction and engineering	Collusive market practices
Legal services	Continued restrictive practices
Insurance	Restricted access to market
High-cube containers	Continuing restrictions
Semiconductors	Limited access to market
TRON (the real-time operating system nucleus)	Government procurement
Optical fibers	Limited access to market
Aerospace	Industrial policy
Auto parts	Limited access to market
Soda ash	Collusive behavior
Distribution system	Variety of biases against imports
Marketing practices	Limits on product promotions
Large-Scale Retail Store Law	Restrictions of these stores

SOURCE: Office of the U.S. Trade Representative, *1989 National Trade Estimate Report on Foreign Trade Barriers*, pp. 97–114.

means that exports must rise, and accomplishing this at a time when the open trading system framework is under attack or replaced by managed trade would be difficult. Consequently the American policy approach toward Japan should continue to be guided by the same principles as in the past. The U.S. goal ought to continue to be a more open Japan.

Evidence that Japan's trade behavior still differs substantially from that of other industrialized countries, and the plethora of issues still on the negotiating agenda, indicate that much remains to be done if greater openness is to be the American objective in dealing with Japan. The following points ought to be part of the U.S. bargaining strategy:

Keep the yen strong against the dollar. This is another way of saying that correcting the macroeconomic fundamentals is a prerequisite for microeconomic progress. This prescription is now becoming commonplace,[33] though it ought to be pursued for domestic reasons, not just because it improves the tenor of bilateral relations. Fiscal deficit reduction in the United States, coupled with continued expansion of domestic demand in Japan, feeds into bilateral microeconomic issues in two ways.

First, keeping the yen strong against the dollar will buttress the reconsideration of protectionism under way in Japan, creating even more constituencies in favor of increased imports. It is unfortunate that a strong currency stemming from large trade surpluses has been the only effective means of getting Japan to alter its stance toward imports, but no realistic alternative exists.

Second, the strong yen means that even without a basic reappraisal of the role of imports, Japan's trade surplus will fall and American exports will rise. These developments will take some of the harsh edge off the discussion of microeconomic problems. The Japanese government may feel that an improved macroeconomic situation will alleviate some of the urgency for removing trade barriers, but that will not be the case.

Maintaining a strong yen and weak dollar does have one disadvantage: the price of American assets appears more attractive to Japanese investors. Thus part of the price of getting Japan to be more open has been the sale of American assets to Japanese investors. Japanese investment in the United States is already rising rapidly and in such a visible fashion (purchasing "trophy" buildings like Rockefeller Center, for example) that it is becoming a major new source of bilateral tension and discussion. But macroeconomic correction requires a strong yen and weak dollar and ultimately will bring a smaller *net* flow of capital from Japan to the United States.

Recognize that problems remain. Macroeconomic adjustment and, in particular, the growth of American exports to Japan induced by dollar depreciation may cause both the Japanese and American governments to relax or assume that the problems have been solved.

Nothing could be further from the truth. Because of the continued operation of Japanese industrial policy, its group dynamics, and traditional political pressure from declining, import-competing industries, access to Japan's markets will remain a problem. The limited growth in intra-industry trade that has occurred despite the appreciation of the yen and overall increases in manufactured imports is strong evidence that problems will persist.

Keep the pressure on Japan. The new atmosphere of openness to imports in Japan is not enough; without pressure, the changes now taking place will favor imports from Japanese-owned or Japanese-controlled manufacturing plants abroad rather than from independent foreign firms. This bias must be countered, and the Japanese must be made aware that protectionist behavior patterns are intolerable. Combined with macroeconomic policies that keep the yen strong, pressure on Japan is more likely to yield favorable results than it was during the first half of the 1980s.

Foreign pressure—*gaiatsu*—as a means to achieve change in Japan is a well-known phenomenon. Kent Calder argues that its importance has grown since the late 1970s as traditional domestic opposition groups pressing for change have become increasingly impotent.[34] Foreign pressure inevitably carries with it the danger of nationalistic backlash, however; people do not like being pushed around by other countries, and a foreign enemy can be a convenient and effective rallying point for domestic opposition. Still, one of the remarkable facts in U.S.-Japan relations has been the durability of favorable Japanese public opinion toward the United States. Despite more than a decade of trade and other economic disputes, general questions on whether people like or respect the United States elicit roughly the same amount of positive response as before.[35] The danger of a backlash, though, is certainly lessened when domestic constituencies support the change being pushed from abroad. Domestic pressures, for example, were instrumental in the positive outcomes achieved on tobacco products.

Several conditions in Japan at the end of the 1980s are favorable for effective foreign pressure on trade matters. Yen appreciation has heightened price disparities between Japan and foreign markets, and increased foreign travel has made Japanese consumers more aware of these disparities. Discount stores would like to improve their competitiveness through the sale of cheaper imported goods. On the theoretical side, intellectuals are reassessing Japan's relationship with the world, and some are pushing the need for greater openness for the sake of harmony (as expressed in the Maekawa Report discussed in chapter 5), while on the practical side, manufacturers favor at least enough change to bring in their own products from abroad more easily. All these developments provide a more fertile field for nurturing alliances with Japanese groups.

The political confusion in Japan during 1989 would seem to militate against the success of such pressure. The Recruit-Cosmos scandal, which toppled Prime Minister Takeshita in the spring of 1989 and made most of the senior leadership of the Liberal Democratic party (LDP) ineligible to succeed him; the success of the opposition parties in the election for the upper house of the Diet in June (in which the LDP lost it majority status for the first time); and the combination of that loss and a sex scandal that toppled Prime Minister Uno after only a few weeks in office—all raise serious concerns about the ability of the Japanese government to make policy decisions. The defection of farmers to the Socialist party in the upper house election signals less willingness on their part at least to accede to foreign pressure. Faced with defection of the farmers, the LDP may be more reluctant to offend small shop keepers—the heart of its urban support base—through progressive changes in the regulation of the distribution sector.

Nevertheless, these weaknesses and problems do not signal an end to the effectiveness of foreign pressure. Political uncertainty in Japan will not last indefinitely, nor are many fundamental policy issues at stake in the turmoil. The big issues are the personal behavior of politicians—both financial and sexual—and not the basic direction of the nation. Once the LDP has repented and reformed to some extent, politics are likely to return to normal. Furthermore, current instability does not negate domestic pressures in favor of openness. The key is how other domestic groups—such as farmers and small shop keepers—will be compensated by the system as reform and change are carried out. Once this critical issue is settled, even the farmers may return to the LDP. Finally, even in the unlikely event that the opposition parties were to win a lower house election in 1990 and form a cabinet, there is no reason to believe they would be more protectionist than the LDP on manufactured imports. Most of these parties have not thought deeply about manufactured trade issues, but to the extent that the Socialists see themselves as the representatives of the worker, they might be more liberal than the LDP.

Thus the political uncertainty that characterized Japan in 1989 does not imply that over the next several years foreign pressure will be a less viable or useful tool to achieve change.

What maintaining pressure on Japan does imply is that bilateral relations will continue to be tense. The Japanese press gives high priority to economic and trade relations with the United States, and as long as the media continue this pattern, problems will remain highly visible.[36] No particular reason exists to believe that tense economic relations will ultimately undermine the strategic relationship. Indeed, the opposite is more likely; failure to deal forcefully and forthrightly with trade problems will undermine the willingness of the American government to maintain a close defense relationship with Japan. Given sufficient time and increased international experience, the Japanese may begin to downplay the coverage given to trade problems and view them less emotionally and in clearer perspective.

Reject broad negotiated outcomes. Some have argued in the press and in Congress that Japan is so different from the United States that America can never hope to achieve satisfactory progress on altering its trade practices.[37] Therefore, they conclude, the only solution is to abandon the principles of market economics and simply mandate numerical outcomes to the Japanese: define an acceptable level for the trade imbalance and then tell the Japanese government to achieve that target or face strong retaliation from the United States. A report from an advisory group of business executives to the U.S. Trade Representative early in 1989 somewhat more cautiously endorsed such a move as well, calling it a "results-oriented" trade policy. Under this approach, the U.S. government would tell the Japanese government what levels of imports of particular products are necessary to demonstrate that the market is more open.[38]

These proposals raise a number of specific problems that go beyond the general objection that they weaken American support for an open trading system. First, with Japan beginning to change its own attitudes under the influence of the strong yen and more exposure to the rest of the world, now is the wrong time to abandon the quest for more open, more freely operating markets in Japan. Second, any system in which Japan must operate an extensive administrative system to govern trade balances will concentrate on restricting exports rather than opening domestic markets. Exporters are large, prof-

itable manufacturers who are easier to deal with than myriad domestic markets and actors, and exporters may even gain (as they
have in the cases of autos and semiconductors) from restraints.
Third, the fact that overall trade balances are determined by macroeconomic factors implies that microeconomic administrative solutions may not work. Unless broad controls on trade also alter the
macroeconomic conditions that caused Japan's trade surpluses in
the first place, the final outcome will be disappointing, with a large
overall trade imbalance continuing at lower levels of both exports
and imports. Fourth, the Japanese government is skilled and experienced at managed trade agreements and the U.S. government is not;
economic benefits under a general system of managed trade are
likely to be skewed toward Japan. This final point is especially true
of the microeconomic version of managed trade proposed in the
business report to USTR. In short, managed overall trade outcomes
would fail as a governing principle.

As a matter of practical reality, managed trade in a few products
may be unavoidable. In those areas in which the Japanese government is determined to pursue industrial policy goals, market access
for foreign products will continue to be difficult, since the removal
of formal or visible import barriers may simply lead to the erection
of informal ones. If foreign firms insist on access to these markets,
results-oriented negotiations may be unavoidable. But accepting this
possibility as an unavoidable necessity in some cases does not mean
that managed trade should become a principle on which to base all
negotiations. Furthermore, when managed trade is unavoidable, it
should be negotiated openly and not through the mechanism of tacit
understandings or secret side letters, as was done in the case of semiconductors.[39]

Use specific and believable sanctions or retaliation. Given their
defensive posture, Japanese negotiators have been tough opponents
who see the defense of existing market regimes as their goal. Their
tactics have included adamant refusal to make concessions until the
last minute; the offer of minor concessions at that point to counterparts desperate to use any excuse to declare the negotiations a success; and blunt, off-the-record threats to undermine other aspects of
the relationship if American pressure is not moderated. The U.S.
government lacks the flexibility of the Japanese government in coordinating its negotiating tactics: the U.S. customs service is bound
to certain procedures by law, and foreign interests have recourse to

customs court if they feel unfairly treated; federal agencies cannot alter regulations without opportunity for all interested parties to present their position; and federal regulatory agencies such as the Federal Communications Commission generally cannot base licensing or product approval decisions on considerations of international trade policy. In Japan, on the other hand, administrative latitude is much wider: government officials can (and do) threaten foreign businesses with prejudicial actions in an attempt to undercut pressure for change; farm organizations threaten to cancel contracts to import American farm products when pressed to open the rice market; and regulations are often vague enough to give officials latitude for arbitrary decisions.

Without resorting to similar arbitrary or behind-the-scenes tactics inimical to American administrative procedures, there are credible ways in which the United States can put pressure on Japan as a negotiating tactic. One effective approach during the Reagan years was use of the GATT dispute settlement mechanism. On beef and citrus, other agricultural products, and leather, adverse decisions by GATT panels or even initiation of GATT procedures was enough to obtain action by Japan. The GATT is a formal international structure for which the Japanese have great respect. To lose a decision represents an international humiliation for the Japanese, especially given the importance of international economic and trade issues in Japan.

U.S. trade law also gives negotiators some leverage to use sanctions against Japan on issues of market access. Although an administration that chose to do so could use the Trade Act of 1988 in an overtly protectionist way, it also serves to enhance the flexibility of the administration in dealing with nations such as Japan. The original semiconductor agreement signed in 1986 can be faulted in several ways, but the retaliation imposed for Japan's failure to abide by it cannot; the agreement was a signed document and overwhelming evidence proved that it was not being implemented. In that situation, imposing punitive 100 percent duties on $300 million worth of imports from Japan was reasonable and represented the sort of bargaining tactic that the Japanese understand and to which they can respond.

Imminent or actual retaliation also furthers negotiating objectives by broadening the discussion within Japan. If the United States levies sanctions on the exports of products other than those directly involved in a dispute, then new participants are brought into the dispute settlement process within Japan. Japanese exporters who find their business adversely affected will blame the target industry for their troubles. They may not sympathize with American desires to penetrate Japanese markets, but they will blame the target industry for failing to get the issue settled well enough to forestall retaliation. Their participation in the resulting policy-setting dynamics pushes in the direction of more open markets.

Saying that sanctions and responses should be part of American negotiating tactics does not mean that they should be a common feature. Some issues can be resolved through low-key discussions, and American businesses must maintain good relations in Japan if they are to expand their sales over the long run. But when gentler tactics fail, there is no reason why American negotiators should not escalate to punitive retaliation. Maintenance of good overall relations with Japan should not preclude this somewhat harsher approach to specific problems, especially if retaliation is part of a strategy to resolve important trade problems that themselves threaten overall relations.

Rate trade problems in order of priority. The Reagan administration approach to trade with Japan was essentially passive—reacting to problems as they arose, without any strong sense of priority. Only when the MOSS talks were organized did a clear sense of priority emerge. To some extent the passive approach cannot be avoided; the government is obligated under U.S. trade laws to investigate complaints filed under the dumping, countervailing duty, unfair trade practices, and other sections of U.S. trade law. Other, seemingly trivial issues (such as aluminum baseball bats) may hold the key for larger negotiating objectives and thus have a rationale that exceeds their direct importance in trade. In dealing with Japan, however, the United States needs a stronger focus on problems related to new emerging technologies and industries because of the attention that these areas receive in Japanese industrial policy.[40] These are the areas where problems of overlapping and mutually reinforcing sets of restrictions on imports are likely to be the strongest, and where new restrictive policies continue to emerge when not aggressively challenged by foreign countries. At the present time the list of industries that ought to be receiving close attention by the federal government includes fiber optics, supercomputers, superconductors, and new materials (kevlar, carbon fiber, and carbon fabric).

The business leaders' advisory committee report submitted to

USTR in 1989 also recommended ranking problems, but with a primary emphasis on "the extent to which an increase in U.S. exports could be expected if Japan were to act like other industrial countries with similar attributes" or have beneficial downstream effects on the U.S. economy.[41] These should be important considerations as well, but basing priorities only on current market potential may miss areas of emerging technology that will have a long-run impact on the economy.

Lobby Japan more effectively. Because of the general failure to disseminate American positions in Japan and to build ties with potentially supportive organizations, those groups and the general public are more easily manipulated by Japanese business interests through fallacious or exaggerated arguments about economic security or appeals to Japanese uniqueness. Embassy and consular officials have furthered U.S. positions somewhat, but their numbers are few, and those with the best ties to political and media groups in the past have tended to be political rather than economic officers, with more interest in defense issues than trade problems. Both government and business need to broaden this outreach and feed more information into the Japanese media on trade and other economic issues.

Now is the time to press hard with lobbying in Japan, for the same reasons that pressure on Japan in general should be effective. Yen appreciation has led to the coalescing of groups that should be more amenable to ideas and personal relationships with American business and government. The political uncertainty in Japan opens further opportunities because a younger generation of politicians, many of whom may be more flexible on trade issues, has moved into positions of importance through the Recruit-Cosmos scandal.

Still, the Recruit-Cosmos scandal is a dismal example of the difficulties of lobbying in Japan, even for a Japanese company. As an upstart firm in a new industry (information services), Recruit saw fit to bribe or donate large sums of money to virtually all of the top leadership of the LDP (plus some bureaucrats) on the assumption that this was the most effective way to ensure policy decisions favorable to its expansion and business success. However, it should be possible to become involved in lobbying without bribery or the excesses exhibited by Recruit Corporation.

Japanese firms and the Japanese government have become adept at lobbying in the United States—to the point that Japanese lobbying has become controversial.[42] Lobbying in an open system like that of the United States is certainly easier than in the more opaque system of Japan, but the latter is by no means impossible. More should be done to alter this imbalance in activity. There are few American studies programs in Japanese universities, only a few retired government officials working as senior advisers to the local subsidiaries of American corporations, and few conferences on bilateral relations funded by American money.

Establish better coordination on trade issues. Trade policy in the U.S. government is fractured and ill-coordinated. Because of the wide range of agencies involved in policy review, differences of opinion are sometimes severe.[43] The persistent and aggressive lobbying effort of the Japanese is quick to take advantage of these disagreements. Conversely, American trade negotiators believe that they have been most successful when the federal government has crafted a consistent position, coordinated with the industry in question. Coordination problems may have been especially severe in the Reagan administration, with some agencies and individuals maintaining an unrealistic belief that Japanese behavior conforms to free trade and free market principles, when the reality has been quite different. Over the course of the eight years of the Reagan administration some learning took place, leading to the agreements within the administration in its final three years to take retaliatory action against Japan when necessary, but further education may be needed.

Avoid bilateralism or regionalism. Creating a free trade area with Japan patterned on the U.S.-Canada agreement makes little sense. The nature of market-access barriers in Japan—informal, ill-defined, and hard to root out—makes them difficult to negotiate away in a broad agreement of this sort. A bilateral mechanism for dispute settlement would also hamper the U.S. government's use of retaliation as a tactical weapon in pressing for market opening in Japan. Furthermore, such an agreement would be bad diplomacy; a deal with Japan would evoke stiff protest from other Asian nations, or heavy demands for equal treatment.[44]

The same objections can be raised to a regional Pacific free trade zone.[45] However, there is a potential problem on the horizon stemming from Japan's newfound interest in Asia. If the Japanese government were to decide that regional groupings are the new global trend, and if the United States shows no interest in cooperating, Japan might unilaterally engage other Asian countries in a dialogue leading toward a preferential trade area without the participation of the United States. Suspicion of Japan's motives on the part of the other countries makes this an unlikely scenario as yet. But a continued rise in their exports to Japan while the United States seeks to reduce its trade deficit, coupled with offers of foreign aid and more direct investment from Japan, could alter their attitudes. If the dynamics of the discussion clearly head toward a closer Pacific economic integration, then the United States cannot afford to be excluded.

The years ahead will be difficult ones as the United States and Japan continue to grapple with rapidly changing world circumstances. Some of the changes set into motion by yen appreciation and dollar depreciation are encouraging. But the set of policies outlined above will be a critical ingredient in ensuring that positive developments continue. Bilateral economic relations with Japan will not be smooth or trouble free in any scenario, and reasonable but tough pressure now is a better course than festering problems and a more serious conflict in the future.

Measuring
Intra-Industry Trade

THE BASIC NOTION of imports and exports of similar products is quite simple, but how to measure this phenomenon accurately is less clear. The standard statistic used to measure a country's intra-industry trade in a particular industry is:

$$IIT_i = [1 - |x_i - m_i|/(x_i + m_i)] \times 100,$$

where x = exports,

$\quad\ m$ = imports, and

$\quad\ i$ = industry i.

This calculation produces a statistic (IIT_i) that varies over the interval [0, 100] in an intuitively obvious way. If either exports or imports equal zero, the resulting index number is zero; no intra-industry trade takes place. If exports exactly equal imports, then perfect intra-industry trade takes place and the index number equals 100. By using the absolute value of the difference between exports and imports, the emphasis is placed on that difference, rather than on distinguishing which is larger; trade in which exports are twice as large as imports yields an IIT index number identical to the case when imports are twice as large as exports.*

---

*To place a nation's trade behavior in proper perspective, one would ideally like to know the shares of exports and imports relative to domestic production of particular products. Unfortunately, data of this type do not exist at a detailed level; nations collect trade data and domestic production data by quite different industry classification schemes. The work by Robert Lawrence discussed in chapter 2 does take such an approach, using a data base that provides trade and production information for 21 industries. (See Robert Z. Lawrence, "Imports in Japan: Closed Markets or Minds?" *Brookings Papers on Economic Activity*, 2:1987, p. 520.) This is still a fairly broad division of industry, but a finer subdivision including domestic production is unavailable.

An average index number for trade in all industries within a nation can be calculated by weighting each industry by its share in total trade (exports plus imports):

$$IIT = \Sigma_i\, [IIT_i \times (x_i + m_i)/(X + M)]$$

where $X = \Sigma_i\, x_i$, and
$\quad\quad M = \Sigma_i\, m_i$.

While the numerical calculations are simple and straightforward, the concept is not so tidy. The first problem is what to use for an industry classification scheme. Furthermore, there are different degrees of specificity in industry classifications. Most of the analysis in this study is based on three- and four-digit industrial classifications in the Standard Industrial Trade Classification (SITC).[1] At the three-digit level, the manufacturing sector is divided into about 110 different industries; moving to the four-digit level produces roughly 400 industries or product groups. Because of the mathematical properties of the IIT statistic, a calculation based on a finer or more detailed industry classification will necessarily produce lower IIT index numbers.

A second problem concerns trade balances. The average level of intra-industry trade can be affected by the overall trade balance of the nation. Overall trade is affected by macroeconomic factors (savings and investment, exchange rates, and interest rates) that have nothing to do with the microeconomic structure of industry trade that is the focus of intra-industry trade studies. If total exports exceed total imports by a wide margin, intra-industry trade is likely to be lower than if total trade is in balance, because the overall imbalance must be reflected in individual products. If, for example, a nation started with balanced overall trade and an intra-industry index of 100 (balanced trade in every industry), and moved to surplus by an increase in exports in every industry, the new calculation of intra-industry trade would be less than 100. However, no clear relationship exists, and it is possible for shifting overall trade balances to produce no change at all in intra-industry trade levels. How to account for overall trade balances is a thorny issue in intra-industry trade studies, and the debate has spawned a number of approaches.[2]

The original solution proposed by Grubel and Lloyd is:[3]

$$IIT_{adj} = IIT \times 1/(1 - k)$$

where $k = |X - M|/(X + M)$.

Thus the average IIT index for a country is adjusted by the absolute size of the overall trade imbalance ($|X - M|$) expressed as a proportion of total trade (exports plus imports, $X + M$). Mathematically, as the trade imbalance rises to infinity, the adjusted intra-industry trade index diminishes to zero, and as the trade imbalance approaches zero (balanced overall trade), the adjusted index number approaches the unadjusted number. The adjusted intra-industry index remains bounded by the interval [0,100]. However, while the adjusted average IIT level for a country is still bounded by this interval, individual industries are not. If the adjustment factor is applied to individual industries, the adjusted index number may exceed 100, making this an unsatisfactory adjustment for individual industries. Furthermore, this adjustment assumes that all products will be affected uniformly by the movement in the overall trade imbalance, an assumption that is quite arbitrary.

A second adjustment has been proposed by Aquino.[4] This more complicated methodology is as follows:

$$IIT_{adj} = 1 - |x_i^* - m_i^*|/(x_i^* + m_i^*),$$

where $x_i^* = x_i \times \frac{1}{2}[(X + M)/X]$, and
$m_i^* = m_i \times \frac{1}{2}[(X + M)/M]$.

This formulation assumes that the adjustment to exports and imports of each individual product should be in proportion to the overall imbalance of trade.[5] While it produces an adjusted figure for each industry or product that is still bounded (to [0,1] or scaled to [0,100]), the procedure is also an arbitrary one. Furthermore, Aquino argued that the adjustment should be based on the overall balance in manufactured goods rather than on the overall trade imbalance. This assumption begins to move away from the notion that an adjustment is justified in order to account for purely macroeconomic influences on the trade balance. Japan, for example, has had large trade surpluses in the 1980s because of macroeconomic factors (an imbalance between total domestic saving and investment),[6] but the distribution of that trade surplus across manufactured goods and nonmanufactured goods (raw materials and food) touches on questions related to intra-industry trade.

Another alternative is to ignore overall trade balances and use unadjusted data. The case for doing so is a strong one, since both the adjustments presented above make simplistic and arbitrary assump-

TABLE A-1. GLOBAL MERCHANDISE TRADE BALANCES, FIVE
COUNTRIES, SELECTED YEARS, 1970–85

Percentages

Year	Japan	United States	France	West Germany	South Korea
			Exports/Imports		
1970	102.3	101.8	94.6	114.3	42.3
1975	96.3	104.0	98.4	120.3	69.9
1980	92.3	87.3	86.0	102.6	79.0
1985	135.8	58.9	93.9	116.0	97.5
			|Exports − imports| / (Exports + imports)		
1970	1.1	9.0	2.8	6.7	40.6
1975	1.9	2.0	0.8	9.2	17.7
1980	4.0	6.8	7.5	1.3	11.7
1985	15.2	25.8	3.2	7.4	1.3

SOURCES: International Monetary Fund, *Direction of Trade Statistics*, 1970–76 ed., pp. 122, 127, 162, 166, 254; 1987 ed., pp. 182, 189, 243, 250, 404.

tions about the influence of the trade imbalance on intra-industry trade. Shifts in the overall trade balance can even be completely unrelated to changes in the level of intra-industry trade. Consider the extreme case of a country that exports only product A and imports only product B. If the values of A and B are equal, the nation will have balanced trade, but zero intra-industry trade. If exports of product A increase, the trade balance moves into surplus, but intra-industry trade remains zero. If the focus of analysis shifts to bilateral intra-industry trade, the adjustment problem is compounded because a change in an overall trade imbalance has unpredictable effects on bilateral trade balances. In considering this problem, two other specialists on intra-industry trade concluded that unadjusted IIT statistics are "not necessarily . . . a biased measure of average IIT in the presence of aggregate trade imbalance; the industry and specialization characteristics of an economy may induce individual industry and aggregate trade flows which are imbalanced but recurring and consistent with macro-equilibrium."[7]

Because adjustment for the trade imbalance is arbitrary, this study sticks to unadjusted data.[8] Overall and bilateral balances for the countries and years used here are presented in tables A-1 and A-2, showing two separate measures of imbalance. For most of these countries, in most of the years, the global imbalances (table A-1) are relatively minor. The measure $|X − M|/(X + M)$ is less than 10 per-

TABLE A-2. BILATERAL MERCHANDISE TRADE BALANCES BETWEEN THE UNITED STATES AND FOUR COUNTRIES, SELECTED YEARS, 1970–85

Percentages

Year	Japan	France	West Germany	South Korea
		Exports/Imports		
1970	74.6	148.4	82.4	162.1
1975	77.5	132.9	90.3	111.1
1980	63.1	134.9	89.4	105.7
1985	31.3	61.2	42.6	55.6
		$\lvert Exports - imports \rvert / (Exports + imports)$		
1970	14.6	19.5	9.6	23.7
1975	12.7	14.1	5.1	5.3
1980	22.7	14.9	5.6	2.8
1985	52.4	24.1	40.2	28.5

SOURCES: International Monetary Fund, *Direction of Trade Statistics*, 1970–76 ed., pp. 254–55; 1988 ed., pp. 406–07.

cent for all countries except Japan and the United States in 1985, and South Korea in 1970, 1975, and 1980. Therefore, if the intra-industry trade calculation is affected by trade imbalances, both Japan and the United States may have results for 1985 that are biased downward by an unusual amount—Japan because of its unusually large surplus and the United States because of its unusually large deficit. South Korea has had a large trade imbalance in the past, which improved over time to a very small deficit by 1985. Thus South Korea may have a level of intra-industry trade that rises over time because of the improving overall trade balance.

The bilateral imbalances for the United States shown in table A-2 are somewhat more variable than the global ones. In trade with France and South Korea, the United States moved from large surpluses to large deficits from 1970 to 1985. But for intra-industry calculations, it is the absolute size of the imbalance that matters, and that measure has been rather stable for trade with France and South Korea. Over the same period the imbalance with Japan and West Germany widened by roughly equal amounts—3.6 times for Japan and 4.2 times for Germany. From 1980 to 1985 U.S. imbalances widened with all the countries shown in the table. The shift for Japan, however, is smaller (2.3 times) than that for West Germany (7.2 times) or South Korea (10.2 times). These shifting bilateral imbalances may cause some reduction in bilateral U.S. intra-industry trade index numbers, with the calculations for U.S. trade with West Germany and South Korea affected the most in the 1980s.

Most of the actual intra-industry trade index numbers calculated in this study for global trade appear to be rather invariant to shifts in overall trade balances. Bilateral index numbers do show some apparent impact in the 1980s.

Tables

TABLE B-1. JAPAN'S IMPORTS OF WOOD AND WOOD PRODUCTS,
SELECTED YEARS, 1970–88

	Value (billions of yen)					Composition (percent)				
Description	1970	1975	1980	1985	1988	1970	1975	1980	1985	1988
Fuel wood and wood charcoal (MT)	1.3	3.7	5.4	2.7	1.7	0.2	0.4	0.3	0.2	0.1
Wood in the rough— coniferous (cu m)	271.9	423.3	641.4	351.1	324.1	44.5	45.6	34.6	32.2	27.5
Wood in the rough— deciduous (cu m)	227.0	245.5	661.2	316.5	220.1	37.2	26.5	35.6	29.1	18.7
Wood, roughly squared (cu m)	2.4	4.6	1.7	0.1	37.5	0.4	0.5	0.1	0.0	3.2
Sawn lumber (cu m)	63.5	91.2	236.3	159.3	312.8	10.4	9.8	12.7	14.6	26.5
Railway ties (cu m)	0.6	0.6	6.2	3.1	1.9	0.1	0.1	0.3	0.3	0.2
Poles, stakes, etc. (MT)	0.1	0.3	1.0	0.9	0.8	0.0	0.0	0.1	0.1	0.1
Chips and particles (MT)[a]	28.8	119.7	214.8	145.1	137.0	4.7	12.9	11.6	13.3	11.6
Milled wood (cu m)	0.6	11.5	39.4	58.4	5.6	0.1	1.2	2.1	5.4	0.5
Veneer (sq m)	1.3	1.8	5.7	8.9	10.1	0.2	0.2	0.3	0.8	0.9
Plywood (sq m)[b]	10.8	8.8	6.7	13.7	75.2	1.8	0.9	0.4	1.3	6.4
Reconstituted wood panels[c]	0.4	0.6	4.5	1.4	8.7	0.1	0.1	0.2	0.1	0.7
Miscellaneous wood products	0.6	9.2	11.9	8.9	17.5	0.1	1.0	0.6	0.8	1.5
Miscellaneous articles of wood	1.0	7.1	19.7	19.2	24.9	0.2	0.8	1.1	1.8	2.1
TOTAL	610.4	927.9	1,856.0	1,089.3	1,178.1	100.0	100.0	100.0	100.0	100.0

SOURCES: Japan Tariff Association, *Japan Exports and Imports: Commodity by Country* (Tokyo), December 1970, pp. 54–135; December 1975, pp. 58–144; December 1980, pp. 23–25; December 1985, pp. 23–25; December 1988, pp. 291–304. Figures are rounded. MT is metric tons; cu m is cubic meters, and sq m is square meters.

n.a. Not available.

Volume (thousands)					Unit price (1980 = 100)				
1970	*1975*	*1980*	*1985*	*1988*	*1970*	*1975*	*1980*	*1985*	*1988*
223	243	342	208	61	38	95	100	82	179
19,386	18,256	18,336	15,592	16,556	40	66	100	64	56
19,838	17,221	19,132	13,306	11,050	33	41	100	69	58
129	172	42	2	1,992	44	66	100	146	46
2,965	2,401	4,567	3,655	8,400	41	73	100	84	72
37	22	126	68	68	34	52	100	92	57
1	2	4	4	6	49	64	100	72	47
3,925	5,534	7,944	6,049	12,792	27	80	100	89	40
8	359	880	1,453	36	169	72	100	90	350
15,472	12,290	27,802	77,361	109,644	41	71	100	56	45
63,642	36,673	14,907	44,044	262,317	38	54	100	70	64
d	d	d	d	d	d	d	d	d	d
d	d	d	d	d	d	d	d	d	d
d	d	d	d	d	d	d	d	d	d
125,648	93,246	101,926	167,980	427,186	. . .	. . .	. . .	. . .	. . .

a. Including wood shavings for liquid clarification and wood wool and flour.
b. Including laminated lumber, inlaid wood, and marquetry.
c. Including fiberboard, hardboard, cellular wood panels, and "improved" wood.
d. Volume and unit-price figures are omitted because of inconsistent measures in these categories.

TABLE B-2. JAPAN'S IMPORTS OF IRON AND STEEL PRODUCTS, SELECTED YEARS, 1970–88

Description	Value (billions of yen)					Composition (percent)				
	1970	1975	1980	1985	1988	1970	1975	1980	1985	1988
Iron ore and concentrates	435.0	651.8	784.8	733.0	367.8	67.1	79.8	74.4	66.0	38.6
Waste, scrap, and intermediate materials	194.3	128.8	142.9	125.2	129.8	30.0	15.8	13.6	11.3	13.6
Ingots, blooms, billets, slag, and coils	2.4	4.3	30.9	96.0	176.2	0.4	0.5	2.9	8.6	18.5
SUBTOTAL	631.6	784.9	958.6	954.1	673.8	97.4	96.1	90.9	85.9	70.7
Bars and rods	0.6	0.2	3.7	3.5	32.5	0.1	0.0	0.3	0.3	3.4
Angles, shapes, and sections	0.7	0.4	0.7	2.1	14.1	0.1	0.0	0.1	0.2	1.5
Iron or steel hoop and strip	0.2	0.2	1.2	0.8	0.0	0.0	0.0	0.1	0.1	0.0
Iron or steel sheets and plates	0.1	0.1	40.1	74.5	132.6	0.0	0.0	3.8	6.7	13.9
Specialty steel (high-speed/bimetal/high-carbon/alloy steel)	3.5	2.6	6.2	11.7	1.1	0.5	0.3	0.6	1.1	0.1
Wire and wire rod	0.8	1.4	1.1	1.8	4.0	0.1	0.2	0.1	0.2	0.4
Railway materials	0.1	0.2	0.1	0.1	0.5	0.0	0.0	0.0	0.0	0.1
Tubes pipes and fittings	2.3	7.3	8.9	11.4	37.4	0.4	0.9	0.8	1.0	3.9
Other shapes and structures	8.3	19.7	34.1	50.1	57.7	1.3	2.4	3.2	4.5	6.1
TOTAL	648.3	817.0	1,054.6	1,110.2	953.6	100.0	100.0	100.0	100.0	100.0

SOURCES: Japan Tariff Association, *Japan's Exports and Imports*, December 1970, pp. 67–68, 178–86, 192–93, 197–98, 200–02; December 1975, pp. 71–72, 192–98, 206–09, 214–18; December 1980, pp. 115–16, 321–33; December 1985, pp. 118–19, 320–32; December 1988, pp. 170, 172, 543–71. Figures are rounded.
n.a. Not available.

	Volume (1,000 tons)					Unit price (1980 = 100)			
1970	1975	1980	1985	1988	1970	1975	1980	1985	1988
102,090	131,753	133,721	124,513	123,688	73	84	100	100	51
8,688	3,493	3,907	4,334	5,001	61	101	100	79	71
76	69	521	1,644	3,449	53	105	100	98	86
110,855	135,314	138,149	130,491	132,138	...	...	...	...	...
14	3	40	41	734	52	83	100	92	48
4	2	4	34	273	79	92	100	30	25
1	1	12	2	0	285	265	100	346	n.a.
2	3	558	1,111	2,160	54	58	100	93	86
30	4	6	24	3	11	57	100	48	40
5	6	1	3	0	9	13	100	31	n.a.
3	1	1	1	0	26	93	100	112	n.a.
30	62	27	44	390	24	36	100	80	29
10	32	48	118	185	119	87	100	60	44
110,953	135,429	138,846	131,868	135,884	...	...	...	...	...

TABLE B-3. JAPAN'S IMPORTS OF COPPER AND COPPER PRODUCTS,
SELECTED YEARS, 1970–88

Description	Value (billions of yen)					Composition (percent)				
	1970	1975	1980	1985	1988	1970	1975	1980	1985	1988
Copper ores and concentrates	180.9	239.9	467.9	291.8	316.1	50.9	73.4	72.0	63.1	61.2
Unwrought copper	170.5	83.1	51.0	12.7	0.0	48.0	25.4	7.8	2.8	0.0
Electrolytic cathode copper	0.0	0.0	102.7	120.5	142.7	0.0	0.0	15.8	26.1	27.6
Waste and scrap	0.0	0.0	18.8	23.9	27.9	0.0	0.0	2.9	5.2	5.4
Master alloys	0.2	1.0	0.2	0.2	1.4	0.1	0.3	0.0	0.0	0.3
SUBTOTAL	351.5	324.0	640.5	449.1	488.1	99.0	99.1	98.6	97.2	94.5
Bars, rods, and sections	0.1	0.2	0.3	3.0	0.9	0.0	0.1	0.0	0.6	0.2
Copper wire	0.0	0.0	0.1	0.5	12.8	0.0	0.0	0.0	0.1	2.5
Alloyed wire	0.1	0.1	0.4	0.4	0.4	0.0	0.0	0.1	0.1	0.1
Plates, sheets, and strips	0.2	0.2	0.7	2.8	3.8	0.1	0.1	0.1	0.6	0.7
Foil	2.4	0.5	1.1	1.2	3.7	0.7	0.2	0.2	0.3	0.7
Powders and flakes	0.2	0.2	0.4	0.4	0.3	0.1	0.1	0.1	0.1	0.1
Tubes and pipes	0.4	1.6	2.2	1.1	3.2	0.1	0.5	0.3	0.2	0.6
Other industrial parts	0.0	0.0	0.4	0.4	0.3	0.0	0.0	0.1	0.1	0.1
Household articles	0.0	0.0	0.7	0.4	0.6	0.0	0.0	0.1	0.1	0.1
Other	0.0	0.0	3.1	3.0	2.7	0.0	0.0	0.5	0.6	0.5
TOTAL	355.0	326.8	649.8	462.1	516.8	100.0	100.0	100.0	100.0	100.0

SOURCES: Japan Tariff Association, *Japan's Exports and Imports*, December 1970, pp. 68–69, 186–87; December 1975, pp. 72, 200–01; December 1980, pp. 115, 333–36; December 1985, pp. 118, 332–35; December 1988, pp. 170, 181, 572–77.
   n.a. Not available.

Volume (metric tons)					Unit price (1980 = 100)				
1970	1975	1980	1985	1988	1970	1975	1980	1985	1988
1,592,911	2,605,399	3,106,131	3,009,703	3,435,612	75	61	100	64	61
312,908	209,707	90,581	41,900	0	97	70	100	54	n.a.
0	0	200,222	351,172	443,872	n.a.	n.a.	n.a.	n.a.	63
0	0	49,929	81,660	108,438	n.a.	n.a.	100	78	68
313	2,544	105	79	4,979	30	19	100	124	13
1,906,132	2,817,650	3,446,968	3,484,514	3,992,901	...	...	...	...	...
47	244	95	7,451	778	45	22	100	12	33
n.a.	n.a.	n.a.	1,367	19,607	n.a.	n.a.	n.a.	n.a.	n.a.
75	48	196	152	592	92	126	100	128	39
162	153	377	3,888	6,690	75	83	100	41	32
1,449	263	523	450	3,526	80	90	100	124	50
210	146	247	316	404	n.a.	n.a.	n.a.	n.a.	58
377	871	1,755	566	2,837	92	143	100	148	89
0	0	221	66	91	n.a.	n.a.	100	393	220
0	0	143	115	245	n.a.	n.a.	100	62	47
0	0	393	434	800	n.a.	n.a.	100	88	43
1,908,452	2,819,377	3,450,919	3,499,318	4,028,472	...	...	...	...	...

TABLE B-4. JAPAN'S IMPORTS OF NICKEL AND NICKEL PRODUCTS, SELECTED YEARS, 1970−88

Description	Value (billions of yen)					Composition (percent)				
	1970	1975	1980	1985	1988	1970	1975	1980	1985	1988
Ores and concentrates	49.4	34.8	44.0	23.1	24.6	62.3	48.7	31.7	21.5	16.9
Matte, speiss, and other intermediate products	12.9	22.0	58.5	39.6	54.6	16.2	30.9	42.1	36.9	37.5
Unwrought nickel, unalloyed	12.6	10.5	23.4	30.5	50.5	15.9	14.8	16.8	28.4	34.7
Unwrought nickel, alloyed	1.3	0.2	1.1	0.8	0.6	1.6	0.3	0.8	0.8	0.4
Waste and scrap	0.0	0.0	1.7	2.0	2.8	0.0	0.0	1.2	1.9	1.9
SUBTOTAL	76.3	67.6	128.8	96.0	133.1	96.0	94.7	92.6	89.5	91.5
Bars, rods, and sections	0.4	0.7	1.3	0.6	0.5	0.5	0.9	0.9	0.6	0.3
Wire	0.6	0.3	0.7	0.6	1.3	0.7	0.4	0.5	0.6	0.9
Foil, flakes, and powders	0.8	0.9	3.6	7.2	7.1	1.0	1.3	2.6	6.7	4.8
Plates, sheets, hoop and strip	0.7	1.2	3.3	1.5	1.7	0.8	1.7	2.3	1.4	1.2
Tubes, pipes, blanks, and hollow bar	0.7	0.7	0.2	0.4	0.2	0.9	0.9	0.1	0.4	0.2
Nickel articles[a]	0.0	0.0	1.2	1.0	1.6	0.0	0.0	0.9	1.0	1.1
TOTAL	79.4	71.4	139.0	107.4	145.5	100.0	100.0	100.0	100.0	100.0

SOURCES: Japan Tariff Association, *Japan's Exports and Imports*, December 1970, pp. 69, 187–88; December 1975, pp. 72, 201–02; December 1980, pp. 126, 336–37; December 1985, pp. 118–19, 335–36; December 1988, pp. 170, 577–78.
n.a. Not available.
a. Not otherwise specified.

	Volume (metric tons)					Unit price (1980 = 100)				
1970	1975	1980	1985	1988	1970	1975	1980	1985	1988
4,670,316	3,396,816	3,952,118	2,976,199	3,269,553	95	92	100	70	68
18,301	27,442	51,571	52,462	58,756	62	71	100	67	82
10,136	8,451	15,202	24,690	34,093	81	81	100	80	96
1,294	188	443	208	235	41	49	100	160	107
0	0	1,824	2,622	3,578	n.a.	n.a.	100	82	82
4,700,047	3,432,897	4,021,338	3,056,181	3,366,214	...	...	...	...	...
156	238	262	136	187	53	57	100	91	56
169	80	142	137	635	64	69	100	83	40
478	580	1,969	4,431	5,423	95	89	100	88	71
288	502	1,214	604	680	87	93	100	95	93
423	256	26	270	40	22	34	100	20	84
0	0	48	36	106	35	23	100	111	58
4,701,563	3,434,553	4,024,999	3,061,794	3,373,286	...	...	...	...	...

TABLE B-5. JAPAN'S IMPORTS OF ALUMINUM AND ALUMINUM
PRODUCTS, SELECTED YEARS, 1970—88

	Value (billions of yen)					Composition (percent)				
Description	1970	1975	1980	1985	1988	1970	1975	1980	1985	1988
Bauxite and concentrates of aluminum	13.2	21.2	35.0	21.3	10.0	20.8	17.8	7.0	3.8	1.3
Refractory construction goods	0.5	0.0	0.1	0.2	0.6	0.7	0.0	0.0	0.0	0.1
Unwrought aluminum	48.0	87.2	335.1	431.6	608.2	75.6	73.0	66.8	76.2	78.5
Aluminum waste and scrap	0.0	0.0	91.2	81.5	89.1	0.0	0.0	18.2	14.4	11.5
SUBTOTAL	61.7	108.5	461.4	534.6	707.9	97.2	90.7	92.0	94.4	91.3
Wrought aluminum: bars and wire	0.4	2.2	9.2	5.7	5.3	0.7	1.8	1.8	1.0	0.7
Wrought aluminum: plates, sheets, and strip	0.8	8.0	18.7	9.5	25.8	1.3	6.7	3.7	1.7	3.3
Foil and powders	0.4	0.6	2.3	2.5	4.8	0.6	0.5	0.5	0.4	0.6
Tube and pipes	0.2	0.3	0.7	0.7	0.9	0.3	0.2	0.1	0.1	0.1
Structures and their parts	0.0	0.0	0.9	1.6	5.5	0.0	0.0	0.2	0.3	0.7
Tanks and other containers	0.0	0.0	0.1	1.0	3.1	0.0	0.0	0.0	0.2	0.4
Wire	0.0	0.0	3.0	2.7	12.2	0.0	0.0	0.6	0.5	1.6
Other articles	0.0	0.0	5.3	8.1	9.7	0.0	0.0	1.1	1.4	1.2
TOTAL	63.5	119.5	501.8	566.3	775.1	100.0	100.0	100.0	100.0	100.0
Reference: Aluminum oxides	9.0	17.4	39.0	2.8	3.7	...	...	...	...	...

SOURCES: Japan Tariff Association, *Japan's Exports and Imports*, December 1970, pp. 69, 99–100, 170, 188–89; December 1975, pp. 72, 103, 182, 202–03; December 1980, pp. 115, 124, 308, 337–40; December 1985, pp. 118, 127, 308, 336–39; December 1988, pp. 170–72, 181, 184, 525–26, 578–82. Figures are rounded.
   n.a. Not available.
   a. Less than 1,000 metric tons.

Volume (1,000 metric tons)					Unit price (1980 = 100)				
1970	1975	1980	1985	1988	1970	1975	1980	1985	1988
3,660	4,600	5,708	3,519	2,164	59	75	100	99	75
a	a	a	a	6	629	239	100	135	20
258	378	910	1,576	2,292	51	63	100	74	72
0	0	276	361	399	n.a.	n.a.	100	68	67
3,919	4,979	6,894	5,456	4,861	...	...	...	...	...
1	6	16	13	11	80	66	100	77	82
2	15	26	18	39	63	74	100	74	92
a	1	3	4	10	106	79	100	91	65
a	a	a	a	a	116	135	100	242	47
0	0	a	a	8	n.a.	n.a.	100	111	40
0	0	a	a	3	n.a.	n.a.	100	36	19
0	0	2	2	11	n.a.	n.a.	100	90	58
0	0	2	3	7	n.a.	n.a.	100	89	55
3,922	5,001	6,944	5,497	4,953	...	...	...	...	...
351	562	749	67	110	49	59	100	81	64

Notes

Chapter One

1. Ellen L. Frost, *For Richer, for Poorer: The New U.S.-Japan Relationship* (New York: Council on Foreign Relations, 1987), p. ix. Frost emphasizes the depth of the relationship, but also recognizes the seriousness of the more caustic rhetoric on both sides.

2. Super 301, which is a revision and strengthening of section 301 of the Trade Act of 1974, deals with unfair trade practices of other countries and provides retaliatory remedies in the case of unsatisfactory progress in removing them. Under the new provision, the U.S. Trade Representative can name countries unfair trading partners; previously only individual products could be cited. Specific barriers listed for these countries must then be negotiated over the subsequent 18 months. If progress in these negotiations proves unsatisfactory, the U.S. government can impose sanctions on imports from the offending country. See Omnibus Trade and Competitiveness Act of 1988, P.L. 100-418, §§1301–03, 102 Stat. 1107, 1164–81 (1988).

3. Exports and imports can be measured in a variety of ways. These figures are from U.S. data, exports measured on a free alongside ship (f.a.s.) basis and imports on a cost, insurance, and freight (c.i.f.) basis.

4. See, for example, Edward J. Lincoln, *Japan: Facing Economic Maturity* (Brookings, 1988); C. Fred Bergsten and William R. Cline, *The United States–Japan Economic Problem* (Washington: Institute for International Economics, 1985); and Bela Balassa and Marcus Noland, *Japan in the World Economy* (Washington: Institute for International Economics, 1988). For a broad study and comparison of macroeconomic models and policy, see Ralph C. Bryant and others, eds., *Empirical Macroeconomics for Interdependent Economies* (Brookings, 1988).

5. For a discussion of this proposition, see Kenneth Flamm and Thomas McNaugher, "Rationalizing Technology Investments," in John D. Steinbruner, ed., *Restructuring American Foreign Policy* (Brookings, 1989). See also Paul Seabury, "Industrial Policy and National Defense," in Chalmers Johnson, ed., *The Industrial Policy Debate* (San Francisco: Institute for Contemporary Studies, 1984), pp. 195–216.

6. Akio Morita and Shintaro Ishihara, *"No" to Ieru Nihon* [A Japan Able to Say "No"] (Tokyo: Kappa Homes, 1989), has a chapter by Sony head Mor-

ita entitled "Mono o Tsukuru koto o Wasureta Amerika" [The America That Forgot How to Make Things].

7. Eileen Marie Doherty, "Battle Lines Forming for Gephardt Debate," *JEI Report,* no. 16B (April 24, 1987), pp. 4–6.

8. Omnibus Trade Act of 1988, §1302, 102 Stat. 1176.

9. Two of the recent studies that describe Japanese protectionism as unchanging are James Fallows, "Containing Japan," *Atlantic Monthly* (May 1989), pp. 40–54; and Karel van Wolferen, *The Enigma of Japanese Power* (Alfred A. Knopf, 1989).

10. Such views have been expressed recently by Fallows, "Containing Japan"; Gregory Clark, "Old Refrain of Free Trade Rings Hollow in Face of Managed Market's Potential," *Japan Economic Journal,* August 5, 1989; and van Wolferen, *Enigma of Japanese Power,* pp. 391–95.

11. Henry Rosovsky, "Trade, Japan and the Year 2000," *New York Times,* September 6, 1985, p. A23; and Henry Kissinger, "The Specter of Protection: Why We Must Reach an Accord with Japan," *Washington Post,* October 8, 1985, p. A19.

12. Advisory Committee for Trade Policy and Negotiations, *Analysis of the U.S.-Japan Trade Problem,* prepared for the U.S. Trade Representative (February 1989).

Chapter Two

1. See, for example, William V. Rapp, "Japan's Invisible Barriers to Trade," in Thomas A. Pugel, ed., *Fragile Interdependence: Economic Issues in U.S.-Japanese Trade and Investment* (Lexington, Mass.: Lexington Books, 1986); C. Fred Bergsten and William R. Cline, *The United States–Japan Economic Problem* (Washington: Institute for International Economics, 1985), pp. 53–72; Bela Balassa and Marcus Noland, *Japan in the World Economy* (Washington: Institute for International Economics, 1988), pp. 49–62; Ryutaro Komiya and Motoshige Itoh, "Japan's International Trade and Trade Policy, 1955–1984," in Takeshi Inoguchi and Daniel I. Okimoto, eds., *The Political Economy of Japan,* vol. 2: *The Changing International Context* (Stanford University Press, 1988); or the more anecdotal approach adopted in Clyde V. Prestowitz, Jr., *Trading Places: How We Allowed Japan to Take the Lead* (Basic Books, 1988). In addition, the Office of the U.S. Trade Representative must report to Congress each year on trade barriers in other nations, including Japan; see Office of the U.S. Trade Representative, *National Trade Estimate Report on Foreign Trade Barriers,* annual editions.

2. For a review of this period in Japan's import policies, see Warren S. Hunsberger, *Japan and the United States in World Trade* (Harper and Row, 1964), pp. 133–41.

3. Ministry of International Trade and Industry (MITI), *Tsūshō Hakusho* [Trade White Paper], 1963 ed. (Tokyo: Ministry of Finance Printing Office, 1963), p. 147; 1964 ed., pp. 107–09.

4. As in the early 1960s, though, the elimination of the beef and citrus quotas will be followed by imposition of high tariff barriers—a jump from 15 percent to 70 percent on beef (in 1991, falling to 50 percent in 1993) and continuation of 20 percent off-season and 40 percent in-season tariffs on oranges. See Susan McKnight, "Japan to Free Imports of Beef and Citrus," *JEI Report*, no. 24B (June 24, 1988), pp. 15–17.

5. Japan Economic Institute, *Yearbook of U.S.-Japan Economic Relations in 1981* (Washington, 1982), pp. 56–57. The initial Japanese position when the problem surfaced in the spring of 1981 was to block all imports of fruits and vegetables from California (including those from outside known areas of infestation). Lengthy negotiations prevented this from happening, although fruits and vegetables from outside infected areas continued to require fumigation, and those shipped through California had to be in certified sealed containers. Melons, strawberries, and lemons were included on the list until 1982, although they are not host to the insect.

6. Bergsten and Cline, *United States–Japan Economic Problem*, pp. 109–16. Their intent was to provide a crude estimate, which was necessarily arbitrary. Their rejection of a large increase in market share for cigarettes, however, was wrong; with the complete removal of barriers on cigarettes, imports (mostly from the United States) have expanded from 1 percent of the market to about 12 percent. Thus their estimate of expanded U.S. sales may be too low.

7. Robert Z. Lawrence, "Imports in Japan: Closed Markets or Minds?" *Brookings Papers on Economic Activity*, 2:1987, pp. 537–38. Lawrence's estimate includes a downward adjustment for an exchange effect (higher imports imply yen depreciation). The initial impact is 58 percent.

8. Gary R. Saxonhouse, "Japan's Intractable Trade Surpluses in a New Era," *World Economy*, vol. 9 (September 1986), p. 246.

9. Robert C. Christopher, *Second to None: American Companies in Japan* (Ballantine Books, 1986).

10. Japanese publications aimed at foreigners have emphasized these success stories. A recent example is Geoffrey E. Duin, "Parker Pen: An Old Japan Hand," *Tokyo Business Today*, July 1989, pp. 50–51. Portrayed as a success, Parker Pen (formerly an American firm sold to British interests in 1985) has a large market share in the high-end pen market, along with several other foreign firms that together dominate this particular market. But the article admits that Japanese firms dominate the middle and low ends of the pen market as well as the enormous mechanical pencil market, so that foreign products make up only a small share of the writing implement market.

11. Mordechai E. Kreinin, "How Closed Is Japan's Market?" *World Economy*, vol. 7 (December 1988), pp. 529–41.

12. Donald J. Daly, "Canada's International Competitiveness," in Alan M. Rugman, ed., *International Business in Canada: Strategies for Management* (Scarborough, Ont.: Prentice-Hall Canada, 1989), p. 46. His observa-

tions on Japan are developed further in "Japanese Manufacturing Competitiveness: Implications for International Trade," Working Paper 53 (University of Toronto-York, University Joint Centre for Asia Pacific Studies, 1988).

13. For an excellent review of the principal writings on the question of Japan's import behavior, see Kenji Takeuchi, *Does Japan Import Less Than It Should?* World Bank Policy, Planning, and Research Working Paper 63 (Washington, July 1988). He reaches no strong conclusions but does review and compare the arguments of the economists considered here.

14. Bergsten and Cline, *United States–Japan Economic Problem*, pp. 78–79. Indeed, because the ratio of total imports to GNP has risen much faster in the United States than in Japan or Europe, they see the United States, rather than Japan, as the outlier.

15. Hollis B. Chenery, "Patterns of Industrial Growth," *American Economic Review*, vol. 50 (September 1960), pp. 624–54; and Hollis B. Chenery and Moises Syrquin, *Patterns of Development, 1950–1970* (Oxford University Press, 1975). Chenery was interested in a wide variety of aspects of the economic development process and not trade per se.

16. Kazuo Sato, "Increasing Returns and International Trade: The Case of Japan," Rutgers University and the East Asian Institute, Columbia University, February 1986.

17. Bela Balassa and Marcus Noland, *Japan in the World Economy*, pp. 239–54. By including GDP per capita, their specification is somewhat closer to the original Chenery model than is Sato's specification.

18. Results summarized in Takeuchi, *Does Japan Import Less Than It Should?* pp. 19–20.

19. Lawrence, "Imports in Japan," pp. 517–54.

20. In particular, Saxonhouse has noted that this approach involves serious questions of simultaneity (since the import shares, export shares, and protection shares are jointly determined). Gary R. Saxonhouse, "Differentiated Products, Economies of Scale and Access to the Japanese Market," Research Seminar in International Economics, Discussion Paper 228, University of Michigan Department of Economics, October 1988, pp. 4–5.

21. All introductory international economics texts explain comparative advantage in its modern form. For one explanation, see Charles P. Kindleberger and Peter H. Lindert, *International Economics*, 6th ed. (Homewood, Ill.: Richard D. Irwin, 1978), pp. 15–57, which gives a history of comparative advantage theory from its origin in the writings of David Ricardo to the present. In its modern form the theory of comparative advantage is often called the Hechscher-Ohlin theory or the Hechscher-Ohlin-Samuelson (HOS) theory.

22. The first articulation of the Saxonhouse position was in "Evolving Comparative Advantage and Japan's Imports of Manufactures," in Kozo Yamamura, ed., *Policy and Trade Issues of the Japanese Economy: American and Japanese Perspectives* (Seattle: University of Washington Press, 1982).

More recent versions include "Japan's Intractable Trade Surpluses in a New Era," and "Comparative Advantage, Structural Adaptation, and Japanese Performance," in Inoguchi and Okimoto, eds., *Political Economy of Japan*, vol. 2, pp. 225–48.

23. Saxonhouse, "Differentiated Products."

24. Some of the very recent analyses that endorse further liberalization of markets are considered in chapter 5.

25. Takashi Eguchi and Manabu Matsuda, *Bōeki Masatsu: Mienai Sensō–Nihon no Taiō to kaiketsu no Michi* [Trade Friction: The Invisible War–The Road for Japan's Response and Solution] (Tokyo: TBS Britannica, 1987), pp. 165–91.

26. Ryutaro Komiya, "Nichibei Keizai Masatsu to Kokusai Kyōchō" [U.S.-Japan Economic Friction and International Cooperation], *Toyo Keizai*, no. 4662 (June 7, 1986), p. 57.

27. Interview with Koji Kobayashi in *Toyo Keizai*, no. 4653 (April 26, 1986), pp. 100–04.

28. Sadayuki Sato, "Nichibei Keizai Masatsu" [U.S.-Japan Economic Friction], in Sadayuki Sato, ed., *Nichibei Keizai Masatsu no Kōzu* [The Composition of U.S.-Japan Economic Friction] (Tokyo: Yūhikaku, 1987), p. 28. Sato is a professor at the Economic Research Institute of Hitotsubashi University, a leading national university specializing in economics and business.

29. Hajime Karatsu, *Tough Words for American Industry* (Cambridge, Mass.: Productivity Press, 1987), p. 33. The Karatsu book was originally published in Japanese under the title *Kūdōka Suru Amerika Sangyō e no Chokugen* [Straight Talk to Hollowing American Industries]. The quotation here is among the milder comments by Karatsu, whose arrogance concerning Japanese superiority and condescension toward the United States are quite extraordinary.

30. Komiya, "Nichibei Keizai Masatsu," pp. 53–56.

31. Reijiro Hashiyama, "Nichibei Masatsu to Nihon no Taiōsaku: Naiju Kakudai dewa Mondai wa Kaiketsu Shinai" [U.S.-Japan Friction and Japan's Policy Response: Demand Expansion Will Not Solve the Problem], *Toyo Keizai*, no. 4738 (July 25, 1987), pp. 66–69.

32. Komiya, "Nichibei Keizai Masatsu," p. 59.

33. Eguchi and Matsuda, *Bōeki Masatsu: Mienai Sensō*, pp. 17–18, 23–28.

34. Yutaka Kosai, "Beikoku Hogoshugi Bōshi e Issō no Shijō Kaihō o!" [Open the Market Much More to Hold Off American Protectionism!], *Toyo Keizai*, no. 4729 (June 6, 1987), pp. 76–79.

35. Japanese discussion of trade liberalization in the 1960s is considered at length in Robert S. Ozaki, *The Control of Imports and Foreign Capital in Japan* (Praeger Publishers, 1972), pp. 55–71. Why the concept of free trade was not widely embraced in Japan is discussed below in chapter 4.

36. See, for example, MITI, *Shōwa 38 Nen Tsūshō Hakusho, Sōron* [1963

International Trade White Paper, Summary Volume] (Tokyo: Ministry of Finance Printing Office, 1963), p. 16; or *Shōwa 39 Nen Tsūshō Hakusho, Sōron* [1964 International Trade White Paper, Summary Volume], p. 12.

37. MITI, *Tsūshō Hakusho, Shōwa 57 Nenban* [International Trade White Paper, 1982 ed.] (Tokyo: Ministry of Finance Printing Office, 1982), pp. 263–72. *Tsūshō Hakusho, Shōwa 60 Nenban* [International Trade White Paper, 1985 ed.], pp. 201–11, makes many similar arguments.

38. "Futatabi Hi o Fuku: Nichibei Tsūshō Masatsu no Kakushin" [Spouting Flames Again: The Core of U.S.-Japan Trade Friction], *Toyo Keizai*, no. 4705 (January 31, 1987). Later in the same article, some grudging credence is granted to some U.S. problems of access to the Japanese market.

39. Shigenobu Yamamoto, *Shijō Kaihō no Tame ni* [In Order to Liberate the Market] (Tokyo: Dōbunkan Shuppansha, 1986), especially pp. 74–115. He is also about the only writer other than Sazanami to mention intra-industry trade (see chapter 3 below).

40. The share of world markets for all devices is based on William F. Finan, "The Outlook for the Semiconductor Device and Equipment Demand, 1988–1992," paper presented at the Semiconductor Equipment and Materials International 12th Annual Information Services Seminar, Newport Beach, Calif., January 15–18, 1989. The share of the world market for one-megabit DRAMS is from *Japan Economic Journal*, February 4, 1989, p. 3. Note that in both cases these market shares are for what is known as the "merchant market," that is, they do not include production that is consumed within the firm rather than sold upon the open market. This factor is significant, since large, vertically integrated firms, such as IBM or Matsushita, consume large quantities of semiconductor devices manufactured by themselves.

41. Saxonhouse, "Differentiated Products," p. 5. He states, "If Japanese trade structure did become more distinctive between 1970 and 1983, this can be more properly attributed to increasing foreign barriers to Japanese exports."

42. Takao Komine, *Keizai Masatsu: Kokusaika to Nihon no Sentaku* [Economic Friction: Internationalization and Japan's Choices] (Tokyo: Nihon Keizai Shimbunsha, 1987), p. 143, picks Japanese successes in the U.S. market as his focus for discussion of microeconomic problems. Hirotomo Ishikawa, *Nichibei Masatsu no Seijikeizaigaku: Tainichi Senryaku Kettei no Mekanizumu* [The Political Economy of U.S.-Japan Frictions: The Decision Making Mechanism toward Japan] (Tokyo: Daiamondo, 1986), pp. 158–67, even puts together a set of indicators to predict fluctuations in bilateral problems, specifying that tension flares up (1) when the bilateral deficit (expressed as a percentage of U.S. exports to Japan) exceeds 20 percent, (2) when the Japanese market share for a particular product in the United States exceeds 10 percent, (3) when exports to the United States grow at an annual rate exceeding 10 percent, (4) when the U.S. unemployment rate exceeds 7 percent, and (5) when large U.S. multinationals face generally unstable con-

ditions. Note that all these items are either American problems or (from a Japanese viewpoint) indicators of simple Japanese economic strength and competitiveness.

43. General Agreement on Tariffs and Trade, *GATT Studies in International Trade: Japan's Economic Expansion and Foreign Trade, 1955 to 1970* (Geneva, 1971), pp. 26–28. The report also notes that in the nine groups with a large share of total OECD exports, Japan had very low levels of intra-industry trade, a point considered in some detail in the next chapter.

44. In 1985 Japan's manufactured exports to the United States were $65.5 billion, 3.6 times larger than West Germany's exports. For motor vehicles, Japan exported $23.4 billion, compared with West Germany's $7.0 billion. Data from UN trade data tapes.

Chapter Three

1. Yoko Sazanami, "Possibilities of Expanding Intra-Industry Trade in Japan," *Keio Economic Studies*, vol. 18, no. 2 (1981), pp. 27–43. She notes some of the features of Japan's trade patterns that will be discussed in this chapter, although her explanations of them differ considerably. The very fact that only one economist has devoted much attention to the issue indicates how little attention or interest is given to intra-industry trade in Japan. The same author has a book on trade, *Kokusai Bungyō to Nihon Keizai* [The International Division of Industry and the Japanese Economy] (Tokyo: Toyo Keizai Shimpōsha, 1980). This book also provides some discussion of intra-industry trade, but most of it is a standard recitation of Japanese trade based on concepts of absolute and comparative advantage and how the industries with international comparative advantage have shifted over time. On intra-industry trade she took an optimistic note (pp. 158–68), hoping for it to rise as the yen appreciated in 1977–78, a point considered below (chapter 5).

2. Donald J. Daly, for example, calculates that Japan's unit labor costs were so far below those of the United States and other industrial nations that its low level of intra-industry trade in the 1970s and the first half of the 1980s is not particularly puzzling. See Donald J. Daly, "Japanese Manufacturing Competitiveness: Implications for International Trade," Working Paper 53 (University of Toronto-York, University Joint Centre for Asia Pacific Studies, 1988).

3. Herbert G. Grubel and P. J. Lloyd, *Intra-Industry Trade: The Theory and Measurement of International Trade in Differentiated Products* (John Wiley and Sons, 1975), pp. 85–115, are careful to note that the concept of intra-industry trade is not in opposition to comparative advantage and comes from relaxation of some of the strict assumptions—such as product homogeneity—that are necessary to construct the theory of comparative advantage.

4. Grubel and Lloyd, *Intra-Industry Trade*, pp. 1–15, discuss the development of empirical studies in the 1950s and 1960s. Among the major early

contributions to the evolution of intra-industry trade studies are P. J. Verdoorn, "The Intra-Block Trade of Benelux," in E. A. G. Robinson, ed., *Economic Consequences of the Size of Nations* (London: MacMillan, 1960); and Bela Balassa, "Tariff Reductions and Trade in Manufactures among the Industrial Countries," *American Economic Review*, vol. 56 (June 1966).

5. F. M. Scherer, *Industrial Market Structure and Economic Performance* (Chicago: Rand McNally College Publishing Co., 1970), pp. 52−54, discusses the problems in defining an industry; Paul Krugman, "New Theories of Trade among Industrial Countries," *American Economic Review*, vol. 73 (May 1983), pp. 343−47, provides an elegant statement on why interest has grown in intra-industry trade.

6. This explanation follows the principal line of reasoning presented by Grubel and Lloyd, *Intra-Industry Trade*, pp. 88−94. Since that time others have offered refinements, but most of them stem from this basic explanation.

7. The extensive nature of this sort of trade is explored at length in Joseph Grunwald and Kenneth Flamm, *The Global Factory* (Brookings, 1985). A product may originate in the United States, be exported for labor-intensive processing abroad, and then return to the United States for further manufacturing, facilitated by favorable treatment under U.S. tariffs.

8. Grubel and Lloyd, *Intra-Industry Trade*, pp. 129−32, discuss the European experience. David Greenaway and P. K. M. Tharakan, "Imperfect Competition, Adjustment Policy, and Commercial Policy," in Greenaway and Tharakan, eds., *Imperfect Competition and International Trade* (Atlantic Highlands, N.J.: Humanities Press International, 1986), provide a review of the academic discussion of the welfare properties of intra-industry trade, upon which this section is based.

9. Robert Z. Lawrence, "Imports in Japan: Closed Markets or Closed Minds?" *Brookings Papers on Economic Activity*, 2:1987, p. 545, pursues this point.

10. This list is based on Rudolf Loertscher and Frank Wolter, "Determinants of Intra-Industry Trade: Among Countries and across Industries," *Weltwirtschaftliches Archiv*, vol. 116, no. 2 (1980), pp. 280−93.

11. Category 732.1 does include vehicles "whether or not assembled," but the term "unassembled" refers to what are known as knockdown kits, or partially assembled vehicles. What would more commonly be considered parts are not included here.

12. L. Gavelin and L. Lundber, "Determinants of Intra-Industry Trade: Testing Some Hypotheses on Swedish Data," in P. K. M. Tharakan, ed., *Intra-Industry Trade: Empirical and Methodological Aspects* (New York: North-Holland, 1983), pp. 181−82. They use an adjustment devised by Grubel and Lloyd for the trade imbalance (see appendix A below) and still find Japan to be far lower than all other countries in their large sample except Australia; they also find that Japan's average level of IIT fell over the period 1970−77.

13. The absolute size of the imbalance expressed as a percentage of total trade (from appendix table A-2) increased 7.2 times for U.S.–West German trade between 1980 and 1985 (from 5.6 percent to 40.2 percent), while that with Japan increased 2.3 times (from 22.7 percent to 52.4 percent). By contrast, the bilateral U.S.–West German index declined only 16 percent (from 43 to 36), while that for U.S.-Japan trade declined 27 percent (from 26 to 19).

14. These industries are road motor vehicles (732), office machines (714), aircraft (734), other electric machinery (729), parts for nonelectric machinery and appliances (719), power generating equipment other than electric (711), machines for special industries (718), organic chemicals (512), telecommunications equipment (724), and scientific, medical, optical, measuring, and control instruments (861). One other category, special transactions not classified as to kind (931), is actually seventh in size but excluded here because it is not a recognizable industry. In 1985 these 10 industries accounted for 61 percent of total U.S. manufactured exports.

15. To test this, the following statistic will have a chi-square distribution:

$$DIFF = \Sigma_i \, (IIT_{iUS} - IIT_{ij})^2 / IIT_{iUS}.$$

The results for the U.S.-Japan calculation as well as the comparison with France and West Germany are as follows: U.S.-Japan, DIFF, 16,707; U.S.-France, DIFF, 2,392; and U.S.-West Germany, DIFF, 2,534. In all three cases, the hypothesis that the intra-industry trade observations come from the same distribution as that of the United States can be easily rejected. (At the 99.5 percent confidence level, the null hypothesis can be rejected when $X^2 > 140$ with 100 or more observations.)

16. Ministry of Finance, Ōkurashō Kokusai Kin'yūkyoku Nenpō [Ministry of Finance, International Finance Bureau Annual Report] (Tokyo, 1988), pp. 524–25.

17. Statistics Bureau Management and Coordination Agency, Japan Statistical Yearbook, 1987 ed., p. 380, reports a total capital stock in chemicals of ¥20.5 trillion, and MITI, Gaishikei Kigyō no Dōkō, vol. 19 (Tokyo: Keibun Shuppansha, 1987), p. 42, reports cumulative FDI in chemicals at ¥687 billion, which yields a 3.4 percent share for foreign ownership. Sales data are for 1984 and the share tends to fluctuate somewhat over time. The sales comparison is biased downward because foreign-owned firms are restricted to those with 50 percent or more foreign ownership only.

Chapter Four

1. The treaties made such an impression that Japan imposed a similar treaty on Thailand in 1877. Jean-Pierre Lehmann, "Variations on a Pan-Asianist Theme: The 'Special Relationship' between Japan and Thailand," in Ronald Dore and Radha Sinha, eds., Japan and World Depression: Then and Now (St. Martin's Press, 1987), p. 181.

2. Chalmers Johnson, *MITI and the Japanese Miracle: The Growth of Industrial Policy, 1925–1975* (Stanford University Press, 1982), especially pp. 17–34, discusses Japan as a "developmental state" in which a strong bureaucracy engages in "plan-rational" policies (rational plans to direct the private sector along a path of industrialization), in contrast to the free-market-oriented model of the United States, which engages in regulation through "market-rational" policies. His distinction between the systems may be somewhat overdrawn, but he gets at an essential difference in the conception of the role of the state in long-term national economic development.

3. Chie Nakane, *Japanese Society* (Penguin Books, 1973), especially pp. 20–23, lays great emphasis on the tendency of social groups in Japan to develop a closed world, building independence for the group. What she describes for households and other social groups can be extended to the nation, with a desire to build group (national) independence by creating or fostering a wide range of domestic industries and pushing foreign firms into the position of outsiders for whom penetration of the group becomes difficult.

4. The full range of postwar industrial policy measures available to the government is discussed in Edward J. Lincoln, *Japan's Industrial Policies* (Washington: Japan Economic Institute, 1984). Johnson, *MITI and the Japanese Miracle*, considers the specific powers and policies of the Ministry of International Trade and Industry, a key (but not sole) player in industrial policy formulation.

5. U.S. Tariff Commission, *Report to the Committee on Finance of the United States Senate and Its Subcommittee on International Trade*, pt. 1: *Trade Barriers—An Overview*, TC Publication 665 (Washington, April 1974), p. 55, notes that world trade grew at an average annual rate of 1.8 percent from 1876 to 1896, 4.3 percent from 1896 to 1926, and a much higher 8.2 percent in the postwar years of 1956 to 1970. The report is careful to note that higher economic growth, not falling trade barriers, is the primary cause of the more rapid expansion of trade, but gives falling barriers some credit (pp. 56–83).

6. Warren Hunsberger, *Japan and the United States in World Trade* (Harper and Row, 1964), p. 130. On Japan's entry into the GATT, see pp. 231–32, 287.

7. As one American economist noted in the 1960s: "It is curious that in the case of Japan there was no systematic advancement of the free trade philosophy until and unless she was reminded by foreign governments of its importance. Even after the policy to move ahead with the liberalization was adopted, there persisted in the country a popular view that Japan was being forced to swallow by foreign pressure something which was really disadvantageous to the country." Robert S. Ozaki, *The Control of Imports and Foreign Capital in Japan* (Praeger Publishers, 1972), p. 60. He does find at least one Japanese advocate of trade liberalization in Hisao Kanamori (head of the Japan Economic Research Center), but the dominant theme in domestic dialogue was one of concern and fear over the effects of liberalization.

8. Writing in 1971 Kiyoshi Kojima, a leading international trade economist, stated that "five or ten years should see [Japan's] heavy industries and chemicals on a sound enough footing, and enable her to join in freer trade and successive tariff reductions without fear." Kiyoshi Kojima, *Japan and a Pacific Free Trade Area* (University of California Press, 1971), p. 31.

9. Japan External Trade Organization (JETRO), *Japan as an Export Market*, JETRO Marketing Series 1 (Tokyo, 1976), p. 8.

10. Takashi Eguchi and Manabu Matsuda, *Bōeki Masatsu: Mienai Sensō—Nihon no Taiō to Kaiketsu no Michi* [Trade Friction: The Invisible War—The Road for Japan's Response and Solution] (Tokyo: TBS Britannica, 1987), pp. 119–22.

11. Yoko Sazanami, *Kokusai Bungyō to Nihon Keizai* [The International Division of Industry and the Japanese Economy] (Tokyo: Toyo Keizai Shimpōsha, 1980), pp. 197–206, does lay out standard arguments on the mutual benefits that come from free trade, as do standard modern economics textbooks (a translated version of Samuelson is quite popular in Japan), but the theory is rarely portrayed as having implications for Japan's own behavior.

12. The 1976 white paper gives some brief mention to intra-industry trade, but as something that will grow in the future between Japan and developing countries, not with developed countries. Elsewhere this report emphasizes comparative advantage as the main determinant of trade structure. MITI, *Tsūshō Hakusho* [Trade White Paper], 1976 ed. (Tokyo: Ministry of Finance Printing Office, 1976), pp. 333–35. The 1978 trade white paper, on the other hand, focuses more heavily on comparative advantage and serves up the failure of foreign firms to try hard enough as a reason for low imports of manufactures. MITI, *Tsūshō Hakusho*, 1978 ed., p. 261. Only in 1979, after the trade surplus had peaked, the second oil shock had begun, and manufactured imports were close to the end of a brief surge, does the trade white paper discuss intra-industry trade. Even in this case, however, the discussion obfuscates the issue and gives a misleading impression that intra-industry trade was rapidly becoming more prevalent. It concludes that such trade would expand with developing countries in the 1980s, in the area of consumer goods, while Japan would have even less such trade in capital equipment (its area of preeminent comparative advantage). MITI, *Tsūshō Hakusho*, 1979 ed., pp. 244–54.

13. Mordechai E. Kreinin, "How Closed Is Japan's Market? Additional Evidence," *World Economy*, vol. 2 (December 1988), pp. 529–41.

14. "All Nippon Airways' Choice of GE Engines Shocks MITI," *Japan Times*, December 17, 1988, p. 3.

15. Shigenobu Yamamoto, *Shijō Kaihō no Tame ni* [In Order to Liberate the Market] (Tokyo: Dōbunkan Shuppansha, 1986), pp. 119–21, identifies *kakō bōeki shugi* (process "trade-ism") as a postwar term. The 1964 *Tsūshō Hakusho* is cited as laying out this concept.

16. Donald J. Daly, "Theory and Evidence on Canada's Comparative Advantage," in K. C. Dhawan, Hamid Etemad, and Richard W. Wright, eds.,

International Business: A Canadian Perspective (Ontario: Addison-Wesley, 1981), p. 38. With the United States set at 100, the index of production of minerals per employed person is 26 in northwestern Europe and 4 in Japan.

17. General Accounting Office, *United States–Japan Trade: Issues and Problems*, GAO ID-79-53 (Washington, September 1979), p. 175. The textbook goes on to note that exports have become larger than imports, and that in the future a better balance between exports and imports should be maintained. As with much of the rest of the dialogue on trade policy, this stresses harmony with the world rather than domestic benefits for Japan.

18. Yamamoto, *Shijō Kaihō no Tame ni*, pp. 118–37, discusses the genesis of policies to promote exports and restrict imports. Ishibashi went on to become prime minister in the late 1950s.

19. Keizai Koho Center, *Japan 1989: An International Comparison* (Tokyo, 1988), p. 68.

20. Many observers have noted the pronounced ascendancy of the workplace over the family in Japanese society. See, for example, Nakane, *Japanese Society*, p. 20, who notes that Japanese enterprise "pervades even the private lives of its employees"; or Karel van Wolferen, *The Enigma of Japanese Power: People and Politics in a Stateless Nation* (Alfred A. Knopf, 1989), pp. 166–67, who sees the workplace as clearly dominant over families in terms of importance as a social unit.

21. Specialized government-sponsored financial institutions exist to meet the needs of small business, but they do not seem to have overcome the bias toward large firms in the financial system. On the biased allocation of credit in the postwar period, see Henry C. Wallich and Mabel I. Wallich, "Banking and Finance," in Hugh Patrick and Henry Rosovsky, eds., *Asia's New Giant* (Brookings, 1976), p. 292. The structure of Japanese financial markets is covered in detail in a number of sources, including Edward J. Lincoln, *Japan: Facing Economic Maturity* (Brookings, 1988).

22. Van Wolferen, *Enigma of Japanese Power*, pp. 50–60, provides an excellent description of how a variety of consumer interests have been defused and co-opted by the granting of token seats on these advisory commissions, the dispatch of retired officials to run organizations nominally opposed to existing government policy, and some measure of flexibility in government policy.

23. Spare use of the court system may also have a cultural basis, since the Japanese dislike open confrontation. There is strong evidence, however, that the government restriction on the supply of legal services leaves a large unmet demand. See John Owen Haley, "The Myth of the Reluctant Litigant," *Journal of Japanese Studies*, vol. 4 (Summer 1978), pp. 359–90. Haley notes that "delay is acute" in the court system, and he finds a significant correlation between the number of trial actions filed each year, the length of trial delay in the preceding year, and the number of lawyers per capita. J. Mark Ramseyer, "Reluctant Litigant Revisited: Rationality and Disputes in Japan," *Journal of Japanese Studies*, vol. 14 (Winter 1988), pp. 111–23,

adds further reasons for the low level of litigation, including a predominance of trials decided by judges rather than juries, the predictability of those judges' decisions, pressure on litigants by trial judges to settle out of court, and high court costs. These are all administrative or institutional features of the legal system unrelated to culture.

24. For example, in 1988, 22.6 percent of Japanese households owned more than one passenger car, compared with 76.7 percent in the United States in 1985. Keizai Koho Center, *Japan 1989*, p. 86; and Bureau of the Census, *Statistical Abstract of the United States* (Department of Commerce, 1987), p. 591. For a recent comparison of housing, see Douglas Ostrom, "Japanese Housing: The International Dimension," *Japan Economic Report*, no. 30A (August 4, 1989). He finds floor area per capita only half the level in the United States, 71 percent of the level in France, and 66 percent of the level in West Germany. For a recent lament on the lack of sewer systems—even in some parts of Tokyo—see the editorial "Ōkii Gesuidō wa Yoi Koto Ka?" [Is a Big Sewer a Good Idea?], *Asahi Shimbun*, August 14, 1989.

25. Edward J. Lincoln, *Japan*, pp. 47–56, discusses the changes in the allocation of public spending in the 1970s in response to changing public attitudes.

26. Economies of scale, or learning-curve economies, and the desirability of low prices for exports to expand production scales have long been the staple of management consulting firms. See, for example, James C. Abegglen and George Stalk, Jr., *Kaisha: The Japanese Corporation* (Basic Books, 1985), especially pp. 42–90.

27. The role of industrial policy in Japan has been extensively analyzed by Chalmers Johnson, beginning with *MITI and the Japanese Miracle*. Some of his critics have noted that the distribution of benefits under the rubric of industrial policy are little different from what happens in other countries through different means—see Philip H. Trezise and Yukio Suzuki, "Politics, Government, and Economic Growth in Japan," in Hugh Patrick and Henry Rosovsky, eds., *Asia's New Giant*, especially pp. 792–811; and Lincoln, *Japan's Industrial Policies*. This criticism does not preclude the possibility of industrial policy working to the detriment of Japan's trading partners.

28. Clyde V. Prestowitz, Jr., *Trading Places: How We Allowed Japan to Take the Lead* (Basic Books, 1988), pp. 122–50.

29. This is the thrust of books such as Ezra F. Vogel, *Japan as Number One: Lessons for America* (Harvard University Press, 1979); Robert B. Reich, *The Next American Frontier* (Times Books, 1983); and Chalmers Johnson, Laura D'Andrea Tyson, and John Zysman, eds., *Politics and Productivity: The Real Story of Why Japan Works* (Ballinger Publishing, 1989). These books portray Japan as a success story written in part by government policymakers, whom U.S. officials should at least consider emulating.

30. In commenting on a paper by Robert Z. Lawrence that dealt with Japan's low level of intra-industry trade, Martin Baily noted that comparative advantage may be the governing model for Japan, and William Branson

noted that, if so, the puzzle is why Japan imports any manufactured goods at all. *Brookings Papers on Economic Activity*, 2:1987, p. 552.

31. Eguchi and Matsuda, *Bōeki Masatsu: Mienai Sensō*, pp. 45–50.

32. Ryuhei Wakasugi, "Strategies to Balance Japan-U.S. Trade," *Economic Eye*, December 1987, pp. 11.

33. Noriyuki Hirai, "Amerika Sangyō no Suitai" [The Decline of American Industry], and Shinjirō Hagiwara, "Rēgan Seiken to Amerika no Kokusai Kyōsōryoku" [The Reagan Administration and American Competitiveness], in Sadayuki Sato, ed., *Nichibei Keizai Masatsu no Kōzu* [The Composition of U.S.-Japan Economic Friction] (Tokyo: Yūhikaku, 1987), pp. 60–61, 77, 107.

34. Sadayuki Sato, "Nichibei Keizai Masatsu" [Japan-U.S. Economic Friction], in Sato, ed., *Nichibei Keizai Masatsu no Kōzu*, pp. 28–30.

35. Some recent exceptions are presented in chapter 5.

36. Yoko Sazanami, "Possibilities of Expanding Intra-Industry Trade in Japan," *Keio Economic Studies*, vol. 18, no. 2 (1981), pp. 27–43.

37. Intra-industry trade is mentioned or discussed briefly in this manner in the following Ministry of International Trade and Industry *Tsūshō Hakusho* [Trade White Papers]: 1963 ed., p. 13 (as something occurring in Europe with no clear discussion of implications for Japan); 1966 ed., p. 172; 1971 ed., pp. 50–57 (primarily talking about other countries); 1972 ed., pp. 281–83; 1973 ed., pp. 192–93; 1974 ed., pp. 397–406; 1975 ed., pp. 289–94; 1977 ed., pp. 420–23, 431–33; and 1979 ed., pp. 240–54. Most of these discussions are quite brief and not part of the paper's major themes.

38. Eguchi and Matsuda, *Bōeki Masatsu: Mienai Sensō*, pp. 165–91, 232. Typical of publications of this sort, they rely on the writings of Americans (C. Fred Bergsten, William Cline, and Gary Saxonhouse), plus a Japanese working at an American consulting firm (Kenichi Ohmae), to demonstrate that Japan's market is open.

39. Akira Ueno, *Yūryō Kigyō no 'Nichibei Keizai Masatsu' Ikinokori Senryaku* [Survival Strategies for Strong Firms Facing "U.S.-Japan Trade Friction"] (Tokyo: Jiji Tsushinsha, 1986), p. 63.

40. See John C. Panzar and Robert D. Willig, "Economies of Scope," *American Economic Review*, vol. 71 (May 1981), pp. 268–72. The theory was designed to explain why multiproduct firms exist, as they do in all economies. Applying this theory to the low level of manufactured imports in Japan, therefore, still involves an unusual pattern; economies of scope would have to be much stronger than in other countries.

41. Kazuo Sato, "Increasing Returns and International Trade: The Case of Japan," revised version of paper presented to the American Economic Association, December 1985, p. 16.

42. Statistics Bureau, Management and Coordination Agency, *Japan Statistical Yearbook*, 1987 ed. (Tokyo: Japan Statistical Association, 1987), p. 544.

43. Bureau of Mines, *Minerals Yearbook*, vol. 1: *Metals and Minerals*, 1986 ed. (Washington: U.S. Department of the Interior, 1988), pp. 353–54, 357–59. Japan is only a minor producer of ore (0.4 percent of the world total), and a smaller producer than the United States of refined copper (9.9 percent of the world total).

44. For Japanese figures, see Japan Aluminum Federation, *Light Metal Statistics in Japan*, 1987 ed. (Tokyo, 1988), pp. 8–9. The terms used here are different from those in table 4-2, but mill products correspond roughly to wrought aluminum, and "other" to finished structural parts and structures. For U.S. figures, see Bureau of Mines, *Minerals Yearbook*, vol. 1, 1986 ed., pp. 102, 104–05. Data show imports as a share of net shipments plus imports minus exports.

45. Sazanami, "Possibilities of Expanding Intra-Industry Trade in Japan," p. 36.

46. Ueno, *Yūryō Kigyō no 'Nichibei Keizai Masatsu' Ikinokori Senryaku*, p. 18, claims that the era of *hakuraihin* is now over, but what Ueno means is not that Japanese expectations of imported products have changed, but that the range of foreign goods qualifying as *hakuraihin* is much more limited because similar Japanese goods are superior.

47. Seibu department store price for GE refrigerator model no. TFX22R, 611 liters, with water and ice on door; U.S. price for the same product quoted by General Electronics, a retail distributor of consumer appliances. The 16-cubic-foot GE refrigerator, available in the United States for $721, cost $2,384 at Seibu. The prices for Johnny Walker Black Label are those at virtually any liquor outlet in Tokyo and compared with retail prices in Washington, D.C.

48. Eguchi and Matsuda, *Bōeki Masatsu: Mienai Sensō*, p. 179.

49. MITI, *Selling to Japan from A to Z* (Tokyo: Manufactured Imports Promotion Organization, 1983), p. 7.

50. Ueno, *Yūryō Kigyō no 'Nichibei Keizai Masatsu' Ikinokori Senryaku*, pp. 84–87. The harshness and forcefulness of Ueno's statements on American corporate failure in approaching the Japanese market and the need for the Japanese government to push this line are quite striking.

51. Robert C. Christopher, *Second to None: American Companies in Japan* (Ballantine Books, 1986), pp. 151–58. Many cases that Americans see as unfair or unethical retaliation by Japanese competitors, though, Christopher passes off as simply products of a different culture, which foreign firms would do better to accept than to challenge.

52. Bureau of Statistics, *Japan Statistical Yearbook*, 1977 ed., p. 44; 1980 ed., p. 48; 1987 ed., p. 61; and U.S. Department of Commerce, *Statistical Abstract of the United States*, 1973 ed., p. 213; 1989 ed., p. 235. Other U.S. data put the number of American citizens departing the country in 1960 at 1.9 million. Department of Commerce, *Statistical Abstract of the United States*, 1973 ed., p. 214.

53. *Asahi Shimbun*, October 1, 1989, p. 1.

54. A group calling itself the "Assembly of the Associations for Appealing to Japanese Consumers' Opinion in the American Media on the Issue of Rice Import Liberalization" placed a full-page ad in the *Washington Post*, July 6, 1989, defending the ban on rice imports. This group claims to include 279 separate groups, including 61 consumer organizations, numerous consumer cooperatives, and a number of labor unions.

55. Van Wolferen, *Enigma of Japanese Power*, pp. 52–53.

56. Yojiro Inui, *Gaikokuhin o Chokusetsu Yasuku Kojin Yu'nyū* [Importing Foreign Products Directly and Cheaply as an Individual] (Tokyo: Seinen Shokan, 1988), pp. 10–11.

57. Izumi Oshima, "Japanese Travellers on a Worldwide Shopping Spree," *Japan Economic Journal*, August 5, 1989, p. 5.

58. Bank of Japan, *Balance of Payments Monthly*, June 1989, pp. 47–48. In the first half of 1989 these payments were 30 percent higher than a year earlier, indicating that the upward trend was continuing.

59. For a general discussion of the structure and performance of Japanese trading companies, see Kiyoshi Kojima and Terutomo Ozawa, *Japan's General Trading Companies: Merchants of Economic Development* (Paris: Organization for Economic Cooperation and Development, 1984); or Alexander K. Young, *Sōgō Shōsha: Japan's Multinational Trading Companies* (Westview Press, 1979).

60. Keizai Koho Center, *Japan 1989*, p. 46. These shares are for fiscal 1987, although they have remained fairly steady over time.

61. Kojima and Ozawa, *Japan's General Trading Companies*, p. 100.

62. In 1979 outstanding trade credit assets in the corporate sector in Japan were 1.3 times larger than those in the United States at then-current exchange rates. Trade credit liabilities were 1.4 times larger. That the absolute size of credit was larger in an economy only half the size of the United States indicates the much greater use of trade credit to provide financing within the corporate sector. Edward J. Lincoln, "Corporate Financing in Japan," *JEI Report*, no. 38 (October 9, 1981), p. 3.

63. Phyllis Ann Genther, "The Changing Government-Business Relationship: Japan's Passenger Car Industry," Ph.D. dissertation, George Washington University, 1986, pp. 187–203.

64. See Eleanor M. Hadley, *Antitrust in Japan* (Princeton University Press, 1970), for an analysis of the distinctions between the prewar *zaibatsu* and the postwar *keiretsu*. The latter are so much looser and more decentralized that they bear only slight resemblance to their prewar predecessors. See Edward J. Lincoln, "Keiretsu," *Council Report* [now *JEI Report*], no. 41 (October 31, 1980), for an update of this analysis.

65. Prestowitz, *Trading Places*, pp. 157–59.

66. For a review of the role of the Fair Trade Commission, see Hadley, *Antitrust in Japan*, pp. 122–24, or Masu Uekusa, "Industrial Organization:

The 1970s to the Present," in Kozo Yamamura and Yasukichi Yasuba, eds., *The Political Economy of Japan*, vol. 1: *The Domestic Transformation* (Stanford University Press, 1987), pp. 477–79.

67. Kenji Sanekata, "Antitrust in Japan: Recent Trends and their Socio-Political Background," *University of British Columbia Law Review*, vol. 20, no. 2 (1986), pp. 396–97.

68. Mary Faith Higgins, "Japanese Fair Trade Commission Review of International Agreements," *Loyola Los Angeles International and Comparative Law Annual*, vol. 3 (1980), p. 46.

69. Sanekata, "Antitrust in Japan," pp. 382–83.

70. In this landmark case the JFTC challenged the legality of administrative guidance by MITI not supported by specific legislative authority. In 1980 the Tokyo High Court upheld at least part of the the JFTC attack on MITI. For a review of this case, see Mitsuo Matsushita, "The Legal Framework of Trade and Investment in Japan," *Harvard International Law Journal*, vol. 27 (Special Issue 1986), pp. 380–83.

71. For a review of this change in the law and the factors leading up to it, see Seichi Yoshikawa, "Fair Trade Commission vs. MITI: History of the Conflicts between the Antimonopoly Policy and the Industrial Policy in the Post War Period of Japan," *Case Western Reserve Journal of International Law*, vol. 15 (Summer 1983), pp. 499–502.

72. Japan Fair Trade Commission, *Kōsei Torihiki Iinkai Nenji Hōkoku: Dokusen Kinshi Hakusho* [Annual Report of the Fair Trade Commission: White Paper on Antitrust], 1988 ed., pp. 202–03.

73. JFTC, *Kōsei Torihiki Iinkai Nenji Hōkoku*, p. 10.

74. Prestowitz, *Trading Places*, pp. 76, 162.

75. Denki Kiki Shijō Chōsakai [Electric Machine Tool Market Study Group], *Denshi Buhin. Zairyō Shijō Yōran 1990 Nenban* [An Outline of the Electronic Parts and Materials Market 1990 Edition] (Tokyo: Kagaku Shimbunsha, 1989), p. 758.

76. Kōjundo Sirikon Mondai Kenkyūkai, *Kōjundo Sirikon Mondai Kenyūkai Chōsa Hōkokusho* [Investigative Report of the High Purity Silicon Problem Study Group] (Tokyo: Shin Kinzoku Kyōkai, 1985), pp. 46–47. These figures are only a crude measure of imports as a share of apparent domestic consumption because of wide variations in inventory behavior from year to year. The shares calculated here are imports divided by the sum of imports plus domestic production (Japan does not export polycrystalline silicon).

77. *Union Carbide* v. *Komatsu and others* (N.D. Cal. filed October 3, 1988).

Chapter Five

1. The very title of one recent offering gives the flavor of the current mood in Japan: Nihon Keizai Shimbunsha, *Shin·Nihon Keizai: Subete ga*

Kawari Hajimeta [The New Japanese Economy: Everything Has Begun to Change] (Tokyo, 1988). The book claims that current shifts and developments in Japan are as fundamental as the Meiji Restoration of 1868, the revolutionary change that created a modern nation-state and propelled Japan onto the path of industrialization.

2. Ministry of International Trade and Industry (MITI), *Tsūshō Hakusho* [Trade White Paper], 1985 ed. (Tokyo: Ministry of Finance Printing Office, 1985), pp. 216, 337. The equations estimating price and income elasticity are of the form manufactured imports = *f* (income, relative prices, and manufactured imports in the preceding period). Income is measured by the index of industrial production rather than GDP or disposable income, and the relative price measure is the price index for manufactured imports divided by the wholesale price index.

3. Robert Z. Lawrence, "Imports in Japan: Closed Markets or Minds?" *Brookings Papers on Economic Activity*, 2: 1987, p. 542.

4. Yoko Sazanami, *Kokusai Bungyō to Nihon Keizai* [The International Division of Industry and the Japanese Economy] (Tokyo: Toyo Keizai Shimpōsha, 1980), pp. 142–44, 156–68, argued in the 1970s that yen appreciation was having and would continue to have the effect of encouraging imports in general and greater intra-industry trade in particular. Writing just before the 1979 oil shock once again postponed change in Japan, she believed that Japan would come into line with the behavior of other nations—and much of what she wrote then sounds very much like what is being written in Japan today.

5. Donald J. Daly, "Japanese Manufacturing Competitiveness: Implications for International Trade," Working Paper 53 (University of Toronto-York, University Joint Centre for Asia Pacific Studies, 1988). Daly emphasizes the persistence of low unit labor costs in Japanese manufacturing during the 1970s and first half of the 1980s as a reason for limited manufactured imports.

6. Among these works are the recent popular book by Karel van Wolferen, *The Enigma of Japanese Power* (Alfred A. Knopf, 1989); Kent E. Calder, *Crisis and Compensation: Public Policy and Political Stability in Japan, 1949–1986* (Princeton University Press, 1988); and Thomas P. Rohlen, "Order in Japanese Society: Attachment, Authority, and Routine," *Journal of Japanese Studies*, vol. 15 (Winter 1989).

7. Ruth Benedict, *The Chrysanthemum and the Sword* (Houghton Mifflin, 1946). This characteristic is known as "situational ethics." Much of Benedict's work on Japan is now considered outdated, but some of her basic observations remain remarkably perceptive.

8. Rohlen, "Order in Japanese Society," p. 32. The notion of the policy process producing stable balances of competing interests was a principal theme of John Creighton Campbell, *Contemporary Japanese Budget Politics* (University of California Press, 1977).

9. Hierarchical structures in Japanese society are the dominant feature in

Chie Nakane's seminal book, *Japanese Society* (Penguin Books, 1973). Rohlen, "Order in Japanese Society," argues that she overemphasizes hierarchy and underemphasizes leaderless groups. Nevertheless, within the group context, hierarchy is generally a useful guide to predicting outcomes.

10. Recent research by sociologists has focused on how nursery school and elementary school education works to shape such behavior patterns. See the symposium in the *Journal of Japanese Studies*, vol. 15 (Winter 1989), and especially the introductory essay by Rohlen, "Order in Japanese Society."

11. Calder, *Crisis and Compensation*, pp. 159–60; and van Wolferen, *Enigma of Japanese Power*, pp. 50–81.

12. Rohlen, "Order in Japanese Society," p. 35.

13. Rodney Clark, *The Japanese Company* (Yale University Press, 1979), p. 50; and Yasusuke Murakami, "The Japanese Model of Political Economy," in Kozo Yamamura and Yasukichi Yasuba, eds., *The Political Economy of Japan*, vol. 1: *The Domestic Transformation* (Stanford University Press, 1987), pp. 33–90. Murakami's approach, in which he uses the Japanese words *ie* (household) and *mura* (village) for group concepts (giving a sense of Japanese uniqueness to his theories), has been controversial. See the symposium on *ie* society in the *Journal of Japanese Studies*, vol. 11 (Winter 1985), and especially Thomas P. Rohlen, "When Evolution Isn't Progressive."

14. Clyde V. Prestowitz, Jr., *Trading Places: How We Allowed Japan to Take the Lead* (Basic Books, 1988); van Wolferen, *Enigma of Japanese Power*; and James Fallows, "Containing Japan," *Atlantic Monthly* (May 1989), all articulate this sense of discouragement about being able to foster change in Japan.

15. T. J. Pempel, "The Unbundling of 'Japan, Inc.': The Changing Dynamics of Japanese Policy Formation," *Journal of Japanese Studies*, vol. 13 (Summer 1987), argues that the political process has changed considerably over the past 30 years. Unfortunately, some of the trends he identifies, such as a proliferation of groups with differing views that must be accommodated in setting public policy, militate against greater openness on trade issues because of the greater difficulty in creating consensus and arranging compensation in a more pluralistic setting.

16. Pempel, "Unbundling of 'Japan, Inc.'"

17. Bank of Japan, *Economic Statistics Annual* (Tokyo, 1989), p. 256.

18. "Yu'nyū Kyūzō: Keizai Seichō Uwamawaru" [The Sudden Increase in Imports: Exceeding Economic Growth], *Nihon Keizai Shimbun*, October 4, 1988, p. 3.

19. MITI, *Tsūshō Hakusho*, 1988 ed., pp. 85, 289. The price elasticities are a cumulative effect over the four previous quarters. Note that the measure on income in these equations is an index of domestic industrial production, rather than any broader measure of domestic income.

20. Economic Planning Agency, *Keizai Hakusho* [Economic White Paper] (Tokyo: Ministry of Finance Printing Office, 1988), pp. 92–94, 383.

From 1.9 through the first quarter of 1983 (that is, using a sample period over which the equation is estimated that extends from the second quarter of 1980 through first quarter of 1983), the EPA finds income elasticity of demand rising to 2.1 by the first quarter of 1988 (that is, this is the result when the sample period is extended to incorporate data through that quarter—which is not the same as saying that elasticity in that quarter was 2.1). Similarly, the price elasticity of demand for imported consumer goods rose from 0.9 to 1.1 for the same periods.

21. Japan Tariff Association, *Japan Exports and Imports: Commodity by Country* (Tokyo, December 1988), p. 3.

22. Data for 1987 that are based on the same classification as the 1985 data show basically the same shifts displayed in figure 5-1, although the improvement is not quite as large.

23. The price of nickel foil, flakes, and powders dropped 29 percent between 1980 and 1988, while ores and concentrates, matte, speiss, and other intermediate products, plus unwrought metal, declined by amounts ranging from 4 percent to 32 percent. Thus unchanged physical volumes of imports of these materials would result in a somewhat smaller value share for foil, flakes, and powders. The large increase in the value of imports, therefore, is a real development, not a result of price movements.

24. On a more optimistic note, a recent newspaper article, *Japan Economic Journal*, July 15, 1989, p. A1, claims that foreign automobiles are aiming at a 10 percent share of the Japanese market.

25. "The Progress of Japan's Structural Adjustment and Prospects for the Industrial Structure (A Summary)," *News from MITI*, NR-354 (88-02), May 1988, p. 5.

26. For a review of the debate over industrial policy, see Edward J. Lincoln, *Japan's Industrial Policies* (Washington: Japan Economic Institute, 1984).

27. Economic Planning Agency, *Keizai Hakusho*, 1984 ed., pp. 179–81, provides a recitation of these explanations, including the large size of the economy (normally inversely related with the ratio of imports to GNP) and Japan's role as a processing nation—importing raw materials and exporting manufactures.

28. MITI, *Tsūshō Hakusho* [Trade White Paper], 1985 ed., pp. 200–33 (especially pp. 200–07), and 1986 ed., pp. 203–22.

29. Prestowitz, *Trading Places*, pp. 272–302.

30. Saburo Okita and others, *Report of the Advisory Committee for External Economic Issues* (Tokyo, April 9, 1985), often called the Okita Report after its chairman. Saburo Okita is a senior and highly respected economist who briefly served as minister of foreign affairs under Prime Minister Ohira in 1979–80.

31. Government–Ruling Parties Joint Headquarters for the Promotion of External Economic Measures, *The Outline of the Action Program for Improved Market Access*, July 30, 1985, p. 2 of the provisional translation by

the Japanese government. The phraseology here sounds virtually identical to the obligatory references to the benefits of liberal trade in the trade white papers of the 1960s.

32. Haruo Maekawa and others, *The Report of the Advisory Group on Economic Structural Adjustment for International Harmony* (Tokyo, April 7, 1986), p. 2.

33. "Premier Asks People to Buy Foreign Goods," *Japan Times*, April 10, 1985. He asked each individual to buy $100 worth of foreign products. MITI followed suit by preparing sample lists of products (separate for men and women) that would sum to $100; see "MITI Prepares Sample Import Shopping Lists," *Japan Times*, April 13, 1985. Shortly thereafter, a cartoon in *Nihon Keizai Shimbun* showed an employee excusing himself from work to go out to do his bit for the national import promotion campaign, and then pictured him drinking "American" coffee (weak coffee with cream) at a local coffee shop (*Nihon Keizai Shimbun*, April 19, 1985). In a similar vein, another cartoon portrayed a worker showing off all the foreign attire he has bought (necktie, suit, shoes, and cufflinks) to a fellow worker. Expecting lavish praise and an invitation to go drinking as a reward for his progressive behavior, he is chagrined when his friend merely gives him a few coins to go buy a can of American beer from a vending machine (*Asahi Shimbun*, April 11, 1985).

34. Economic Planning Agency, Sōgō Keikaku Kyoku [Planning Bureau], *21 Seiki e no Kihon Senryaku: Keizai Kōzō Chōsei to Nihon Keizai no Tenbō* [Fundamental Strategies for the 21st Century: The Future of the Japanese Economy and Economic Structural Change] (Tokyo: Toyo Keizai Shimpōsha, 1987), pp. 87–93. The term used for government cooperation is *seisaku doryoku*, which means to make great efforts in policy. It is significant that the EPA sees an important and necessary role for the government in allowing or making these changes in Japan.

35. Economic Planning Agency, *Sekai to Tomo ni Ikiru Nihon: Keizai Un'ei 5-ka Nen Keikaku* [Japan Living Together with the World: A Five-Year Plan for Economic Management] (Tokyo: Ministry of Finance Printing Office, 1988), pp. 22–23. This plan is known as the Hiraiwa Report after Gaishi Hiraiwa, chairman of Tokyo Electric Power, who headed the advisory commission that discussed and approved the plan. The Japanese original uses the terms *issō susume* and *sekkyokuteki* for the two emphasized terms in the quotation. The themes of greater openness and government policy action to achieve that goal are developed in somewhat greater detail in an attached report by the Kokusai Keizai Bukai (Subcommittee on the International Economy), especially pp. 193–95. The only cautionary note is that the membership of this subcommittee contains mostly familiar names from the rather small set of well-known internationalists in Tokyo (including Shijuro Ogata of the Japan Development Bank, Hiroto Ohyama of NHK, Yotaro Kobayashi of Fuji Xerox, and Professor Iwao Nakatani of Osaka University). The report itself, however, should not be seen as the product of this liberal

group; as an official government document, it must have at least the tacit approval of all involved ministries.

36. Economic Planning Agency, *Keizai Hakusho,* 1988 ed., pp. 88–127, especially pp. 113–15.

37. MITI, *Tsūshō Hakusho,* 1988 ed.

38. MITI, Minister's Secretariat, *Nihon no Sentaku: 'Nyū Gurōbari-zumu' e no Kōken to 'Shin-Sangyō Bunka Kokuka' no Sentaku* [Japan's Choices: Choices Concerning Contributions to the "New Globalism" and the "New National Industrial Culture"] (Tokyo: Tsūshō Sangyō Chōsakai, 1988), p. 43. Unlike most of the other recent sources cited here, this one presents the need to open markets with the more traditional and condescending explanation of helping the United States to export more rather than as a means of promoting greater economic efficiency in Japan. Similar to the EPA long-term economic plan, this report was discussed and approved by an advisory committee of familiar international figures (Professor Heizo Takenaka, Tadashi Yamamoto of the Japan Center for International Exchange, Professor Akihiro Tanaka, Akira Kojima of Nihon Keizai Shimbun, Hideo Sugiura of Honda Motor Co., and others).

39. Kōsei Torihiki Iinkai [Japan Fair Trade Commission], *Kōsei Torihiki Iinkai Nenji Hōkoku: Dokusen Kinshi Hakusho* [The JFTC Annual Report: The Antitrust White Paper], 1987 ed. (Tokyo: Kōsei Torihiki Kyōkai, 1987), pp. 38–52.

40. MITI, *Yu'nyū Brandohin Naigai Kakaku Hikaku Chōsa* [Price Comparison Survey of Imported Brand Name Items] (Tokyo, March 27, 1989). The cities included New York, Paris, Düsseldorf, Sydney, and Seoul, but not such geographically close and open markets as Hong Kong and Singapore. The product list appears to include only non-Japanese items, avoiding the embarrassing revelation that prices even for Japanese goods are lower abroad. Furthermore, possible defects in the Japanese distribution sector are not included in the list of causes for the differentials. The original survey is in Sangyō Kōzō Shingikai Ryūtsū Bukai (Distribution Subcommittee, Industrial Structure Council) and Chūshō Kigyō Seisaku Shingikai Ryūtsū Shōiinkai (Distribution Subcommittee, Medium and Small Business Policy Council), *90 Nendai Ni Okeru Ryūtsū no Kihon Hōkō Ni Tstuite (Chūkan Tōshin): 90 Nendai Ryūtsū Bijon Zuhyōhen)* [On Fundamental Directions of Distribution in the 1990s (Interim Report): The 1990s Distribution Vision (Tables Section)] (Tokyo: MITI, June 9, 1989), pp. 57–58.

41. Economic Planning Agency, *Bukka Repōto '89* [Commodity Price Report, 1989] (Tokyo, September 1989), p. 33.

42. U.S. Department of Commerce/MITI Price Survey, n.p., n.d

43. Sangyō Kōzō Shingikai Ryūtsū Bukai and Chūshō Kigyō Seisaku Shingikai Ryūtsū Shōiinkai, *90 Nendai Ryūtsū Bijon,* pp. 47–58. The proposed changes include expediting the review of applications (to eight months in principle), reducing mandatory closing days from 44 (or more) to 30, and abolishing closing time requirements.

44. Keizai Koho Center, *Deregulating Distribution: Keidanren Proposals for Transport, Trade, Retailing, and Farming and Food Processing*, KKC Brief 48 (July 1988). This appears to be a very mild position, and in typical Japanese fashion, it involves no changes in the language of the law itself. All these changes can be handled as administrative decisions even though they could have a considerable impact on the profits and market share of the superstores.

45. Oroshiurigyō Yu'nyū Sokushin Kyōgikai [The Wholesale Industry Committee for Promotion of Imports], *Ryūtsugyō Yu'nyū Sokushin Seminā: Jisshi Hōkokusho* [Distribution Sector Import Seminars: Report on Results], March 1988. As of March 1988 the seminars, held in cities across Japan, had attracted 2,090 attendees (p. 12).

46. "'Yu'nyū O'miai': Kōhyō" [Import Arranged Marriages: Favorable Impressions], *Asahi Shimbun*, November 5, 1988, p. 9. The service was begun in July 1988, and by the date of the article, JETRO claimed it had brought together 403 foreign companies representing 625 products with 3,743 domestic companies, although no firm contracts had been signed yet.

47. Kenji Takeuchi, "Effects of Japanese Direct Foreign Investment on Japan's Imports of Manufactures from Developing Economies," paper presented at the Fourth Biannual Conference on U.S.-Asian Economic Relations, Columbia University, June 1989, p. 22.

48. See, for example, "Kaigai Shinshutsu Masatsu Taiō kara Endaka Taiō e" [New Investment Overseas: From Dealing with Friction to Dealing with Yen Appreciation], *Toyo Keizai*, no. 4668 (July 12, 1988), which notes that in the first half of the 1980s, the locus of investment was shifting from developing countries to industrial countries because the main motivation was to combat real or threatened protectionism, whereas yen appreciation is ushering in a new era of cost-motivated investment. Problems involved in managing investment are a major theme. Also, "Yushutsu Sangyō ni Osoi Kakaru Kokusai Bungyō e no Shiren" [The Ordeal of Export Industries under Attack from the International Division of Industry], *Toyo Keizai*, no. 4653 (April 26, 1988), expects moderation in the rise of direct investment because of the employment system in Japan. An article detailing NEC's response, "Nippon Denki Yushutsu no Hanbun o Genchi Seisan e" [Half of NEC's Exports Will Be Replaced by Local Production], *Toyo Keizai*, no. 4668 (July 12, 1986), still placed heavy emphasis on protectionism as a motive for overseas investment. But the sense of a new era of heavy foreign investment, both to serve local markets and to export back, is conveyed by the title of a recent book cited above, Nihon Keizai Shimbunsha, *Shin·Nihon Keizai: Subete ga Kawari Hajimeta* [The New Japanese Economy: Everything Has Begun to Change].

49. Japanese firms can ameliorate the problems of breaking the web of existing ties through compensation—continuing to use Japanese suppliers when they invest overseas, or offering to continue buying if the suppliers will also move overseas. These issues were considered briefly in chapter 2.

50. "Mitsui's Strategies for Globalization," *Mitsui Trade News,* vol. 25 (September–October 1988), p. 3.

51. Government–Ruling Parties Joint Headquarters, *Outline of the Action Program,* pp. 32–33.

52. "Yu'nyū Daikōzui III: Kyūsoku ni Tayōka, Takakuka Shitsutsu Nyū Yu'nyū Bijinesu Kaikaki e" [The Big Flood of Imports III: The Flowering of Increasingly Diverse and Multifaceted New Import Businesses], *Toyo Keizai,* no. 4735 (July 4, 1987), pp. 15–16.

53. David Flath, "Why Are There So Many Retail Stores in Japan?" Working Paper 17, Center on Japanese Economy and Business, Columbia University, n.d., suggests that the system may not be so inefficient. The small size of retailers and the existence of multiple layers of wholesalers is a response to a variety of factors, including high population density, the smallness of dwelling units, relatively low automobile ownership, and a propensity for very fresh fish and vegetables.

54. Akira Goto, "Ryūtsū Keiretsuka to Shijō Keizai" [Development of Distribution Groups and Market Economics], in Mitsuo Matsushita, ed., *Ryūtsūkeiretsuka to Dokkinhō: Kasen Taisaku wa Dō Susumu* [Development of Distribution Groups and the Antimonopoly Law] (Tokyo: Nihon Keizai Shimbunsha, 1977), pp. 9–40. He downplays the importance of these manufacturer-controlled distribution chains, pointing out that in the 1970s the vast number of wholesale firms operated independently of such explicit groupings. But the issue was serious enough to prompt a report by the Fair Trade Commission—"Dokkinkon Shiryō: Ryūtsū Keiretsuka o Meguru Dokkinhōjō no Mondai" [Antimonopoly Data: Problems in Distribution Groupings from the Standpoint of the Antimonopoly Law], *Kosei Torihiki,* no. 300 (October 1975).

55. Japan Fair Trade Commission, *Kōsei Torihiki Iinkai Nenji Hōkoku: Dokusen Kinshi Hakusho* [Annual Report of the Fair Trade Commission: White Paper on Antitrust], 1988 ed., pp. 272–73. Resale price maintenance is now allowed for cosmetics and pharmaceuticals only, including in 1988 some 2,042 individual cosmetic products and 102 nonprescription pharmaceutical products.

56. This pattern is discussed in Edward J. Lincoln, *Japan: Facing Economic Maturity* (Brookings, 1988), p. 170.

57. See Edward J. Lincoln, "The Zebra's Stripes, or A Tale of Distributus Japonicus and the Economists," in Michael G. Harvey and Robert F. Lusch, eds., *Marketing Channels: Domestic and International Perspectives* (University of Oklahoma Press, 1982), pp. 152–65. The original law applied to all stores greater than 1,500 square meters, a minimum size that was reduced to 500 square meters (5,387 square feet) through a revision of the law in 1977. Approval involves dealing with local councils, on which sit representatives of local retail shops.

58. Lincoln, "Zebra Stripes," pp. 6–10.

59. Calder, *Crisis and Compensation,* p. 327.

60. Calder, *Crisis and Compensation*, pp. 345–46.

61. Yuko Inoue, "Licenses Snag Liquor Imports," *Japan Economic Journal*, July 9, 1988, p. 3. In 1973, 7.2 percent of these stores had liquor licenses, a figure that rose to only 8.7 percent by March 1988.

62. Some products from Sears have been available since the early 1970s through a special mail-order corner in the Seibu department store network, but this remained a small curiosity. The selection was limited, prices were high, and Seibu handled the ordering. The new development is truly an individual effort, although other large retail outlets are now establishing mail-order corners where people can peruse foreign catalogs and order with the assistance of the store. Note that this pattern is quite different from that in the United States, where large distributors handle the importation and then offer foreign goods in retail outlets or through domestic mail-order catalogs, taking advantage of the economies of scale in transportation, handling, and customs inspection.

63. Yojiro Inui, *Gaikokuhin o Chokusetsu Yasuku Kojin Yu'nyū* [Importing Foreign Products Directly and Cheaply as an Individual] (Tokyo: Seinen Shokan, 1988). Inui founded an organization in Osaka called the Mēru Ōdā Kenkyūkai (the Mail-Order Study Group) in 1978.

64. Japan External Trade Organization, *Saishin Kaigai Katarogu Shoppingu Gaido* [Latest Foreign Catalog Guide] (Tokyo, 1988). It provides both an illustrated listing of American and European mail-order catalogs and instructions on how to order and how to deal with the postal systems and customs. For packages too large to come through the mail, the minimum customs handling fee per shipment is ¥20,000–¥30,000 ($160–$240).

65. Michael D. Evans, "Newly Industrialized Economies Store: Shopwise in Tokyo," *City Life News*, October 1, 1988, p. 5; and Nippon Hoso Kyokai (NHK), *Sekai no Naka no Nihon: Ajia Kara no Chōsen* [Japan in the World: The Challenge from Asia] (Tokyo: Japan Broadcasting Publishing Association, August 1988), p. 24. As of the summer of 1988, the Inbix chain had 13 stores nationwide. None of the Japanese interviewed for this project could positively identify where the Tokyo branch of this chain was; that information finally came from the American embassy.

66. "Endaka Kaisō! Yu'nyūsha Shijō no Nyū Wēbu" [The High Yen Revolution! The New Wave in the Imported Car Market], *Toyo Keizai*, no. 4698 (January 3, 1987), pp. 130–31. Specifically, BMW has managed to get existing Japanese auto showrooms to add their imported cars. Earlier, imports had been handled exclusively by a minuscule number of specialized imported car dealers.

67. These activities had their origin in the Action Program announced in 1985. Government–Ruling Partners Joint Headquarters, *Outline of the Action Program*, p. 2–1.

68. MITI, *Ōte Kourigyō no Endaka Katsuyō Jōkyō ni Tsuite* [Concerning the Conditions of Actualization of Yen Appreciation at Large-Scale Retail Businesses], internal MITI report dated February 1988, p. 3. "Yu'nyū Daikō-

zui II: Kaihatsu Yu'nyū ga Kasoku Suru Hyakkaten, Sūpā no Ajia Ryūtsū-ken" [The Big Flood of Imports II: The Acceleration of Development Imports from the Asian Sphere by Department Stores and Superstores], *Toyo Keizai*, no. 4735 (July 4, 1987), p. 14, supports the contention that many of these fairs emphasize folk crafts and exotic presents (*o-miyage*), but praises Sogo department store for establishing a corner for Thai manufactured goods tailored to the Japanese market.

69. MITI, *Ōte Kourigyō no Endaka Katsuyō Jōkyō ni Tsuite*, p. 60. Note, however, that the size of the purchasing-sales offices was not specified in this survey.

70. MITI, *Tsūshō Hakusho*, 1988 ed., discusses the rising trend toward *kaihatsu yu'nyū*, along with direct imports by retail establishments (completely circumventing wholesalers) and parallel imports (circumventing sole distributors). "Yu'nyū Daikōzui II: Kaihatsu Yu'nyū," pp. 10–14, is devoted to explaining this trend.

71. MITI, *Ōte Kourigyō no Endaka Katsuyō Jōkyō ni Tsuite*, p. 75.

72. "Ajia no Seiki: Nihon no Yakuwari" [The Asian Century: Japan's Role], *Toyo Keizai*, no. 4689 (November 15, 1986), p. 14.

73. "Kan·Tai no Saiyakushin de Nihon o Fukumu Shinkeizaiken Keisei e" [Toward the Formation of a New Economic Area including Japan, under the Onslaught of Taiwan and South Korea], *Toyo Keizai*, no. 4698 (January 3, 1987), pp. 104–05.

74. NHK, *Sekai no Naka no Nihon: Ajia Kara no Chōsen* [Japan in the World: The Challenge from Asia] (Tokyo: Japan Broadcasting Publishing Association, 1988).

75. *Ekonomisuto, Rinji Zokan* [Economist, Special Edition], November 2, 1987. See especially the article by Kim Do-Jung, "Kan-Nichi Suihei Bungyō Jidai ga Tōrai Suru" [Arrival of the Era of the Korea-Japan Horizontal Division of Industry], pp. 76–82.

76. Japan Economic Foundation, *Journal of Japanese Trade and Industry*, March–April 1988, pp. 12–25.

77. Yukiko Fukagawa, "Ajia no Dainamizumu o Torikomu Nihon: Nihon·ASEAN·NICs no Shin Sangyō Chizu" [Japan Grasping Asian Dynamism: The New Industrial Map of Japan-ASEAN-NICs], *Ekonomisuto*, July 4, 1988, pp. 86–91. This article stresses the shift of Japanese manufacturing operations from the NICs to ASEAN (especially Thailand and Malaysia) because of rising wage costs.

78. *Toyo Keizai*, no. 4698 (January 3, 1987), pp. 130–31.

79. *Ekonomisuto*, July 4, 1988, p. 167.

80. "Yu'nyū Daikōzui I: Hirogaru Seihin Yu'nyū Kyūzō no Impakuto" [The Big Flood of Imports I: The Impact of the Widening Rapid Increase in Manufactured Goods], *Toyo Keizai*, no. 4735 (July 4, 1987), p. 7.

81. Izumi Oshima, "Chocolate Imports Irk Domestic Candy Makers," *Japan Economic Journal*, July 29, 1989, p. 3.

82. MITI, *Ōte Kourigyō no Endaka Katsuyō Jōkyō ni Tsuite*, pp. 35–47.

83. "Yu'nyū Daikōzui I," *Toyo Keizai*, no. 4735, pp. 6-7.

84. Ministry of Finance, *Zaisei Tokei* [Fiscal Statistics], fiscal 1988 ed., p. 126. The data used for fiscal 1988 represent the initial budget, and the actual results could differ. Fiscal 1986 is the last year for which final results are available.

85. MITI, *Ōte Kourigyō no Endaka Jōkyō ni Tsuite*, data from an unfolioed inserted page.

Chapter Six

1. Miyohei Shinohara, a leading academic economist in Japan during the 1950s and 1960s, clearly expresses such justifications. See Shinohara, *Industrial Growth, Trade, and Dynamic Patterns in the Japanese Economy* (University of Tokyo Press, 1982), especially pp. 24-26.

2. This questioning began with Ezra F. Vogel, *Japan as Number One: Lessons for America* (Harvard University Press, 1979); and Chalmers Johnson, *MITI and the Japanese Miracle: The Growth of Industrial Policy, 1925-1975* (Stanford University Press, 1982); a recent statement on the need for the United States to adopt a more coordinated industrial policy in response to Japan's successful example comes from Chalmers Johnson, Laura D'Andrea Tyson, and John Zysman, eds., *Politics and Productivity: The Real Story of Why Japan Works* (Ballinger, 1989); and John Zysman and Stephen S. Cohen, *The Mercantilist Challenge to the Liberal International Trade Order*, Committee Print, Joint Economic Committee, 97 Cong. 2 sess. (GPO, December 1982).

3. "Yu'nyū Daikōzui II: Kaihatsu Yu'nyū ga Kasoku Suru Hyakkaten, Sūpā no Ajia Ryūtsūken" [The Big Flood of Imports II: The Acceleration of Development Imports from the Asian Sphere by Department Stores and Superstores], *Toyo Keizai*, no. 4735 (July 4, 1987), p. 14.

4. Yukiko Fukugawa, "Ajia no Dainamizumu o Torikomu Nihon: Nihon-ASEAN-NICs no Shin Sangyo Chizu" [Japan Grasping Asian Dynamism: The New Industrial Map of Japan-ASEAN-NICs], *Ekonomisuto*, July 4, 1988, pp. 86-90.

5. "Nō Moa Japan!: Beikoku no Kankoku-Taiwan Tataki to Nihon" [No More Japans! Japan and the United States Policy of Beating Up South Korea and Taiwan], *Toyo Keizai*, no. 4737 (July 18, 1987), pp. 4-17. The article is actually somewhat more innocuous than the title, dealing with the decision of the U.S. Trade Representative to forestall trade problems with South Korea and Taiwan by making them open up their markets earlier. But the tone of the title and much of the writing is one of American fear of having to deal with more successful industrial countries across the Pacific.

6. Roundtable discussion with Toshio Watanabe, Naoki Tanaka, and Masao Okonogi, "Kankoku ga Senshin Koku ni Naru Hi" [The Day South Korea Becomes an Advanced Country], *Ekonomisuto, Rinji Zokan* [Economist, Special Edition], November 2, 1988, pp. 16-25.

7. Kokumin Keizai Kenkyūkai [official name in English: Research Institute on the National Economy], *Chōki Keizai Yosoku: 2000-Nen no Nihon Keizai, Higashi Ajia Kōiki Keizaiken no Kanōsei* [Long-Term Economic Forecast: The Japanese Economy in the Year 2000—The Possibility of a Broad Economic Area in East Asia] (Tokyo, August 1988), especially pp. 9–15.

8. Bank of Japan, "Ajia Shokoku no Hatten to Nichi, Bei, Ajia Keizai no Kimmitsuka" [The Development of Asian Countries and the Integration of Japan, the United States, and Asia], *Chōsa Geppō* [Monthly Studies], August 1988.

9. Ministry of International Trade and Industry (MITI), Minister's Secretariat, *Nihon no Sentaku: 'Nyū Gurōbarizumu' e no Kōken to 'Shin-Sangyō Bunka Kokka' no Sentaku* [Japan's Choices: Choices Concerning Contributions to the "New Globalism" and the "New National Industrial Culture"] (Tokyo: Tsūshō Sangyō Chōsakai, 1988), pp. 46–47, 50–53. This book is a very liberal document for Japan, and the list of participants on the committee that discussed and approved the report includes many well-known international figures, as pointed out in chapter 5, note 38. The United States and the European Community abolished generalized system of preferences (GSP) status for the Asian NICs in 1988, on the grounds that GSP was designed to assist the poorest countries, a category to which they no longer belong.

10. Noriko Tamachi, interview with Choi Chong-Soo, "Ajia Chiiki wa Wagakuni ni Nani o Kitai Suru ka" [What Does Asia Expect from Our Country?], *ESP*, no. 198 (October 1988), pp. 50–53. He sees a free trade area as unrealistic because of the wide disparities in economic development, not because of any fear of being more closely tied to Japan.

11. See Harry Harding and Edward J. Lincoln, "The East Asian Laboratory," in John D. Steinbruner, ed., *Restructuring American Foreign Policy* (Brookings, 1989), pp. 211–18, for a discussion of the United States as the regional peacekeeper.

12. Detail on the specific issues is scattered through Clyde V. Prestowitz, Jr., *Trading Places: How We Allowed Japan to Take the Lead* (Basic Books, 1988), and a synopsis of a number of major negotiating areas can be found in the Advisory Committee for Trade Policy and Negotiations (ACTPN), *Analysis of the U.S.-Japan Trade Problem*, prepared for the U.S. Trade Representative, February 1989 (hereafter *ACTPN Report*). See also the review of Japanese import barriers in Kenji Takeuchi, "Problems in Expanding Japan's Imports of Manufactures from Developing Economies: A Survey," International Economics Department, World Bank (Washington, May 1989); and Bela Balassa and Marcus Noland, *Japan in the World Economy* (Washington: Institute for International Economics, 1988), pp. 49–62.

13. Osamu Fujizawa, "Kinzoku Batto o Megutte" [The Metal Bat Problem: Its Real Meaning in U.S.-Japan Relations], *Tsūsan Jyānaru* [MITI Jour-

nal], vol. 15 (March 1983), pp. 42–47. It is unclear from this account whether the bat causing the injury that led to the standards was Japanese or foreign— probably a deliberate ambiguity, since this publication comes from MITI and Mr. Fujizawa was a MITI official.

14. This latter argument was made with great seriousness to the author in 1982 at a meeting at Keidanren by a mid-level executive of a Japanese firm.

15. Prestowitz, *Trading Places*, pp. 97–98.

16. Fujizawa, "Kinzoku Batto o Megutte."

17. This discussion of tobacco products is based on the *ACTPN Report*, pp. 89–92.

18. *ACTPN Report*, p. 91.

19. United States–Japan Advisory Commission, *Challenges and Opportunities in United States–Japan Relations: A Report Submitted to the President of the United States and the Prime Minister of Japan*, Washington, September 1984, p. 37. Even this bilateral, cooperative report noted that "previously announced measures appear to be repeated in later packages, and explanations of what has been added are often highly technical and raise questions as to why a previous measure was only half a step in the first instance" (p. 38).

20. U.S. MOSS Negotiating Team, *Report on Telecommunications Market-Oriented Sector Selective (MOSS) Discussions* (Washington: U.S. Department of the Treasury, August 1986), pp. 3–4.

21. Japan Economic Institute, *JEI Report*, no. 2B (January 17, 1986).

22. See the *ACTPN Report*, p. 94, on the 1987 dispute and pp. 116–17 on the cellular telephone dispute.

23. U.S. and Japan MOSS Negotiating Teams, *Report on Medical Equipment and Pharmaceuticals Market-Oriented Sector Selective (MOSS) Discussions* (Washington: U.S. Department of the Treasury, January 1986), p. 1.

24. *JEI Report*, no. 2B.

25. Prestowitz discusses this particular problem extensively. American intervention resulted in the use of copyright law (as in the United States) rather than patent law to provide intellectual property right protection for software. Prestowitz, *Trading Places*, pp. 287–95.

26. *ACTPN Report*, p. 95.

27. *JEI Report*, no. 2B.

28. *ACTPN Report*, p. 96.

29. *JEI Report*, no. 2B.

30. Prestowitz, *Trading Places*, p. 299, has done so in print, others privately. An extensive report by the U.S. General Accounting Office, *U.S.-Japan Trade: Evaluation of the Market-Oriented Sector Selective Talks*, GAO/NSIAP-88-205 (Washington, July 1988), calls the talks a qualified suc-

cess in terms of achieving removal of some trade barriers that were real and pernicious, but it notes the difficulty of measuring success in any quantitative terms.

31. Japan Economic Institute, *U.S.-Japan Economic Relations Yearbook, 1984–1985* (Washington, 1986), pp. 15–16.

32. Office of the U.S. Trade Representative, *1989 National Trade Estimate Report on Foreign Trade Barriers*, p. iii. Japan occupies 18 pages, while the next longest chapters are Brazil, Canada, Chile, the Federal Republic of Germany, and Korea, all with 10 pages each.

33. See Edward J. Lincoln, *Japan: Facing Economic Maturity* (Brookings, 1988); Balassa and Noland, *Japan in the World Economy*, pp. 135–55; Francis McNeil and Seizaburo Sato, *The Future of U.S.-Japan Relations: A Conference Report* (New York: Council on Foreign Relations, 1989), pp. 19, 22, 24; Japanese-American Study Committee on Comprehensive Security, *Creative Engagement: Strategies for United States–Japan Global Cooperation toward the 21st Century* (Honolulu: Pacific Forum, 1988); and John D. Steinbruner, ed., *Restructuring American Foreign Policy* (Brookings, 1989), pp. 12–25.

34. Kent E. Calder, *Crisis and Compensation: Public Policy and Political Stability in Japan, 1949–1986* (Princeton University Press, 1988), pp. 117, 126.

35. A survey in the spring of 1989 sponsored by MITI found 65 percent of Japanese respondents expressed a favorable attitude toward the United States. Kokusai Keizai Kōryū Zaidan, *Nichibei Kankei ni Tsuite no Seron Chōsa (Nichibei Pāsepushion Chōsa)* [Public Opinion Survey on U.S.-Japan Relations (Survey of U.S.-Japan Perceptions)] (Tokyo, 1988), p. 7.

36. Just to give one example, Clayton Yeutter's appointment as secretary of agriculture in the Bush cabinet was front-page news, and an accompanying news analysis speculated on whether the appointment was good or bad for Japan. *Asahi Shimbun*, December 16, 1988, pp. 1, 9.

37. Henry Rosovsky, "Trade, Japan and the Year 2000," *New York Times*, September 6, 1985, p. A23; and Henry Kissinger, "The Specter of Protection: Why We Must Reach an Accord with Japan," *Washington Post*, October 8, 1985, p. A19.

38. *ACTPN Report*, p. xiii. This proposal proved quite controversial, but in fairness, it was only one of many proposals—including a primary emphasis on macroeconomic adjustment in the United States (especially through federal budget deficit reduction).

39. Prestowitz, *Trading Places*, pp. xxx.

40. Prestowitz, *Trading Places*, p. 322, speaks of the need for a "comprehensive agenda in which trade and domestic programs mesh" in these new, high-technology areas.

41. *ACTPN Report*, p. xvi.

42. "Japan's Influence in America," *Business Week*, July 11, 1988, pp. 64–75.

43. Prestowitz, *Trading Places*, pp. 230–37.

44. For a review of the arguments on a free trade area with Japan, see U.S. International Trade Commission, *Pros and Cons of Initiating Negotiations with Japan to Explore the Possibility of a U.S.-Japan Free Trade Area Agreement*, USITC Publication 2120 (Washington, September 1988).

45. Issues concerning such a broader arrangement are considered in U.S. International Trade Commission, *Pros and Cons of Entering into Negotiations on Free Trade Area Agreements with Taiwan, the Republic of Korea, and ASEAN, or the Pacific Rim Region in General*, USITC Publication 2166 (Washington, March 1989).

Appendix A

1. Because new products and industries are constantly evolving, this industry classification has been periodically revised. The statistical data used here are based on Revision 2 of the SITC codes. There is now a new revision available, which should reflect product divisions in high-technology industries more accurately, but earlier data based on this revision were unavailable for historical comparison.

2. This issue and the various approaches to it are summarized in David Greenaway and Chris Milner, *The Economics of Intra-Industry Trade* (Basil Blackwell, 1986), chap. 5, "Measures of Intra-Industry Trade."

3. Herbert G. Grubel and P. J. Lloyd, *Intra-Industry Trade: The Theory and Measurement of International Trade in Differentiated Products* (John Wiley and Sons, 1975), pp. 22–23.

4. Greenaway and Milner, *Economics of Intra-Industry Trade*, pp. 69–70.

5. If overall trade is balanced, then the quantity $1/2 [X + M/X]$ equals 1, so that the adjusted IIT index number equals the unadjusted 1. As trade becomes unbalanced, the export and import figures for an individual product are adjusted separately (with a trade surplus, for example, causing the export figures to be adjusted downward and the import figures adjusted upward).

6. See Edward J. Lincoln, *Japan: Facing Economic Maturity* (Brookings, 1988), pp. 69–129, for a discussion of these factors.

7. Greenaway and Milner, *Economics of Intra-Industry Trade*, p. 68.

8. Yoko Sazanami, "Possibilities of Expanding Intra-Industry Trade in Japan," *Keio Economics Studies*, vol. 18, no. 2 (1981), adopts the same approach, arguing that adjustment "may conceal the major characteristics of Japanese trade" (p. 31).

Index